Cambridge English

EMPOWER

STARTER
STUDENT'S BOOK

A1

Adrian Doff, Craig Thaine
Herbert Puchta, Jeff Stranks, Peter Lewis-Jones
with Rachel Godfrey

Contents

4

Listen.

Read.

Write.

Teacher

Watch.

Look at the pictures.

Work in pairs.

CAN DO OBJECTIVES

■ Say your name and country
■ Talk about people you know
■ Meet and greet new people

UNIT 1
Hello!

GETTING STARTED

▶ 1.3

a 💬 Look at the picture. What countries can you see?

b 💬 What other countries do you know in English?

1A I'm from Mexico

1 READING AND GRAMMAR

be: I / you / we positive and questions

a ▶ **1.4** Listen. Then say *Hi, I'm …* or *Hello, I'm …* and say your name.

Hi, I'm Ruben.

Hello, I'm Harumi.

b ▶ **1.5** Read and listen to conversations 1–3. Match the conversations with groups of people a–c in the picture below.

c Complete the sentences in the table.

I / we	you
I _____ Camila. (= *I am* …) We _____ from the USA. (= *we are* …)	_____ you from England? How _____ you?

d ▶ Now go to Grammar Focus 1A Part 1 on p.114

e Sound and spelling Long and short sounds

   1 ▶ **1.9** Listen to the words. Notice the long (—) and short (^) sounds.

     a I̅'m   b We̅'re   c frôm   d thê

   2 💬 Practise saying the words.

f 💬 Practise the conversations in 1b.

   1 Work in pairs. Practise Conversation 1.
   2 Work in groups of three. Practise Conversation 2.
   3 Work with a new partner. Practise Conversation 3.

g 💬 Practise the conversations in 1b again. Use your own name.

1
V Hi, I'm Vilma. What's your name?
C I'm Camila.
V Hi, Camila. Nice to meet you.

2
H Hello, I'm Harumi.
K Hi. I'm Katy.
P And I'm Paul. Hi.
H Are you from England?
P No, we're from the USA.

3
L Hi, Ruben. How are you?
R Hi, Li. I'm fine. How are you?
L Fine, thanks.

2 LISTENING AND GRAMMAR *be: I / you / we* negative

a ▶1.10 Read and listen to the conversation. Choose the correct answers.

CLARA Are you Sasha?
SASHA Yes, that's right.
CLARA Hi, I'm Clara.
SASHA Oh, hi. Are you a student here?
CLARA No, I'm not a student. I'm your teacher!
SASHA Oh … sorry.

1 Sasha is:
  a a student. b a teacher.
2 Clara is:
  a a student. b a teacher.

b Complete the sentences in the table.

Positive (+)	Negative (−)
I'm____ a student. (= *I am*)	I'm _____ a student. (= *I am not*)
We _____ from England. (= *we are*)	We _aren't_ from England. (= *we are not*)

c ▶ Now go to Grammar Focus 1A Part 2 on p.114

d Read the sentences. Make them true for you.
  1 I'm a student.
  2 We're teachers.
  3 I'm from England.
  4 I'm Laura.
  5 We're from Tokyo.

e 💬 Tell a partner your sentences in 2d. Are they the same?

3 VOCABULARY AND READING Countries

a ▶1.12 Match the countries in the box with maps 1–8. Listen and check.

the UK   China   the USA   Spain   Japan   Russia   Brazil   Mexico

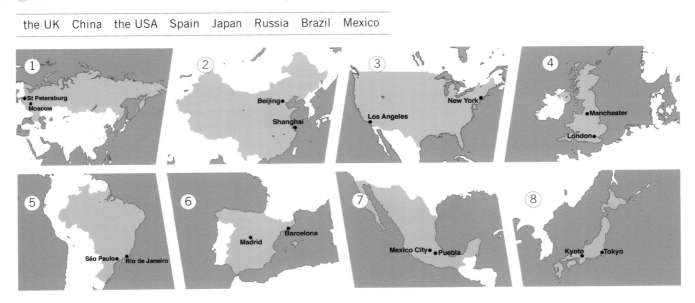

b ▶1.13 Complete the sentences with the correct country. Listen and check.

OUR STUDENT GROUP

❝ I'm Vilma. I'm from Rio de Janeiro, in ¹_____. ❞

❝ Hi, I'm Paul. I'm from ²_____. I'm from New York. ❞

❝ Hello. I'm from Puebla, in ³_____, and my name's Camila. ❞

❝ Hi, I'm Li. I'm from Beijing, in ⁴_____. But I'm not in Beijing now. I'm a student in Shanghai. ❞

❝ My name's Harumi. I'm from Tokyo, in ⁵_____. ❞

❝ I'm Sasha. I'm from ⁶_____. I'm a student in Moscow. ❞

❝ I'm from Barcelona, in ⁷_____, and my name's Ruben. ❞

❝ Hello. I'm a teacher and my name's Clara. I'm from Manchester, in ⁸_____. ❞

c ▶ Now go to Vocabulary Focus 1A on p.132

d Choose a city and a country in 3a. Write it on a piece of paper.

  Moscow, Russia.

e 💬 Give your piece of paper to the teacher and take a new one. Try to find the student with the information on your piece of paper.

  Are you from Russia?
  No, I'm not. I'm from Mexico.

4 SPEAKING

▶ Communication 1A
Student A go to p.103.
Student B go to p.108.

1B He's Brazilian

Learn to talk about people you know
- **G** be: he / she / they
- **V** Nationalities

1 VOCABULARY Nationalities

a 💬 Do you know the people in pictures a–h? Ask your partner.

> Do you know Maria Sharapova?

b Match the nationalities with pictures a–h.

| A|mer|i|can Chi|nese Mex|i|can Ru|ssian |
| Spa|nish Brit|ish Jap|an|ese Bra|zil|i|an |

c ▶1.15 **Pronunciation** Listen to the words in 1b. How many syllables are in each word?

A|mer|i|can = 4 syllables

d ▶1.16 Listen and notice the stressed syllable.

e ▶1.15 Listen to the words in 1b again. Underline the stressed syllables. Then listen and repeat.

f ▶ Now go to Vocabulary Focus 1B on p.132

Rafael Nadal – tennis player

Shinji Kagawa – football player

Maria Sharapova – tennis player

Li Na – tennis player

Neymar – football player

Kelly Smith – football player

Bob and Mike Bryan – tennis players

Javier Hernández and Guillermo Ochoa – football players

2 GRAMMAR *be: he / she / they positive*

a ▶1.18 Match 1–3 with a–c. Listen and check.

1 Maria Sharapova is a tennis player.
2 Shinji Kagawa is a football player.
3 Bob and Mike Bryan are tennis players.

a He's Japanese.
b They're American.
c She's Russian.

b Complete the table.

+	
she is …	she's …
he is …	¹_____ …
they are …	²_____ …

c ▶ Now go to Grammar Focus 1B Part 1 on p.114

d Write two sentences about 1–3.

1 Rafael Nadal
2 Li Na
3 Javier Hernández and Guillermo Ochoa

e Tell a partner your sentences in 2d. Are they the same?

3 LISTENING

a ▶1.20 Read and listen to Liz talk about the people on her winter holiday. Complete 1–6 with the words in the box.

American   Alexander   Penny   Russian   Mexican   Anna

LIZ This is ¹_____.
MARK Is she Spanish?
LIZ No, she isn't Spanish. She's ²_____.
MARK OK. And who's this?
LIZ This is ³_____.
MARK Is he Brazilian?
LIZ No, he isn't Brazilian. He's ⁴_____.
MARK Oh, really.
LIZ And these are my friends, ⁵_____ and Simon. They're married.
MARK Are they English?
LIZ No, they aren't English. They're ⁶_____ – from New York.

b Tell a partner about two of your friends. What nationality are they?

4 GRAMMAR

be: he / she / they negative and questions

a Complete the tables with the words in the box.

they   isn't   is   are   aren't   she

+	–
She's Russian. They're Chinese.	She _____ Russian. They _____ Chinese.

?
_____ _____ Russian? _____ _____ Chinese?

b ▶ Now go to Grammar Focus 1B Part 2 on p.114

c ▶1.24 Complete the sentences. Listen and check.

1 **A** _____ he Mexican?
  B No, _____ _____.
2 **A** _____ they American?
  B Yes, _____ _____.
3 **A** _____ she Chinese?
  B No, _____ _____.
4 **A** _____ they Brazilian?
  B No, _____ _____.
5 **A** _____ he British?
  B Yes, _____ _____.

d Practise saying 1–5 in 4c with a partner.

Language Plus *this / these*

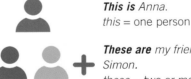

This is Anna.
this = one person

These are my friends, Penny and Simon.
these = two or more people

5 SPEAKING

▶ Communication 1B Student A go to p.103. Student B go to p.108.

1C Everyday English
Nice to meet you

1 LISTENING

a 💬 Look at picture a. Is she in a new place?

b ▶️ **1.25** Watch or listen to Part 1 and check your answer in 1a.

c ▶️ **1.25** Watch or listen to Part 1 again. Complete the sentences with words in the box.

> Hi   Good morning

RECEPTIONIST _____, Electric Blue Technology.
SOPHIA _____, my name's Sophia Taylor. It's my first day.

Sophia

2 USEFUL LANGUAGE Greeting people

a Complete 1–3 with the words in the box.

> evening   morning   afternoon

7 am – 12 pm = ¹_____
12 pm – 5 pm = ²_____
5 pm – 10 pm = ³_____

b ▶️ **1.26** Pronunciation Listen. How many syllables are in the words and expressions?

hi (1)   good|mor|ning   good|eve|ning
hel|lo   good|af|ter|noon

c ▶️ **1.26** Listen to the words and expressions in 2b again. Underline the stressed syllables.

hel<u>lo</u>

d 💬 Look at the times with a partner. Use the correct expression.

1 8 pm   3 11 am   5 6 am
2 3 pm   4 10 pm   6 1 pm

> Good morning.
>
> Good afternoon.

3 LISTENING AND USEFUL LANGUAGE
Meeting new people 1

a ▶️ **1.27** Watch or listen to Part 2. Sophia meets the manager of Electric Blue Technology. What's his name?

☐ Daniel   ☐ Darren   ☐ David

b ▶️ **1.28** Listen to the sentences. <u>Underline</u> the words you hear. Are both options in 1–2 possible?

1 *I'm* / *My name's* Sophia Taylor.
2 *I'm* / *My name's* David.

c ▶️ **1.29** Pronunciation Listen and notice the main stress.

A How <u>are</u> you?
B I'm <u>good</u>, thank you. And <u>you</u>?
A I'm <u>fine</u>, thanks.

d 💬 Practise the conversation in 3c with a partner.

e ▶️ **1.30** Put the expressions in the table. Listen and check.

> I'm fine, thanks.   I'm OK, thank you.
> Oh, not bad, thanks.   I'm good, thank you.

A ☺	B 😐

f 💬 Practise the conversation in 3c again, but change roles and use expressions in 3e to reply.

4 LISTENING AND USEFUL LANGUAGE
Meeting new people 2

a ▶ 1.31 Watch or listen to Part 3. Are Sophia and Megan friends?

b ▶ 1.31 Watch or listen to Part 3 again. Underline the correct answer.
1 **MEGAN** Nice to *meet / see* you too, Sophie.
2 **DAVID** So, this is your *home / office*.
3 **MEGAN** OK. So, … this is your *desk / chair*.

c ▶ 1.32 Put the conversation in the correct order. Listen and check.

☐ **MEGAN** Nice to meet you too, Sophie.
☐ **SOPHIA** Nice to meet you, Megan.
☐ **DAVID** This is Megan Jackson.

d 💬 Work in groups of three. Practise the conversation in 4c. Use your names.

This is Hassan.

Nice to meet you, Hassan.

Megan

5 PRONUNCIATION Tone

a ▶ 1.33 Listen to phrases 1–5. Does the tone change or stay the same →?
1 Hello.   3 I'm well.   5 Thank you.
2 How are you?   4 Nice to meet you.

b ▶ 1.33 Listen to the phrases in 5a again and repeat.

6 SPEAKING

a ▶ 1.34 Complete the conversation. Listen and check.

LARISSA Hi.
AMIRA Good evening.
KARL Hello.
LARISSA I'm Larissa and this ¹_____ Amira.
KARL Nice to meet you. I'm Karl.
AMIRA Nice to ²_____ you too. How are you?
KARL I'm good. And ³_____?
AMIRA I'm fine.
LARISSA I'm ⁴_____ too.

b 💬 Work in groups of three. Practise the conversation in 6a. Use your names.

7 WRITING

a Read Sophia's profile. What information about her is new?

ELECTRIC BLUE
TECHNOLOGY:
Our people in London

Hi, my name's Sophia Taylor. I'm from Toronto in Canada. I'm in an office with Megan Jackson.

b ▶ Now go to Writing Plus 1C on p.154 for Capital letters and full stops.

c Write a profile about you and your English class. Here are some ideas:

Hi/Hello, my …
I'm from … in …
I'm in a class with … in room …

d Read other students' profiles. Is everyone from the same place?

🔄 **Unit Progress Test**

CHECK YOUR PROGRESS

You can now do the Unit Progress Test.

UNIT 1
Review

1 GRAMMAR

a <u>Underline</u> the correct answer.

1 Hello. I *'m* / *are* Anna.
2 'Are you students?' 'Yes, *we're* / *we are*.'
3 You *am not* / *aren't* a teacher.
4 '*Am I* / *I am* right?' 'Yes, you are.'
5 Where *are you* / *you are*?
6 We *'re* / *am* at home.

b Add *is*, *isn't*, *are* or *aren't*.

1 'Is your name Sandy?' 'No, it _____.'
2 'Are Javier Hernández and Guillermo Ochoa from Mexico?'
  'Yes, they _____.'
3 'Is Rafael Nadal Spanish?' 'Yes, he _____.'
4 '_____ New York and Washington in the USA?'
  'Yes, they are.'
5 'Are your friends football players?' 'No, they _____.'
6 '_____ your teacher English?'
  'No, she _____.'

c 💬 Ask and answer the questions in 1b.

d Correct the sentences.

> They's Spanish.
> *They're Spanish.*
1 No, he aren't from China.   4 What your name?
2 You are OK?   5 I not am Brazilian.
3 Yes, I are.   6 Who she?

2 VOCABULARY

a Write the names of the countries.

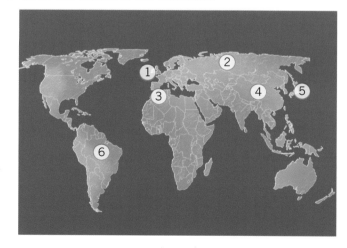

1 i t n a B i r _____
2 a s i R s u _____
3 i p S a n _____
4 h i C a n _____
5 a n a J p _____
6 l a r B i z _____

b Complete the nationalities.

> Spa<u>nish</u> _____

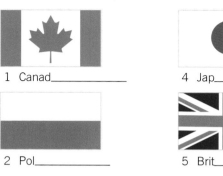

1 Canad_____   4 Jap_____

2 Pol_____   5 Brit_____

3 Amer_____   6 Ital_____

3 SOUND AND SPELLING

a ▶1.35 Do these words have long (—) or short (^) sounds? Write — or ^. Practise saying the words.

1 we're   4 is   7 from
2 he   5 you're   8 she
3 it   6 not

b ▶1.36 Look at the information in the table.

/r/	no /r/ sound
Russia	are
Cla**r**a	a**r**en't
Ame**r**ica	you**r**
f**r**om	teache**r**
room	mo**r**ning
right	afte**r**noon
B**r**azil	chai**r**

c ▶1.37 Tick (✓) the sentences with a /r/ sound. Practise saying the sentences.

1 ☐ I'm right.   5 ☐ She's from Brazil.
2 ☐ He's a teacher.   6 ☐ The chairs are small.
3 ☐ Good morning.   7 ☐ How are you?
4 ☐ This is my room. 8 ☐ Laura's American.

🔄 REVIEW YOUR PROGRESS

How well did you do in this unit? Write 3, 2, or 1 for each objective.
3 = very well   2 = well   1 = not so well

I CAN ...

say my name and country	☐
talk about people I know	☐
meet and greet new people	☐

CAN DO OBJECTIVES

- Talk about your home town
- Talk about possessions and common objects
- Ask for and give personal information

UNIT 2
All about me

GETTING STARTED

▶ 1.38

a 💬 Look at the picture and answer the questions.

1 Is it a ... ?
- hot country
- big city
- new house

2 What country do you think it is?

3 Count (1, 2, 3 ...):
- the windows on the blue house
- the people in the family
- the chairs
- the tables
- the TVs
- the cars

4 What other things do they have?

b 💬 What things in the picture do you have?

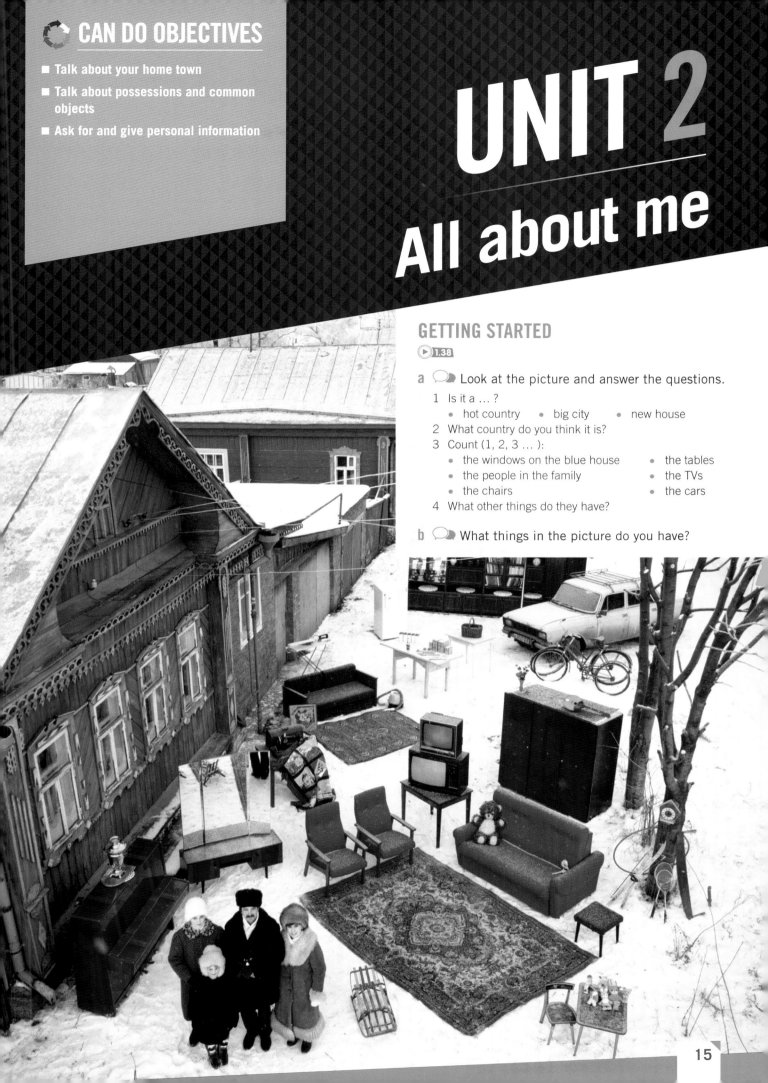

2A It's a very big city

Learn to talk about your home town
G *be*: it's / it isn't; Possessive adjectives
V Common adjectives

1 LISTENING

a 🔊 **1.39** Match the words in the box with pictures a–c. Listen and check.

> town   village   city

💬 Which are you from?

b 🔊 **1.40** Listen and match pictures a–c with the names in the box.

> Katia   Yuri   Carlo

c 🔊 **1.40** Listen again. Complete the sentences with the words in the box.

> is (x2)   it   it's   isn't (x2)

Conversation 1
A Is ¹_____ a big city?
B No, no. It ²_____ a city.
Conversation 2
A ³_____ a big city.
B Yes, it ⁴_____.
Conversation 3
A ⁵_____ it a city?
B No, it ⁶_____.

2 GRAMMAR *be*: it's / it isn't

a Complete the table with *it* or *it's*.

+	Ravello is in Italy.	_____ in Italy.
–	Ravello isn't in Russia.	_____ isn't in Russia.
?	Is Ravello in Italy?	Is _____ in Italy?

b Complete the sentences with *he's*, *she's* or *it's*.
1 Giovanna's from Ravello in Italy. _____ a village near Naples.
2 Yulia's from Vyborg. _____ Russian.
3 Ricardo's Spanish. _____ from Madrid.
4 Akiro's from Sôka in Japan. _____ a small city near Tokyo.
5 Selim's from Bursa in Turkey. _____ a big city near Istanbul.

c 🔊 **1.41** Listen and check.

d ▶ Now go to Grammar Focus 2A Part 1 on p.116

Language Plus *in / near*

*Naples is **in** Italy.*

*Ravello is **near** Naples.*

e Write sentences about you.

> I'm from …   It's a (village / town / city) (in / near) …

f 💬 Tell a partner your sentences.

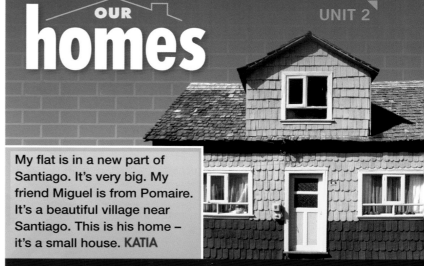

OUR homes

3 READING AND VOCABULARY
Common adjectives

a ▶ 1.44 Read and listen to *Our homes*. Complete the table.

	home		home
Katia	big flat	Miguel	
Carlo		Pietro and Susanna	
Yuri		Nina	

b **Sound and spelling** /h/

1 ▶ 1.45 Listen to the words. Which word has no /h/ sound?

home	hi	who	what	how	hotel

2 💬 Practise saying the words with /h/.

c ▶ 1.46 Complete the sentences with the words in the box. Listen and check.

big	small	old	new

1 It's a _____ house.   2 It's a _____ flat.

3 It's a _____ city.   4 It's an _____ house.

d ▶ Now go to Vocabulary Focus 2A on p.134

4 GRAMMAR
Possessive adjectives

a Read *Our homes* again. Complete the table.

Pronoun	Possessive adjective
I	_____
you	your
he	_____
she	her
we	our
they	_____

My flat is in a new part of Santiago. It's very big. My friend Miguel is from Pomaire. It's a beautiful village near Santiago. This is his home – it's a small house. **KATIA**

My flat in Ravello is big, old and beautiful. My friends Pietro and Susanna are from Naples. This is their home. It's a big flat in a nice part of town. **CARLO**

My home is a small house in an old part of Vyborg. My friend Nina is from St Petersburg. This is her home. It's a small flat and it's old and beautiful. **YURI**

b Complete the sentences.

1 Javier is from Barcelona. _____ home is in a nice part of the city.
2 Are you from Berlin? Where's _____ flat?
3 We're from Bogotá, in Colombia. _____ home is near a big hotel.
4 Sarah is from England. _____ village is near Hastings.
5 Pedro and Eva are from Mexico City. _____ flat is very big.

c ▶ Now go to Grammar Focus 2A Part 2 on p.116

d Complete the sentences about a friend.

My friend _____ is from _____. His / Her home is _____.

e 💬 Tell a partner about your friend's home.

5 SPEAKING

▶ Communication 2A
Student A go to p.103.
Student B go to p.109.
Student C go to p.113.

1 VOCABULARY Common objects 1

a ▶1.49 Match 1–10 in picture a with the words in the box. Listen and check.

a computer   a newspaper   a knife   a phone   a key
a watch   an umbrella   a ticket   a book   a bottle of water

b 💬 Two objects in 1a are not OK in an airport. What are they?

Language Plus *a / an*

We use *a* before most nouns.   • *a key*   • *a book*
We use *an* before *a, e, i, o, u*.   • *an **u**mbrella*   • *an **i**ce cream*

c 💬 Cover the words in the box in 1a. Ask a partner questions about the objects in the picture.

What's this?   It's a watch.

d ▶ Now go to Vocabulary Focus 2B Common objects 1 on p.133

2 LISTENING AND GRAMMAR Plural nouns

a ▶1.51 Listen to the conversation with John Munroe. Tick (✓) the words you hear.

☐ newspapers
☐ computers
☐ phones
☐ watches
☐ umbrellas
☐ bottles
☐ books
☐ knives

b Complete the table.

Singular (= 1)	Plural (= 2+)
a key	keys
a newspaper	_____
a watch	_____
a knife	_____

c Most nouns add *-s* in the plural. How are the plurals of *watch* and *knife* different?

d Sound and spelling /s/, /z/ and /ɪz/

1 ▶1.52 Listen and practise these sounds. Which word has an extra syllable in the plural?
1 /s/ book**s**   2 /z/ key**s**   3 /ɪz/ watch**es**

2 ▶1.53 Listen to these words. Which word has an extra syllable in the plural? Listen again and repeat.

knives   bottles   tickets   apples   villages   phones

e 💬 Work in pairs.

Student A: say a singular word.
Student B: say the plural.

Then swap roles.

f ▶ Now go to Grammar Focus 2B on p.116

3 GRAMMAR *have*

a ▶1.54 Look at the X-ray picture and complete the conversation. Listen and check.

A What's in your bag?
B Mm, I have a ¹b_____, and my ²k_____s, and an ³u_____.
A Do you have a ⁴p_____?
B Yes. Oh, and a ⁵b_____ of w_____. Sorry!

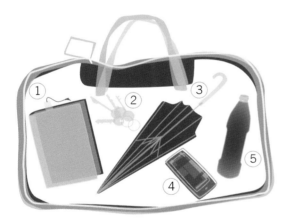

b ▶1.55 Listen to the forms of *have*.

+	?
I **have** a book.	**Do** you **have** a book?

c ▶1.55 Pronunciation Listen again. Do the words *do* and *you* have a long (—) or a short (˄) sound? Practise saying the sentences.

d 💬 Ask a partner about objects 1–5 in 3a. Ask about:
1 here (in class)
2 at home

Do you have an umbrella here?   No.

Do you have an umbrella at home?   Yes.

4 VOCABULARY   Numbers 1

a ▶1.56 Listen and repeat the numbers.

b Match the words in the box with numbers 1–12 in 4a.

seven   two   nine   four   eight   eleven
three   six   one   ten   twelve   five

c 💬 Work in pairs.

Student A: say a number.
Student B: say the next number.

Then swap roles.

d ▶ Communication 2B Student A go to p.104. Student B go to p.108.

e ▶ Now go to Vocabulary Focus 2B Numbers 1 on p.146

5 SPEAKING

a Write three things you have in your bag.

a computer   six apples

two bottles of water

b 💬 Guess what is in your partner's bag.

Do you have a phone?   Yes.

Do you have a knife?   No!

Learn to ask for and give personal information

P Tone in questions
W A form

1 LISTENING

a Think about a good home for you. Tick <u>four</u> boxes.

1 ☐ a house   3 ☐ old
  ☐ a flat   ☐ new
2 ☐ in a village   4 ☐ near a park
  ☐ in a city   ☐ near shops

b 💬 Tell a partner about your home in 1a.

> A good home for me is …

c ▶1.59 Watch or listen to Part 1. Answer the questions.

1 Who asks questions, Sophia or the woman?
2 What kind of home does Sophia need, a flat or a house?

d ▶1.59 Watch or listen to Part 1 again. Tick (✓) the correct answer.

1 Sophia's surname:
  a ☐ Tailor   b ☐ Taylor
2 Her address in London:
  a ☐ Alpha Hotel   b ☐ Alfa Hotel
3 Her phone number:
  a ☐ 07832 674893   b ☐ 07832 647893

2 USEFUL LANGUAGE Asking for and giving personal information

a ▶1.60 <u>Underline</u> the correct answer. Listen and check.

1 A What's your surname?
  B *It's / I'm* Robinson.
2 A What's your address?
  B *It's / It's on* 7 King Street.
3 A What's your phone number?
  B *They're / It's* 0124 352738.
4 A What's your email address?
  B *He's / It's* chrisrobinson@powermail.com.

b ▶1.61 Listen to the answers to questions 3 and 4 in 2a again. Tick (✓) the correct answer.

1 a ☐ oh-one-two-four-three-five-two-seven-three-eight
  b ☐ oh-twelve-four-three-five-two-seven-three-eight

2 a ☐ chris-robinson-from-powermail-point-com
  b ☐ chris-robinson-at-powermail-dot-com

c ▶1.62 <u>Underline</u> the correct word. Listen and check your answer.

RACHEL Sophia Taylor. *What / How* do you spell that?
SOPHIA T-A-Y-L-O-R.

d ▶1.63 Pronunciation Listen to the questions. Notice the main stress in each question.

1 How do you <u>spell</u> that?
2 Can you <u>spell</u> that?
3 Sorry, what's the <u>spelling</u>?

▶1.63 Listen again and repeat.

e ▶ Now go to Writing Plus 2C Part 1 on p.154 for The alphabet.

f 💬 Ask a partner his / her surname. Then ask how to spell it.

g ▶ Communication 2C Student A go to p.104. Student B go to p.109.

3 LISTENING

a (▶)**1.65** Watch or listen to Part 2. What does Sophia think? Tick (✓) the correct sentence.

1 ☐ The flat's really nice.
2 ☐ The flat isn't very nice.

b (▶)**1.65** Watch or listen to Part 2 again. Tick (✓) the correct information about the flat.

1 ☐ small ☐ big
2 ☐ good for one person ☐ good for two people
3 ☐ near a supermarket ☐ near a park

4 PRONUNCIATION Tone in questions

a (▶)**1.66** Listen to the questions. Does the tone go up ↗ or down ↘ at the end?

1 What's your surname?
2 What's your phone number?

b (▶)**1.66** Listen again and repeat the questions.

c 💬 (▶)**1.67** Practise asking the questions with a partner. Then listen and check the tone.

1 What's your address?   3 What's the spelling?
2 Where are you from?

5 SPEAKING

a 💬 Talk to different students. Ask about:

• names (first name and surname)   • address
• phone number   • email address

Write down the information. Ask about the spelling.

What's your surname?

It's Mishkin.

Can you spell that, please?

M-I-S-H-K-I-N.

6 WRITING

a Read about Sophia. What's the new information?

Local Rentals: Customer Information	
First name:	Sophia
Surname:	Taylor
Address:	Alpha Hotel, High Street
Phone number:	07832 647893
Email:	sophiat@electricblue.com

b ▶ Now go to Writing Plus 2C Part 2 on p.154 for Spelling.

c Complete the form with your information.

Local Rentals: Customer Information	
First name:	
Surname:	
Address:	
Phone number:	
Email:	

🔄 **Unit Progress Test**

CHECK YOUR PROGRESS

You can now do the Unit Progress Test.

UNIT 2
Review

1 GRAMMAR

a Correct the <u>underlined</u> word.

> <u>It's</u> big houses. *They're*
1 This is Katia and this is <u>she</u> house.
2 'Excuse me! Is this <u>you</u> bag?' 'Yes, it is! Thank you.'
3 Hiro's from Sōka. <u>She's</u> a small city in Japan.
4 It <u>not</u> a big flat.
5 They live in Madrid. This is <u>they</u> home.
6 'Hi, we're from New York. <u>We</u> city is big!'

b Complete the sentences with the plural form of the nouns in brackets.

1 They're my _____. (key)
2 Are they your _____? (knife)
3 I have two _____. (watch)
4 Are they your _____? (bottle of water)
5 Oxford and Cambridge are _____ in the UK. (city)
6 Where are the _____? (book)

c Complete the sentences with the words in the box.

| are his is they |
| they're it's isn't |

1 I'm from Ravello. _____ a village in Italy.
2 The men _____ at home.
3 'Are they big houses?' 'Yes, _____ are.'
4 _____ my books.
5 _____ it a city?
6 This is John and this is _____ flat.
7 'Is Madrid in Italy?' 'No, it _____.'

2 VOCABULARY

a Match 1–6 with the opposite adjectives in the box.

| boring difficult good |
| happy old ~~small~~ wrong |

> big   small
1 easy   _____
2 bad   _____
3 right   _____
4 sad   _____
5 interesting _____
6 new   _____

b Complete the crossword with the objects in pictures 1–8.

3 SOUND AND SPELLING

a ▶1.69 Look at the words in the box. Is the final sound /s/, /z/ or /ɪz/? Complete the table. Practise saying the words.

| ~~phones~~ villages keys addresses houses |
| flats umbrellas tickets books computers |

/s/	/z/	/ɪz/
	phones	

b ▶1.70 Tick (✓) the words with a /h/ sound. Practise saying the words.

☐ hello	☐ is	☐ how	☐ watch
☐ her	☐ home	☐ who	☐ happy
☐ our	☐ house	☐ she	☐ right
☐ his	☐ where	☐ phone	

⟳ REVIEW YOUR PROGRESS

How well did you do in this unit? Write 3, 2, or 1 for each objective.
3 = very well   2 = well   1 = not so well

I CAN ...

talk about my home town	☐
talk about possessions and common objects	☐
ask for and give personal information	☐

● **CAN DO OBJECTIVES**

■ Say what you eat and drink
■ Talk about food and meals
■ Order and pay in a café

UNIT 3
Food and drink

GETTING STARTED
▶ 1.71

a 💬 Look at the picture and answer the questions.

1 What food can you see in the fridge?
2 Do you have the same food in your fridge?
3 Which food in this fridge do you like?
4 Which food in this fridge don't you like?
5 When do you eat the food in the fridge?

b 💬 What other food do you know in English?

23

3A Do you like fish?

Learn to say what you eat and drink
G Present simple: *I / you / we / they*
V Food 1

1 VOCABULARY Food 1

a ▶1.72 Match pictures 1–7 with the words in the box. Then listen and check.

| fruit rice meat bread vegetables eggs fish |

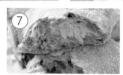

b ▶1.72 Pronunciation Listen to the words in 1a again. Which word has more than one syllable? <u>Underline</u> the stressed syllable.

c 💬 Say two things you like ☺.

> I like fruit and I like fish.

d Sound and spelling /iː/, /ɪ/ and /aɪ/

1 ▶1.73 Listen and practise these sounds.

1 /iː/ m<u>ea</u>t 2 /ɪ/ f<u>i</u>sh 3 /aɪ/ <u>I</u>'m

2 ▶1.74 What sound do the **marked** letters have in the words in the box? Listen and add the words to the sound groups below.

| big **ea**t nine sister it's me |
| China five his t**ea**cher Hi |

Sound 1 /iː/	Sound 2 /ɪ/	Sound 3 /aɪ/
meat	fish	I'm

3 💬 Practise saying the words.

e ▶ Now go to Vocabulary Focus 3A on p.142

2 READING AND GRAMMAR
Present simple: *I / you / we / they* positive and negative

a Which words in 1a can you see in pictures 1–3? Which word <u>isn't</u> in the pictures?

b ▶1.77 Read and listen to texts a–c. Match them with the families in pictures 1–3.

FOR ONE WEEK

a "They eat a lot of fruit and vegetables every day. And they eat meat with rice. They like eggs, but they don't eat bread or fish. They don't like fish."

b They eat meat and eggs every day, but they don't eat fish. And they don't eat vegetables, but they eat fruit. They really like bread.

c They eat a lot of rice and vegetables. They like fruit and they eat bread. They don't eat fish or meat. They are vegetarians.

① ☐

Tang family, China

c Complete the table.

+			–			
I We They	eat like	meat. fish.	I We They	_____ _____	eat like	meat. fish.

d <u>Underline</u> the correct words.

1 The Tang family *eat / don't eat* fish.
2 The Ruiz family *eat / don't eat* bread.
3 The Donati family *like / don't like* meat.
4 The Tang family *eat / don't eat* a lot of eggs.
5 The Donati family *like / don't like* vegetables.

e 💬 Which family's food would you like to have for a week? Why?

② ☐

Donati family, Italy

③ ☐

Ruiz family, Guatemala

3 LISTENING AND GRAMMAR Present simple: *I / you / we / they* questions

a ▶ 1.78 Listen to a conversation with Rajit. Tick (✓) the food he eats.

✓ bread ☐ vegetables ☐ meat
☐ fish ☐ rice ☐ fruit

Rajit

b ▶ 1.78 Listen again. Complete the conversation.

A Rajit, what do you eat in a week?
B Oh lots of things. I eat rice every day, and bread. I eat a lot of fruit. I eat fish …
A ¹ _____ you eat meat?
B No, I don't like meat.
A Do you ² _____ vegetables?
B Oh yes, I like vegetables. I eat a lot of vegetables.
A Do you ³ _____ them every day?
B Yes. They're very good for me.

c ▶ 1.79 Complete the questions in the table. Then listen and check.

+	–	?
I eat fish. We like fruit.	I don't eat fish. We don't like fruit.	_____ you _____ fish? _____ you _____ fruit?

d ▶ Now go to Grammar Focus 3A on p.116

e 💬 Practise the conversation in 3b with a partner.

4 SPEAKING

a 💬 Ask and answer questions with a partner. Complete the table with their answers.

Do you eat meat?　　Yes, (I do).

Do you eat bread every day?　　No, not every day.

Do you like fish?　　No, I don't like fish.

	yes / no?	every day?	like?
meat			
fish			
rice			
bread			
vegetables			
fruit			
eggs			

b 💬 Write words for three drinks. Then ask your partner questions.

Do you drink cola?　　Do you like milk?

3B I always have dinner early

1 READING

a Tick (✓) the boxes about your breakfast.

b 💬 Talk about your answers in 1a with a partner.

> I have coffee – I don't have ice cream.

For my breakfast, I have ...

	YES	NO		YES	NO
coffee			tea		
bread			fruit		
ice cream			fish		
cold pizza			nothing		

c 💬 Look at the pictures. What's the number one breakfast in the UK?

☐ fruit   ☐ cereal

☐ toast   ☐ eggs

d Read the text and find the answer to 1c.

THE NUMBER ONE BREAKFAST

In the UK, people like different food for breakfast. They sometimes eat a hot breakfast with eggs, but toast is the number one breakfast food. The number two breakfast food is cereal with cold milk and number three is fruit.

e 💬 What's the number one breakfast food in your country? What's the number one drink?

> I think _____ is the number one breakfast food in my country.

2 VOCABULARY Food 2; Time

a Match sentences 1–3 with pictures a–c.

1 I have lunch at *twelve / one* o'clock.
2 They have dinner at *six / seven* o'clock.
3 In my family we have breakfast at *seven / eight* o'clock.

a in the morning

b in the afternoon

c in the evening

b ▶ Now go to Vocabulary Focus 3B Food 2 on p.143

c ▶1.84 Listen to sentences 1–3 in 2a. Underline the correct words.

d ▶1.85 Match the clocks with the times. Listen and check.

- ☐ (a) quarter past four
- ☐ four o'clock
- ☐ (a) quarter to five
- ☐ half past four

e 🗨 Point to a clock in 2d for a partner to say the time.

f ▶ Now go to Vocabulary Focus 3B Time on p.146

g **Sound and spelling /ɑː/ and /ɔː/**

1 ▶1.87 Listen and practise these long sounds.

1 /ɑː/ p**a**st h**a**lf   2 /ɔː/ f**our** qu**ar**ter

2 ▶1.88 What sound do the **marked** letters have in the words in the box? Listen and add the words to the sound groups below.

cl**a**ss **a**ll f**a**ther **a**fternoon w**a**ter d**au**ghter

Sound 1 /ɑː/	Sound 2 /ɔː/
past	four

3 🗨 Practise saying the words.

h ▶ **Communication 3B** Student A go to p.103. Student B go to p.108.

3 LISTENING

a ▶1.89 Listen to three people talk about dinner. Match 1–3 with a country in the box.

Poland   Spain   the USA   Russia   Mexico   China

b ▶1.89 Listen again. Complete the table.

Name	Dinner time	Food
Julie		
Misha		
Bianca		

c 🗨 Do you like the same food as Julie, Misha and Bianca?

4 GRAMMAR Adverbs of frequency

a ▶1.90 Listen and complete the sentences with the words in the box.

always   usually   sometimes   never

1 **JULIE** We _____ have rice with meat and vegetables.
2 **MISHA** I _____ have dinner early.
3 **BIANCA** People _____ have dinner early in Spain.
4 **BIANCA** I _____ have bread and cheese.

b Complete 2 and 4 with words in the box in 4a.

1 always (100%)   3 sometimes (50%)
2 _____ (80%)   4 _____ (0%)

c ▶ Now go to Grammar Focus 3B on p.118

d Put the words in brackets in the correct place in the sentences.

1 I have breakfast at 9:00 at weekends. (sometimes)
2 I have a sandwich for lunch. (usually)
3 I have breakfast. (never)
4 In the evening, I have dinner at about 7:00. (always)

e 🗨 Which sentences in 4d are true for you?

Language Plus *What time ... ? / When ... ?*
What time *do you have dinner?* = **When** *do you have dinner?*

5 SPEAKING

a Answer questions 1–4. Write another question with your own idea.

1 In the morning, do you eat breakfast?
2 In the evening, do you eat a big meal?
3 What time do you have lunch?
4 What do you eat for lunch?

b 🗨 Ask and answer the questions in 5a with other students. Who has the same answers as you?

> Jaime and I never eat breakfast.

1 LISTENING

a 💬 What food on the menu do you like? Tell a partner.

MENU
—— SANDWICHES: ——
cheese, tomato, egg 3.00
—— CAKE: ——
banana, chocolate 3.00
—— DRINKS: ——
tea, coffee, orange juice 2.50

b ▶️2.2 **Pronunciation** Listen. This word has two syllables:

coff | ee

▶️2.3 Which words have two syllables? Listen and check.

sandwich   banana   orange   tomato

c ▶️2.3 Listen to the words in 1b again. <u>Underline</u> the stressed syllable.

<u>cof</u>fee

d 💬 Practise saying the words in 1b with a partner.

e Find 1–3 in pictures a–c.
1 a piece of chocolate cake   2 a key   3 ten pounds

f ▶️2.4 Watch or listen. Put pictures a–c in the correct order.

g ▶️2.4 Watch or listen again. Are the sentences true or false?
1 Sophia has a new flat.
2 Sophia has a cup of tea.
3 Sophia likes her flat.
4 The text message is from Sophia's cousin.

2 PRONUNCIATION Sentence stress

a ▶️2.5 Listen to 1–3. Is the pronunciation of *of* the same?
1 of   2 a cup of tea   3 a glass of cola

b ▶️2.6 Listen to these phrases. Which other word isn't stressed?
a cup of coffee   a piece of banana cake

c 💬 Practise saying the phrases in 2b.

d 💬 Work in pairs. Practise more phrases with *a cup / a glass / a piece of …* . Use the menu in 1a or your ideas.

a

b

c

4 SPEAKING

a 💬 Work with a partner. Student A: you work in a café. Student B: you're a customer. Use the menu on p.28 and the conversation map below.

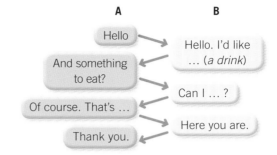

A | B
Hello → Hello. I'd like … (*a drink*)
And something to eat? ← → Can I … ?
Of course. That's … ← → Here you are.
Thank you. ←

b 💬 Swap roles and repeat the conversation.

3 USEFUL LANGUAGE
Ordering and paying in a café

a ▶2.7 Listen and complete the sentences.
1 **MEGAN** I'd _____ a cup of coffee, please.
2 **SOPHIA** Can I _____ a cup of tea, a cup of coffee and a piece of chocolate cake, please?

▶2.7 Listen again and repeat.

b ▶2.8 Put the words in the correct order. Listen and check.
1 have / I / a cup of / can / coffee / please ?
2 please / an egg sandwich, / I'd like .
3 two / can / have / we / tomato sandwiches ?

c 💬 Practise saying the sentences in 3b with a partner.

d ▶2.9 Put the conversation in the correct order. Listen and check.
☐ A cheese sandwich, please.
☐ Of course. That's £6.00, please.
☐ Certainly. And to eat?
☐ Here you are.
☐ Can I have a glass of cola, please?
☐ Thank you.

e 💬 Practise the conversation in 3d with a partner. Change the drink, food and price.

> Can I have a cup of tea, please?

5 WRITING

a Read the text message. Who is it from? Who is it for?

> Hi, James. I'm in a café with Sophia. She's my new friend at work. She's from Canada. She has a new flat here in London! Talk to you later. Megan.
>
> Delivered

b ▶ Now go to Writing Plus 3C on p.155 for Contractions.

c Write a text message to a friend. Here are some ideas:

Hi, …
I'm … (*at school* / *at work* / *in a café* / *in a restaurant*) with …
He's / She's … (*Spanish* / *a student* / *very nice*)
Talk (to you) / See you soon / later.

d Read a partner's text message. Who does he / she write about?

🔄 Unit Progress Test

CHECK YOUR PROGRESS

You can now do the Unit Progress Test.

UNIT 3
Review

1 GRAMMAR

a Write present simple sentences and questions with the words and phrases.

> (–) I / have / lunch at home.
> *I don't have lunch at home.*
1 (?) you / like / eggs
2 (+) we / eat / bread every day.
3 (–) I / drink / juice.
4 (–) we / eat / meat.
5 (+) you / like / fruit.
6 (?) they / eat / fish

b <u>Underline</u> the correct answer.

1 *Always I / I always* have a sandwich for lunch.
2 I *drink sometimes / sometimes drink* cola.
3 I *eat usually / usually eat* lunch at home.
4 I *never / never don't* drink milk.
5 *Never I have / I never have* dinner at 9:00.
6 I *don't sometimes / sometimes don't* have breakfast.

c 💬 Are the sentences in 1b true or false for you? Tell a partner.

d Correct the sentences.

> I not like rice.
> *I don't like rice.*
1 No, we not do.
2 Always I have breakfast.
3 We not eat fish.
4 I drink usually water.
5 You like tea?
6 Yes, do I.

2 VOCABULARY

a Complete the groups with words in the box.

coffee	dinner	fish	cakes	juice	banana

1 water, milk, _____
2 tea, _____
3 orange, apple, _____
4 breakfast, lunch, _____
5 meat, eggs, _____
6 ice cream, biscuits, _____

b 💬 Which is your favourite group in 2a?

c Look at 1–6 in the picture and complete the food words.

1 b_____   4 a_____s
2 r_____   5 o_____s
3 m_____   6 e_____s

3 SOUND AND SPELLING

a ▶ 2.10 Which sounds are the **marked** letters – /ɪ/, /iː/ or /aɪ/? Tick (✓) a or b. Practise saying the sentences.

> It's a biscuit.
> a ☐ /iː/ /iː/ /iː/
> b ✓ /ɪ/ /ɪ/ /ɪ/

1 T**ea**, pl**ea**se.
  a ☐ /iː/ /iː/
  b ☐ /ɪ/ /ɪ/
2 I'd like ice cr**ea**m.
  a ☐ /aɪ/ /aɪ/ /aɪ/ /iː/
  b ☐ /iː/ /iː/ /iː/ /aɪ/

3 W**e** drink milk.
  a ☐ /aɪ/ /aɪ/ /iː/
  b ☐ /iː/ /ɪ/ /ɪ/
4 R**i**ce **i**s n**i**ce.
  a ☐ /aɪ/ /ɪ/ /aɪ/
  b ☐ /iː/ /iː/ /iː/

b ▶ 2.11 Tick (✓) the words with the /ɔː/ sound. Practise saying the words.

1 ☐ water   5 ☐ potato
2 ☐ tomato   6 ☐ orange
3 ☐ glass   7 ☐ quarter
4 ☐ morning   8 ☐ all

🔄 REVIEW YOUR PROGRESS

How well did you do in this unit? Write 3, 2, or 1 for each objective.
3 = very well   2 = well   1 = not so well

I CAN ...

say what I eat and drink	☐
talk about food and meals	☐
order and pay in a café	☐

○ **CAN DO OBJECTIVES**

■ Talk about your life and ask about others'
■ Talk about your family
■ Ask and talk about photos

UNIT 4
My life and my family

a

GETTING STARTED

▶ 2.12

a 💬 Look at the picture and answer the questions.

1 Look at person a. Can you see ... ?
   • her parents   • her brother   • her child
2 Do you think this family all live together in one house?
3 Who in the picture ... ?
   • works   • studies
4 What do you think the people in the picture do next?

b 💬 Who lives in your home?

31

4A What do you study?

Learn to ask and talk about your life
- **G** Present simple: *Wh-* questions
- **V** Common verbs

1 VOCABULARY Common verbs

a ▶️ 2.13 Match sentences 1–5 with pictures a–e. Listen and check.

1 I **study** at university.
2 I **work** in an office.
3 I **speak** Japanese.
4 We **live** in London.
5 We **go** to the gym every day.

b 💬 Which sentences in 1a are true for you?

c ▶ Now go to Vocabulary Focus 4A on p.136

2 READING

a Read Matt's blog. Which sentence is true?

1 'I live and I work in London.'
2 'I live in Barcelona and I work in London.'
3 'I speak Spanish very well.'

b Read Matt's blog again. What does he say about these things?

1 flats in London
2 flats in Barcelona
3 number of days at work (in London)
4 number of days at work (in Barcelona)
5 Spanish classes
6 Barcelona

c 💬 What do you think of Matt's life?

Language Plus *study*

study
... at university / school / an English language school
... English / Spanish / Arabic
... a subject (*art*, *maths*)

d Write sentences about you.

I live ...   I work / study ...   I study English ...

e 💬 Tell a partner your sentences in 2d.

こんにちは

BREAKFAST IN BARCELONA AND LUNCH IN LONDON – JUST A NORMAL DAY FOR MATT!

HERE'S HIS STORY:

I work in London. Flats are very expensive there. In Barcelona, in Spain, flats aren't very expensive and they're nice and big. So I work in London, but I live in Barcelona! I fly from Barcelona to London on Monday. I work there for three days and I stay with my sister. Then I fly to Barcelona again and I work at home two days a week. I don't speak Spanish very well, so I study Spanish at a language school and I go to classes on Saturday. I love Barcelona – it's a beautiful city and it's great to live here!

3 LISTENING

a ▶ 2.15 Listen to Tom and Miriam. Who lives in Auckland but works in Wellington?

b ▶ 2.15 Listen again. <u>Underline</u> the correct answers.

1 Miriam is *Brazilian* / *a New Zealander*.
2 Her home's in *Brazil* / *New Zealand*.
3 Her job *is* / *isn't* near her home.
4 She *is* / *isn't* married.
5 Miriam and Bernardo speak *English* / *Portuguese* together.

4 GRAMMAR
Present simple: *Wh-* questions

a ▶ 2.16 Complete the questions in the table. Listen and check.

Yes/No questions	
_____ you work at home?	Yes, I work two days at home. No, I work in an office.
Wh- questions	
Where _____ you live? When _____ you have dinner? What _____ you study at university?	I live in Auckland. I have dinner at 8:00. I study Italian.

b ▶ Now go to Grammar Focus 4A on p.118

c ▶ 2.19 Put the words in the correct order to make questions. Listen and check.

1 you work / do / in an office ?
2 do / where / you work ?
3 where / you live / do ?
4 university / study at / do you ?
5 do / speak Spanish / you ?

d ▶ 2.19 **Pronunciation** Listen to the questions in 4c again. Notice the stressed words.

1 Do you <u>work</u> in an <u>office</u>?

e ▶ 2.19 Tick (✓) the words we stress. Then listen to the questions in 4c again and repeat.

1 ☐ question word (e.g. *where*)
2 ☐ *do*
3 ☐ main verb (e.g. *work*)
4 ☐ preposition (e.g. *in*)

f 💬 Ask and answer the questions in 4c with a partner.

5 SPEAKING

▶ Communication 4A
Student A go to p.104.
Student B go to p.109.

4B She has a sister and a brother

1 READING AND LISTENING

a Match sentences 1–6 with pictures a–f.

1 Film stars and brothers, Liam and Chris Hemsworth.
2 Colombian pop star Shakira with her parents.
3 Football player Cristiano Ronaldo as a boy with his father and his two sisters.
4 Hillary Clinton with her husband, Bill Clinton, and their daughter, Chelsea.
5 Will Smith with his wife, Jada, and Will's three children.
6 Actor George Clooney as a child with his sister, Adelia, and his mother.

b ▶ 2.20 Listen and check.

c 💬 What other things do you know about the people in the pictures?

2 VOCABULARY Family and people

a Complete the table. Use words from 1a.

👩	👨
mother	father
_____	son
wife	_____
_____	brother

b Which word in the sentences in 1a means … ?

1 mother and father   2 boys and girls

c Look at the family tree. Which people … ?

1 are married   3 have a sister
2 have a brother   4 have a child / children

d 💬 Work in pairs.

Student A: choose a person from the family tree.
Student B: ask questions to guess who Student A is.

Then swap roles.

Are you married?   Yes.

Do you have children?   Yes.

e ▶ Now go to Vocabulary Focus 4B Family and people on p.135

f Sound and spelling /ð/

1 ▶ 2.23 Listen and practise this sound.
/ð/ mother

2 ▶ 2.24 /ð/ is usually spelled *th*. Listen to the words and repeat.

this   that   father   they   brother   then

3 💬 Practise saying the words.

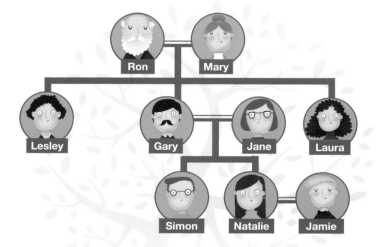

1991

f 1995

3 READING AND VOCABULARY Numbers 2

a Read *An international family*. Are the sentences true or false?

1 Pablo and Alicia have two small children.
2 María is married and lives in Turkey.
3 Only Pablo and Alicia live in Mexico.

An international

family

Pablo and Alicia Moreno are married. Pablo is from Spain and Alicia is from Buenos Aires, in Argentina, but they live in New York. Their family is very international!

Alicia has a sister and a brother. Her sister Daniela is 46. She lives in Buenos Aires and her mother lives there too. Her brother Carlos is 37. He lives in Brazil and he works in São Paulo.

Alicia and Pablo have two children. Their son Alex is 19. He's at university in Mexico and he lives there too. Their daughter María is 24. She lives in Istanbul with her Turkish husband, Mehmet.

b Where do they live? Write the names of countries.

1 Daniela   4 María
2 Carlos   5 Mehmet
3 Alex

c Daniela is forty-six. How old are … ? (Write the numbers in words.)

1 Carlos   2 Alex   3 María

Language Plus *How old … ?*

How old is *she?*
She's *25.*

How old are *her children?*
They're *three and five.*

Note: We use *be*, not *have*, to ask about age.

d ▶ Now go to Vocabulary Focus 4B Numbers 2 on p.146

e 💬 Write the names of three famous people. How old are they? If you don't know, guess! Read out the names. What do other students think?

Madonna.   I think she's 50.

4 GRAMMAR
Present simple: *he / she / it positive*

a Look at the verbs in the table and answer the questions.

1 How are the verbs in A different from the verbs in B?
2 How is *has* different?

I / we / you / they	he / she
A I **work** in an office. We **have** two children. They **live** in New York.	B He **works** in São Paulo. She **has** a sister and a brother. She **lives** in Buenos Aires.

b Complete the sentences with verbs from 4a.

1 He _____ in an office.
2 He _____ at home with his parents.
3 Her mother _____ a flat in New York.

c ▶ Now go to Grammar Focus 4B on p.118

d ▶ Communication 4B Student A go to p.103. Student B go to p.109.

5 SPEAKING

a 💬 Tell your partner about your family. Use the verbs in the box. Listen, but don't make notes.

have   go   study   live   work

My brother has two children – a boy and a girl.

b 💬 Say what you remember about your partner's family. Are you correct?

35

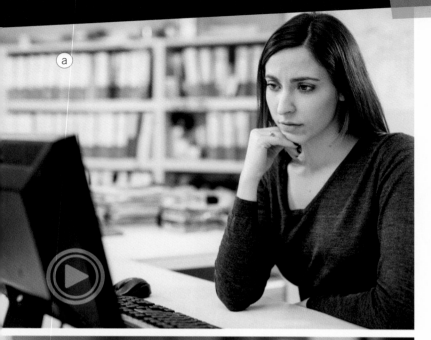

1 LISTENING

a 💬 Ask and answer the questions.
   1 Do you have photos of family and friends with you?
   2 Where do you have them, on your phone or in your wallet?
   3 How often do you look at them?

b 💬 Look at picture a and answer the questions.
   1 Is Sophia happy or sad?
   2 Why does she feel happy / sad?

c ▶2.27 Watch or listen to Part 1. Are your ideas in 1b correct?

d ▶2.28 Watch or listen to Part 2. Answer the questions.
   1 How many people does Sophia talk about?
   2 How many people does Megan talk about?

e ▶2.28 Complete the information about Sophia and Megan's families with the words in the box. Then watch or listen to Part 2 again and check your answers.

---

sister   cousin   teacher   hotel   computers
supermarket

Sophia's mother's a ¹_____ and her father's the manager of a ²_____. She has a ³_____, Jackie. Jackie has two girls, Kylie and Amanda.

Megan has a brother, Mike. He works with ⁴_____ and is married to Helen. She's the manager of a ⁵_____. Megan also has a ⁶_____, James.

f 💬 Talk about a favourite photo of your family. Who's in it?

2 USEFUL LANGUAGE Asking and talking about photos

a Look at expressions 1–7 from Part 2. Do we use them to … ?

   a ask about photos
   b talk about your photos
   c talk about another person's photos

   1 This is my mother.
   2 Do you have photos of your family?
   3 Nice picture!
   4 Can I see them?
   5 Who's this?
   6 They're lovely.
   7 This is my sister, Jackie.

b ▶ 2.29 Look at expressions 1–4. Are they in group a, b or c in 2a? Listen and check your answers in 2a and 2b.

   1 This is a picture of my town.
   2 It's really nice.
   3 Do you have any pictures of your home?
   4 These are my friends, Sayeed and Mona.

c ▶ 2.30 **Pronunciation** Listen to the sentence. Answer the questions. Listen again and repeat.

            This is my mother.

   1 Do the first two words join?
   2 Is the pronunciation of *s* the same in *this* and *is*?

d ▶ 2.31 Complete the conversation with expressions in the box. Listen and check.

> Great photo!   Can I see them?
> He's funny.
> Do you have any photos of your friends?

  A ¹ _____
  B Yes, I do.
  A ² _____
  B Sure. This is a photo of my friend, Marco.
  A ³ _____
  B And this is me with my friend, Emilio.
  A Yes, I know Emilio. ⁴ _____
  B You're right – he's really funny.

e 💬 Practise the conversation in 2d. Take turns to be A and B.

3 PRONUNCIATION Sound and spelling: /tʃ/ and /dʒ/

a ▶ 2.32 Listen and practise these sounds.

   1 /tʃ/ tea**ch**er   pi**c**ture   2 /dʒ/ mana**g**er   **J**ames

b ▶ 2.33 Listen to the **marked** sounds in the words. Which one is different in each group?

   1 **ch**ips   **j**eans   ques**t**ion
   2 lar**ge**   **j**ob   **ch**oose
   3 oran**ge**   **ch**eap   ma**tch**
   4 pa**ge**   **ch**eese   **G**ermany

c 💬 Practise saying the words in 3b.

4 SPEAKING

▶ **Communication 4C** Student A go to p.105. Student B go to p.109.

5 WRITING

a Read Sophia's information about her sister. What information is new?

> < PREVIOUS   NEXT >

This is my sister Jackie with her two beautiful daughters, Kylie and Amanda. They live in a new house in Toronto – it's very nice. Her husband Tom isn't there, because it's his photo! They're a great family.

b ▶ Now go to Writing Plus 4C on p.155 for Word order.

c Write about your photo from 1f. Here are some ideas:

  This is my … with …   He's / She's / They're …
  They live … It's nice / lovely / great!

d Read about your partner's photo. How many people does he / she write about?

Unit Progress Test

CHECK YOUR PROGRESS

You can now do the Unit Progress Test.

UNIT 4
Review

1 GRAMMAR

a Look at the words and write present simple questions.

> where / you / live   *Where do you live?*
1 what / your name
2 when / you / have lunch
3 what time / you / go to work
4 where / your friends / from
5 what / you / study
6 where / your school

b 💬 Ask and answer the questions in 1a.

c Correct the <u>underlined</u> words.

> My son <u>like</u> football. *likes*
1 Yoshi <u>work</u> in Berlin.
2 Our daughter <u>eat</u> rice every day.
3 My city <u>haves</u> two universities.
4 Naif <u>go</u> to school at 8:30.
5 My dad <u>teachs</u> Spanish.
6 My brother <u>studys</u> Russian.

d <u>Underline</u> the correct answer.

1 When *are* / *'s* / *do* you work?
2 María *is live* / *live* / *lives* in Istanbul.
3 Where *are* / *is* / *do* you from?
4 What *are* / *is* / *do* you have for breakfast?
5 What *are* / *is* / *do* their names?
6 What time do you *gos* / *go* / *goes* to school?

2 VOCABULARY

a Cross out the answer which is NOT possible.

> I work *in a factory* / *in an office* / *tennis.*
1 I meet *my friends for coffee* / *to the gym* / *people at work* every day.
2 I play *home* / *football* / *the guitar.*
3 I live in *Italian* / *a small house* / *a big city.*
4 I teach *at university* / *to the cinema* / *young children.*
5 I study *English* / *at university* / *to school.*
6 I speak *Spanish* / *Russia* / *Chinese.*

b 💬 Which information in 2a is true for you? Tell a partner.

c Complete the numbers.

> 29 ___twenty-___nine
1 31 _____one
2 24 _____four
3 75 _____five
4 82 _____two
5 96 _____six
6 53 _____three
7 48 _____eight
8 67 _____seven
9 100 a _____

d Match 1–6 with the words in the box.

| baby | boy | girl | men | woman | women |

3 SOUND AND SPELLING

a ▶2.34 <u>Underline</u> ONE or TWO /ð/ sounds in each sentence. Practise saying the sentences.

1 These are my friends.
2 I study there.
3 This is my father.
4 They're at the cinema.
5 They teach at the university.
6 I like their daughter.

b ▶2.35 Look at the information in the table.

/tʃ/	/dʒ/	/s/
tea**ch**	mana**g**er	**s**tudy
pi**c**ture	**g**ym	offi**c**e
child	**J**ulia	**c**inema

c ▶2.36 Are the **marked** sounds the same (S) or different (D)? Practise saying the sentences.

> We're on pa**g**e **s**eventy-two.   D
> The offi**c**e is number **s**ixty-three.   S
1 **G**ary is a mana**g**er.
2 **J**ohn speaks **G**erman.
3 It's a pi**c**ture of the **g**ym.
4 Is the univer**s**ity ni**c**e?
5 It's a que**s**tion about **ch**ildren.
6 It's a **s**mall **c**inema.

CAN DO OBJECTIVES

- Describe a town
- Talk about hotels and hostels
- Ask about and say where places are

UNIT 5
Places

GETTING STARTED

▶ 2.37

a 💬 Look at the picture of a hotel and tick (✓) the things you think are in each room.

- ☐ a bed
- ☐ a chair
- ☐ a TV
- ☐ a phone
- ☐ a computer
- ☐ pictures

b 💬 Talk about the questions.

1 What are the good things and bad things about this hotel room?
2 What other buildings do you think are near these rooms?
3 Would you like to stay in this hotel?

5A There are lots of old houses

Learn to describe a town
- **G** *there is / there are*: positive
- **V** Places in a town

VERY HOT!

Ghadames is a beautiful old city in Libya. There are lots of old houses, shops and cafés – so what's different? Ghadames is in the Sahara. It's very hot in the day (sometimes 55°C). The houses have very thick walls and they're always cool. In the old town there are streets for men and children and there are different streets (on the roofs of the houses) for women.
Now, there's a new town with new houses and flats, but in summer lots of people go to live in the old houses because they aren't hot.

Ghadames

VERY COLD!

Esperanza Base is Argentinian and it's in Antarctica. It's cold in summer (0°C) and very cold in winter (-10°C). There are homes for about 100 people there. There are ten families with children, there's a school and there are two teachers. There's also a bank and a hospital. There are a few cars, but there's only one road – it's 1.5 km long!

Esperanza Base

1 READING

a 💬 Look at the pictures of Ghadames and Esperanza Base. Which place is … ?
- an old city
- in a hot country
- in a cold country

b Read about the two places and check your answers in 1a.

c Are the sentences about Ghadames (G) or Esperanza Base (EB)?
1 'It's always cold here.'
2 'Our new flat is very hot in summer.'
3 'It's so small – you never get lost.'
4 'The men and women don't always walk together.'
5 'The school is small, but it's very good.'

d 💬 Do you think Ghadames and Esperanza Base are nice places to live? Why / Why not?

Language Plus *a few*, *lots of*

a few cars

lots of cars

a few houses

lots of houses

2 GRAMMAR
there is / there are: positive

a Complete the sentences. Check your answers in the texts in 1b.
Singular: There ¹_____ a new town / a school.
Plural: ²_____ are lots of old houses / two teachers.

b ▶2.38 **Pronunciation** Listen and write the sentences. How many words are there in each?

c ▶ Now go to Grammar Focus 5A on p.120

d Write two true sentences about your street. Use *there's* or *there are*.

e 💬 Tell a partner your sentences in 2d.

3 VOCABULARY Places in a town

a ▶ 2.40 Match the words in the box with the places in pictures a–f. Listen and check.

café shop restaurant
school bank hotel

b Which places in 3a are these?

1 'My daughter goes there every day from 8:00 to 4:00.'
2 'We go there for dinner every Saturday night.'
3 'I often drink coffee there with my friends.'
4 'You're in room 305. Here's your key.'
5 'They have fruit and vegetables and also newspapers and magazines.'
6 'I'd like £500, please.'

c ▶ Now go to Vocabulary Focus 5A on p.148

d Sound and spelling /uː/ and /ʌ/

1 ▶ 2.42 Listen and practise these sounds.

1 /uː/ sch**oo**l   2 /ʌ/ l**u**nch

2 ▶ 2.43 What sound do the **marked** letters have in the words in the box? Listen and add the words to the sound groups below.

Russia f**oo**d n**ew** t**wo** wh**o** m**o**ther
umbrella b**ea**utiful s**o**metimes

Sound 1 /uː/	Sound 2 /ʌ/
school	lunch

3 💬 Practise saying the words.

4 LISTENING

a ▶ 2.44 Listen to a conversation about places in a town. Look at the map and match 1–5 with the words in the box.

bookshop café bank restaurant food shop

b ▶ 2.44 Listen again. Are the sentences true or false?

1 There are lots of shops in New Street.
2 Nice people work in the bookshop.
3 The café is Italian.
4 The coffee and cakes in the café aren't good.
5 It's a Chinese restaurant.
6 The restaurant is cheap.

c 💬 What is the same about the town on the map and your town?

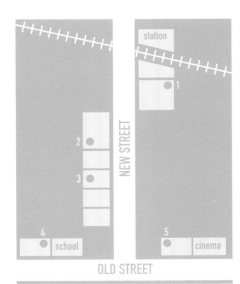

5 SPEAKING

a Think of a street in the town where you are now. Make notes. Use words from this lesson.

There's a …   There are …   It's in …   It's near …

b 💬 Describe your street, but don't say its name. Do other students know the name of the street?

41

1 VOCABULARY Hotels

a ▶2.45 Match the words in the box with pictures 1–5. Listen and check.

> bath   room   bed   TV   shower

b **Sound and spelling /ʃ/**

1 ▶2.46 Listen and practise this sound.

/ʃ/ **sh**ower

2 ▶2.47 Listen to the words in the box. Underline the /ʃ/ sound in each word.

> shop   fish   sure   Russia

3 💬 Practise saying the words.

c ▶ Now go to Vocabulary Focus 5B on p.149

d ▶2.49 **Pronunciation** Listen to the words. Notice the stressed syllables. Practise saying them.

hostel   hotel

e 💬 Which things in pictures 1–5 in 1a aren't in a hostel room?

hostel room

2 READING

a 💬 Look at pictures 1–3 of Turkey. Choose adjectives to talk about them. Compare your ideas with your partner.

- beautiful
- great
- nice
- boring
- exciting
- interesting
- old
- big

b Read Sandra's review of a hostel in Turkey. Does Sandra like the hostel?

c Read the review again. Tick (✓) what's in the hostel.

second floor	☐ small rooms	☐ big rooms	☐ café
first floor	☐ restaurant	☐ TV room	☐ small rooms
ground floor	☐ café	☐ kitchen	☐ TV room

d 💬 Would you like to stay at the hostel? Why / Why not?

HOLIDAY REVIEWS

The Cave Hostel

This is a great hostel in Göreme, in Turkey. It's in Cappadocia, a very old part of the country. You can do lots of things here. My favourite thing is going in a hot air balloon. You can see really beautiful places from the air.

The hostel has different rooms with different prices. On the first floor, there are small rooms for two people with baths. On the second floor, there are big rooms with six beds in them. They're very cheap, but there isn't a shower or a bath in the big rooms. There aren't any blankets or pillows – you pay for those. There isn't a restaurant or café in the hostel, but there's a kitchen on the ground floor. There aren't any TVs in the rooms, but there's free wi-fi. It's a very simple place to stay, but it's clean. And the people are very friendly. Faruk, the manager, sings karaoke really well!
Sandra

3 GRAMMAR
there is / there are: negative

a ▶2.50 Complete the sentences with *isn't* or *aren't*. Listen and check.

  1 There _____ any blankets.
  2 There _____ a restaurant.

b Find more examples of *there isn't* and *there aren't* in Sandra's review.

c Think about the town or city you're in now. Tick (✓) the sentences that are true. Correct the false sentences.

  1 ☐ There's a big museum in this town / city.
  2 ☐ There are lots of shops here.
  3 ☐ There aren't any hostels.
  4 ☐ There are two stations.
  5 ☐ There aren't any parks.

d 💬 Read your sentences and listen to your partner's sentences. Are they the same?

There aren't any museums in this town.

No, there is a museum in this town – on Cromwell Road.

4 LISTENING

a ▶2.51 Listen to a hostel receptionist and Barry, a guest. Is Barry happy with the hostel?

b ▶2.51 Listen again. Tick (✓) the things in the hostel.

  ☐ free rooms   ☐ café   ☐ wi-fi
  ☐ car park   ☐ kitchen ☐ showers

c 💬 Why do people like hostels? Why do people like hotels?

5 GRAMMAR
there is / there are: questions

a ▶2.52 Complete the questions. Listen and check.

  1 Singular: _____ _____ a car park here?
    Yes, there's a car park here.
  2 Plural: _____ _____ any cafés near here?
    Yes, there are cafés near here.

b ▶ Now go to Grammar Focus 5B on p.120

c Write questions using *Is there ... ?* and *Are there ... ?* about your partner's town, city or street. Here are some ideas:

  • cafés   • swimming pool • cinema
  • supermarket   • hospital   • restaurants

d 💬 Ask your partner about their town, city or street.

Are there any cafés in your town?

Yes, there are two cafés.

Is there a supermarket in your street?

No, but there are two shops.

6 SPEAKING

▶ Communication 5B
Student A go to p.105.
Student B go to p.110.

5C Everyday English
Is there a supermarket near here?

1 LISTENING

a 💬 Ask and answer the questions.

1 What food shops or markets are there near your home?
2 Do you go to these shops or markets? How often?
3 Is the food good / expensive?

b ▶2.55 Watch or listen to Part 1. Answer the questions.

1 Does Megan like Sophia's flat?
2 What does Sophia need?
3 Does Sophia know where to buy food near her flat?

2 PRONUNCIATION Emphasising what you say 1

a ▶2.56 Listen to the sentence.

MEGAN It's a really nice flat, Sophia.

▶2.57 Listen to the sentence again. Is *really* more or less stressed the second time?

b Tick (✓) the correct rule.

We say *really* with a strong stress to:
1 ☐ speak loudly
2 ☐ make the meaning stronger

c ▶2.58 Listen to the sentences. Underline one word with strong stress in each sentence.

1 My country is very hot in summer.
2 James's new car is really fast.
3 This film is so boring.

d ▶2.58 Listen again and repeat.

3 LISTENING

a ▶2.59 Watch or listen to Part 2. Answer the questions.

1 Do Sophia and Megan find a shop?
2 Who do they meet in the street?

b ▶2.59 Watch or listen to Part 2 again. Are the sentences true or false?

1 Sophia thinks a café is a shop.
2 James sees Megan and Sophia first.
3 James lives in the next street.
4 There's a supermarket in the next street.
5 There's a shop near James's flat.

4 USEFUL LANGUAGE Asking and saying where places are

a ▶2.60 Complete the questions with words in the box. Listen and check.

near   where   there

1 _____'s your flat?
2 Is _____ a supermarket near here?
3 Are there any shops _____ here?

b ▶2.61 Match the two possible answers in a–c with questions 1–3 in 4a. Listen and check.

a Yes, there are. There's one in this street. /
No, sorry, there aren't.
b Yes, there's one near my flat. / No, sorry, there isn't.
c It's in the next street. / It's in this street.

c ▶2.62 Put the conversation in the correct order. Listen and check.

A ☐ Great, thank you. And is there a good restaurant in this part of town?
A ☒1 Excuse me, can you help me?
A ☐ OK, thanks for your help.
A ☐ Are there any good cafés near here?

B ☐ Yes, there's one in the next street – Café Milano.
B ☐ No, I'm sorry, there aren't any restaurants near here. But there's one near the station.
B ☐ Yes, of course.
B ☐ No problem.

d 💬 Practise the conversation in 4c with a partner.

5 SPEAKING

▶ Communication 5C Student A look at the information below. Student B go to p.111.

a **Conversation 1.** You're on a street you don't know. Ask Student B about:
• a hotel • cafés

b **Conversation 2.** Now you're on a street you know. Use the information to answer Student B's questions.
• a bank: in the next street
• shops: not near here – near the hospital

6 WRITING

a Read part of an email from Sophia to her parents. She writes about her new flat. Does she only write about the good things?

> My new flat is great. It's big and it's in a nice part of town. The flat is near my office and there's a beautiful park in the next street. There isn't a supermarket near me, but there's a shop in the next street.

b ▶ Go to Writing Plus 5C on p.156 for *and* and *but*.

c Write about your part of town. Use *there's / there isn't / there are / there aren't*. Use *and* and *but*.

d Read about your partner's part of town. Is it the same?

 Unit Progress Test

CHECK YOUR PROGRESS

You can now do the Unit Progress Test.

UNIT 5
Review

1 GRAMMAR

a Correct the sentences.

> There an Italian restaurant. *There's an Italian restaurant.*
1 There is a museum in this street?
2 Yes, there's.
3 There are a shower.
4 There aren't a free rooms.
5 Is there swimming pool in the hotel?
6 No, there not is.

b Complete the sentences.

1 Is _____ a bank near here?
2 Are there _____ bottles of water in the room?
3 _____ there a supermarket in this street?
4 Is there _____ TV in the room?
5 _____ there any cafés near here?
6 Is there _____ teacher in the room?

c 💬 Ask and answer the questions in 1b.

2 VOCABULARY

a What are these places? Use the words to complete the crossword.

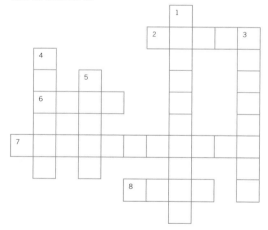

b Write the words.

1 d e b _____

5 o r o m _____

2 w e r h o s _____

6 w o t e l _____

3 i p o w l l _____

7 i w-i f _____

4 t h a b _____

8 k a n b l e t _____

3 SOUND AND SPELLING

a ▶2.63 Complete the table with the words in the box. Practise saying the words.

~~up~~ ~~you~~ umbrella lovely Russia beautiful new brother school mother museum pool

/uː/	/ʌ/
you	up

b ▶2.64 Look at the information in the table.

/ɒ/	/aʊ/	/əʊ/
sh**o**p	sh**ow**er	pill**ow**
h**o**spital	fl**ow**er	kn**ow**
h**o**t	t**ow**el	h**o**tel

c ▶2.65 Are the **marked** sounds the same (S) or different (D)? Practise saying the words.

> t**ow**n – sh**o**p D
1 h**o**t – h**o**tel
2 sh**ow**er – h**ow**
3 **O**K – kn**ow**
4 g**o** – pill**ow**
5 h**o**t – t**ow**el
6 fl**ow**er – h**o**spital

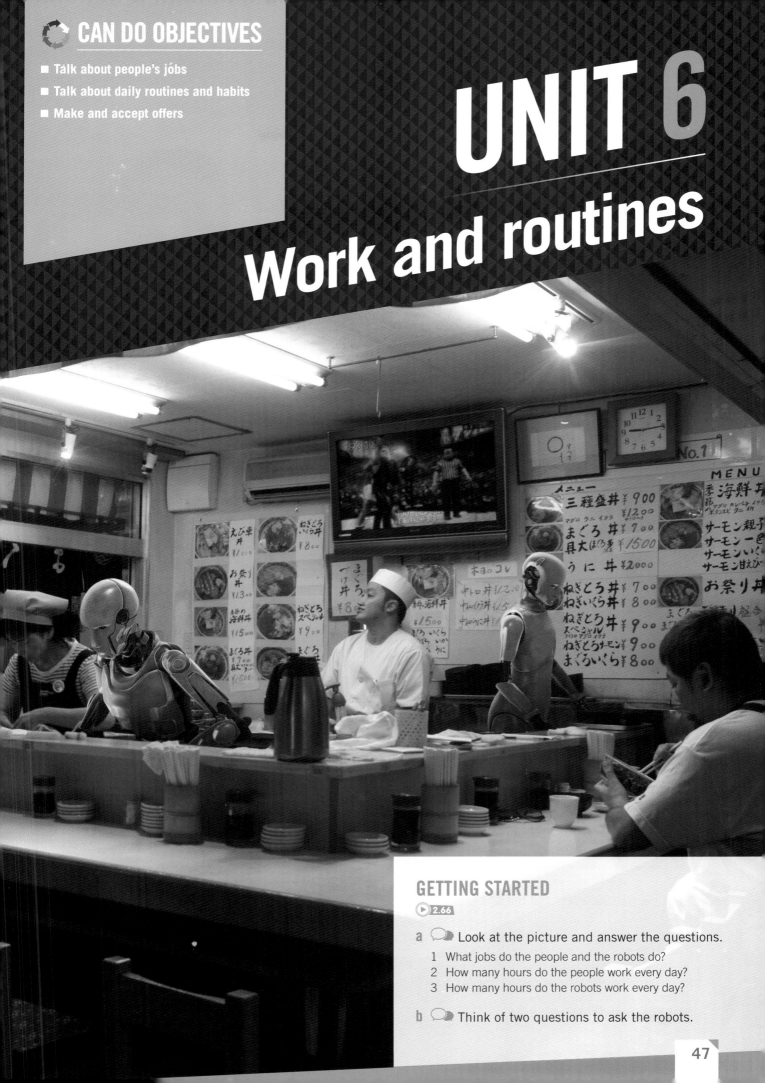

CAN DO OBJECTIVES

- Talk about people's jobs
- Talk about daily routines and habits
- Make and accept offers

UNIT 6
Work and routines

GETTING STARTED

▶ 2.66

a 💬 Look at the picture and answer the questions.

1 What jobs do the people and the robots do?
2 How many hours do the people work every day?
3 How many hours do the robots work every day?

b 💬 Think of two questions to ask the robots.

Learn to talk about people's jobs

Ⓖ Present simple: *he / she / it* negative
Ⓥ Jobs

Home   News   **About**

JOBS INTERNATIONAL

HELP AROUND THE WORLD ...
Welcome to *Jobs international*. Our people go around the world and help others. Meet two of them.

LUIZA *I'm a doctor from Brazil and I work in a small hospital in Ghana. I love the work here because it's very interesting. I do different things every day. And the people are so friendly. Life isn't always easy here, but it's great to help people.*

FRED *I'm a teacher at a school in Samoa, but I'm from Australia. I teach English here and after school I play sports with the children. They love rugby and volleyball. The children are really happy – a lot of fun. This is a really good job.*

1 READING

a 💬 Look at the pictures. What places are in the pictures? What jobs do people do there?

b Read about Luiza and Fred on the *Jobs international* website. Are your ideas in 1a correct?

c Read the website again. Are the sentences true or false?

1 *Jobs international* people don't work in their home countries.
2 Luiza works in a big hospital.
3 Her work is sometimes boring.
4 She likes the people in Ghana.
5 Fred goes home after classes.
6 His students like playing sport.

d Write questions for Luiza and Fred.

What ... do? → *What do you do?*
1 Where ... work?
2 ... like the people?
3 ... like the job?

e 💬 You are Luiza or Fred. Ask and answer the questions in 1d.

What do you do?   I'm a teacher.

Language Plus *work / job*

She **works** in a hospital.	work = verb
I like my **work**.	work = noun
It's a good **job**.	job = noun (*doctor, teacher*)

2 LISTENING AND VOCABULARY Jobs

a Match the words in the box with pictures a–h.

football player   student   receptionist   waiter   taxi driver   factory worker   office worker   shop assistant

b ▶2.67 **Pronunciation** Listen to the two-word jobs in 2a. Which word is stressed?

1 ☐ the first word
2 ☐ the second word

💬 Practise saying the words.

c ▶2.68 Listen to four people talk about their job. What do they do?

1 _____   3 _____
2 _____   4 _____

d ▶2.68 Listen again. Complete the sentences with the words in the box.

study   play (x2)   sit   meet (x2)

1 **DIANA**   I _____ all day, but I _____ some interesting people and go to lots of different places. I don't work at night.
2 **FELIPE**   I _____ in a team and the weekend is the most important time of the week in my job. I don't _____ games in the week – well, sometimes on Wednesdays.
3 **FATIMA**   I _____ business at university. It's really interesting.
4 **SHONA**   I work in a shop and _____ a lot of different people.

e 💬 Which job do you like in 2c? Which job don't you like? Say why.

f ▶ Now go to Vocabulary Focus 6A on p.151

3 GRAMMAR Present simple: *he / she / it* negative

a ▶2.70 Complete the sentences with *does* or *doesn't*. Listen and check.

DIANA I don't work at night.
1 She _____ work at night.
FELIPE I don't play games in the week.
2 He _____ play games in the week.

b ▶ Now go to Grammar Focus 6A on p.120

c Complete the sentences with the correct form of the verbs in brackets.

1 Alex is a taxi driver. He _____ in the morning. (not work)
2 Sam is a bank worker . He _____ his job. (not like)
3 Lucy is a shop assistant. She _____ much each day. (not sit)
4 Matteo is a waiter. He _____ on Monday. (not work)

d Sound and spelling /ɜː/

1 ▶2.72 Listen to the words. Do the **marked** letters sound the same?

wo**r**k   uni**ver**sity

2 ▶2.73 Listen to the words in the box. Which words have the sound /ɜː/?

fi**r**st   ve**r**b   n**ear**   g**ir**l   re**ce**ptionist   wo**r**ld

3 Which letter often comes after the vowel to spell the sound /ɜː/?

4 💬 Practise saying the words with /ɜː/.

4 SPEAKING

▶ Communication 6A Student A go to p.105. Student B go to p.110.

A Good Night's Sleep

People say it's good to sleep for eight hours every night … but is it true? Some people sleep for only five or six hours and they feel fine in the morning. And some people sleep twice every night …

Anneli Hanka, 24, Finland
I always **wake up** at about 4:00 in the morning. I don't want to sleep, so I **get up** and I do yoga. Then I **go to bed** again. Then I get up at 8:00 in the morning and I go to work. I feel fine – I never feel tired.

Beatriz Romero, 32, USA
I finish work at 6:00 in the evening and I arrive home at 6:30. I read a book or phone a friend. Then I go to bed for three hours. My husband works in a restaurant and he gets home at about 12:00 at night. So I get up, and we have dinner and then we watch TV until about 3:00. Then I sleep until 7:00.

1 READING AND VOCABULARY Daily routine

a Talk about when you do these things. Use the phrases in the box.

in the morning	in the afternoon	in the evening	at night

1 have dinner
2 go to English class
3 work
4 have coffee
5 read a book
6 sleep

b Read about Beatriz and Anneli. Match what they say with pictures a and b.

c Match the **marked** words in the text with pictures 1–3.

d Complete the verb phrases with the words in the box. Then read the text again to check your answers.

have	watch	go	arrive / get	finish

1 _____ to work
2 _____ home
3 _____ dinner
4 _____ TV
5 _____ work

e ▶ Now go to Vocabulary Focus 6B on p.137

f Ask and answer the questions with a partner.

1 Do you sleep … ?
  • for eight hours   • for five or six hours
  • twice every night
2 When do you usually … ?
  • wake up   • get up   • go to bed
3 When do you usually … ?
  • go to work or school   • finish work or school
  • get home in the evening

Language Plus *for, from … to … , until*

8 hours
11:00 pm   7:00 am

*I sleep **for** eight hours.*
*I sleep **from** 11:00 **to** 7:00.*
*I sleep **until** 7:00.*

g **Sound and spelling** Consonant groups

1 ▶2.76 These words start with two consonant sounds together. Listen and practise saying them.
sleep   **br**eakfast   **tw**elve

2 ▶2.77 Listen to the words in the box. Underline the two consonant sounds that are together.

play	small	bread	fruit	flat	study	speak

3 Practise saying the words.

2 LISTENING

a ▶2.78 Listen to an interview with Paul. What are his answers to the questions?

1 Do you go to bed early?
2 When do you wake up?
3 What do you do then?
4 What about your wife? Does she wake up?

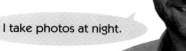

I take photos at night.

Paul

b 💬 Talk about the questions with a partner.

1 What do you think about Paul's daily routine?
2 What do you think about his photos? Think of adjectives to talk about them.

3 GRAMMAR Present simple: he / she / it questions

a Complete the questions in the table with *do* or *does*.

you	he / she / it
___Do___ you go to bed early?	_____ she wake up?
When _____ you wake up?	When _____ he get up?

b ▶ Now go to Grammar Focus 6B on p.122

c ▶2.81 Pronunciation Listen to the questions with *when* in 3a and notice the stressed words. Tick (✓) the words we stress.

1 ☐ question word (*when*)
2 ☐ *do*
3 ☐ *up*

d Write questions about Beatriz and Anneli on page 50.

1 What time / Beatriz / finish work?
2 Where / her husband / work?
3 What time / he / get home?
4 When / Anneli / wake up?
5 What / she / do then?
6 How / she / feel in the morning?

e 💬 Ask and answer the questions in 3d with a partner.

f 💬 Ask about your partner's routine.

- the morning
- meals
- work / school / university
- the evening
- sleep

When do you get up?   I get up at 7:30.

g 💬 Work with a new partner. Ask questions about their <u>first</u> partner's routine.

When does Liza get up?   Liza gets up at 7:30.

4 SPEAKING

▶ Communication 6B Student A go to p.105. Student B go to p.113.

Learn to make and accept offers

P Emphasising what you say 2
W An email about your day

1 LISTENING

a It's your first week in a new flat. Tick (✓) four things you need.

1 ☐ a bowl   4 ☐ a spoon
2 ☐ a glass   5 ☐ a knife
3 ☐ a cup   6 ☐ a plate

b 💬 Tell a partner your ideas in 1a. Do you need the same things?

c ▶2.82 Watch or listen to Part 1. Answer the questions.

1 Who do Megan and Sophia meet?
2 Where do they all go?

d ▶2.82 Watch or listen to Part 1 again. <u>Underline</u> the correct word.

1 The flowers are for *Megan* / *Sophia*.
2 Megan and James want *tea* / *coffee*.
3 Sophia needs another *cup* / *spoon*.
4 Sophia wants to go shopping *today* / *tomorrow*.

2 USEFUL LANGUAGE Making and accepting offers 1

a ▶2.83 Complete the conversations with the words in the box. Listen and check.

thanks   please   like (x2)

1 **SOPHIA** Would you _____ a cup of coffee?
  JAMES Yes, _____.
2 **SOPHIA** … I have biscuits! Would you _____ one, Megan?
  MEGAN No, it's OK, _____.

b ▶2.83 Pronunciation Listen to the mini-conversations in 2a again. Do you hear a /l/ or a /d/ sound in *would*? Listen again and repeat.

c ▶2.84 Put A's questions in the correct order in the conversation. Listen and check.

A like a / would you / cup of tea ?
B Yes, please.
A piece of cake / you like a / and would ?
B No, it's OK, thanks.

d 💬 Practise the conversation in 2c with a partner. Ask about different food and drinks.

Would you like a glass of orange juice?

Yes, please.

Would you like a sandwich?

No, thanks.

3 LISTENING AND USEFUL LANGUAGE
Making and accepting offers 2

a ▶️2.85 Watch or listen to Part 2. Answer the questions.

1 What does James want to do?
2 Do Sophia and Megan want him to help?

b ▶️2.86 Complete the sentences with words in the box. Listen and check.

can   help   I'll

1 I _____ go with you.
2 I'll _____ you buy things.
3 _____ come with you.

c ▶️2.87 Do these replies answer yes or no? Listen and check.

That's great, thanks.   Don't worry, it's OK.
Thanks, but I'm fine.   Thank you, that's very kind.

d ▶️2.88 Complete the conversation with the words in the box. Listen and check.

great   can   help   right   supermarket

A I need to go to the ¹_____.
B I ²_____ come with you.
A That's ³_____! And I need to make dinner.
B I'll ⁴_____ you.
A All ⁵_____, thank you very much.

e 💬 Practise the conversation in 3d with a partner.

f 💬 Use different words and expressions to make a new conversation.

> I need to go to the shops.
>
> I'll go with you.

4 PRONUNCIATION
Emphasising what you say 2

a ▶️2.89 Listen to the sentences and notice the strong stress. Then listen again and repeat.

1 I can go with you.   2 I'll come with you.

b ▶️2.90 Listen to the mini-conversations. Underline the strong stress.

Conversation 1
A I can't do this exercise.
B Joe can help you.
Conversation 2
C I need to get to the station this afternoon.
D I'll drive you.

c 💬 Practise the mini-conversations in 4b with a partner.

5 SPEAKING

a 💬 You're in a café with your partner. Use the ideas below to make a conversation.

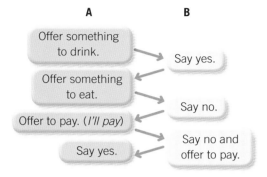

6 WRITING

a Read part of an email from Sophia to her sister. She writes about a day in her life in London. Where do Sophia and Megan have coffee? Why?

> I walk to work every day because my flat is near the office. I start work at 8:30 and I finish at 5:30. I work with Megan. We go out to a café for coffee every day because the coffee machine in the office isn't very good. We also have lunch there. They have nice sandwiches and chocolate cake – my favourite! Megan always says, 'I'll pay.' She's very nice.

b ▶ Now go to Writing Plus 6C on p.156 for *because* and *also*.

c Write about a day in your life. Use *because* and *also*.

d Read about your partner's day. Do you do the same?

🔄 **Unit Progress Test**

CHECK YOUR PROGRESS

You can now do the Unit Progress Test.

UNIT 6
Review

1 GRAMMAR

a Tick (✓) the sentences that are correct. Correct the mistakes.

> My sister doesn't lives at home.
  My sister doesn't live at home.

> ✓ I don't study Russian.

1 ☐ She don't like cake.
2 ☐ Marcus doesn't meets many people.
3 ☐ This town doesn't have a university.
4 ☐ I work not on Fridays.
5 ☐ We don't talk much at work.
6 ☐ Isabella speaks not French.

b Complete the sentences with *do, don't, does* or *doesn't*.

1 _____ your sister work in a bank?
No, she 2 _____.

3 _____ you meet people at work?
Yes, I 4 _____.

5 _____ you and your friends play football?
No, we 6 _____.

c Write present simple questions with the words and phrases.

> what time / you / get up
  What time do you get up?

1 what / you / eat in the morning
2 where / your brother / work
3 you / speak / English
4 your teacher / speak / French
5 what time / the lesson / start
6 when / it / finish

d 💬 Ask and answer the questions in 1c.

2 VOCABULARY

a Complete the job words.

1 w_____s   2 t___i d___r   3 d____r
4 r_____t   5 t____r   6 c___f

b Complete the table with the words and phrases in the box.

| arrive | get | start | to bed | lunch | shower | ~~to school~~ |

go	*to school* / to work 1 _____
wake 2 _____	up
3 _____ finish	work
have	breakfast / 4 _____ / dinner a 5 _____ a coffee
6 _____ / get	home

c 💬 What do you do every day? Tell a partner.

3 SOUND AND SPELLING

a ▶2.91 Look at the information in the table.

/ʌ/	/ɔː/
up, l**u**nch, c**u**p, r**u**gby c**o**me, l**o**vely, w**o**rry	sp**or**t, b**or**ing f**our** sm**all**, **al**ways

b ▶2.92 Are the **marked** sounds the same (S) or different (D)? Practise saying the words.

1 **al**ways – b**or**ing
2 sm**all** – l**u**nch
3 l**o**vely – r**u**gby
4 f**our** – c**u**ps
5 sp**or**t – w**o**rry
6 c**o**me – **u**p

c ▶2.93 Match the words that start with the same consonant group. Practise saying the words.

| bread | class | ~~flowers~~ | player | sport | start | twenty |

> **fl**at – ___*flowers*___
1 **tw**elve – _____
2 **st**udy – _____
3 **pl**ate – _____
4 **cl**ock – _____
5 **br**eakfast – _____
6 **sp**oon – _____

CAN DO OBJECTIVES

- Talk about things you want to buy
- Talk about the clothes that people wear
- Ask about and pay for things in a shop

UNIT 7
Shopping and fashion

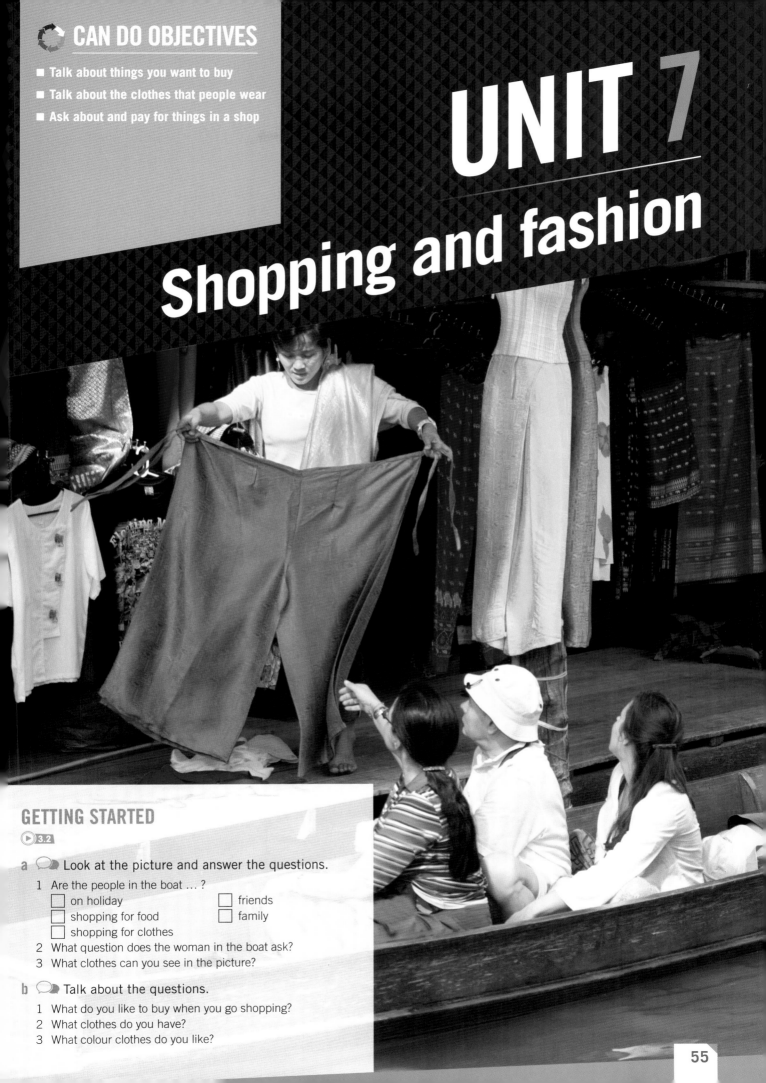

GETTING STARTED

▶ 3.2

a 💬 Look at the picture and answer the questions.

1 Are the people in the boat … ?
- [ ] on holiday
- [ ] shopping for food
- [ ] shopping for clothes
- [ ] friends
- [ ] family

2 What question does the woman in the boat ask?

3 What clothes can you see in the picture?

b 💬 Talk about the questions.

1 What do you like to buy when you go shopping?
2 What clothes do you have?
3 What colour clothes do you like?

55

1 READING AND VOCABULARY Common objects 2

a Read about three places to shop. Which place is in the picture?

b Which place is good for these people?

1 'I want a new bed for my flat.'
2 'I love old books and magazines.'
3 'I always finish work at 7:00 pm.'
4 'I think old lamps are beautiful.'

c Look at the picture and read about The Saturday Market again. Find the words for objects a–f.

d 💬 Talk with other students about which object you would like to buy in the picture. Say why. Which object do most people want?

e ▶ Now go to Vocabulary Focus 7A on p.133

f Sound and spelling /b/, /p/, /g/ and /k/

1 Complete the words in the table. They are all common objects.

Sound 1 /b/	Sound 2 /p/	Sound 3 /g/	Sound 4 /k/
_ag foot_all	_lant _late _icture	_lass _uitar	_up suit_ase _lo_ _

2 ▶3.4 Listen and check.

3 Which sound is spelled in different ways in the table?

4 💬 Practise saying the words.

g 💬 Work in pairs.

Student A: you have a market stall. Write five things you sell. Don't show Student B. Student B: what does Student A sell?

> Do you sell guitars?   No, sorry.

> Do you have glasses?   Yes, I do. Here you are.

SHOPPING

Places to go

Books & Co.
Open 9 am–6 pm

A very interesting bookshop. They sell old and new books and they also have magazines, pictures, old photographs and music. If you like old books and pictures, this is the place for you.

The Saturday Market
Open 6 am–4 pm

Here you can buy something for your home or you can just look around. They sell lots of old things. You can buy clocks, radios, suitcases, lamps, pictures, chairs … anything!

The Mega Home Store
Open 8 am–8 pm

A great place to buy things for your home. They sell beds, pillows, tables, chairs and lamps. Everything is new, but it isn't expensive. There's also a good café with drinks, pizzas and sandwiches.

2 LISTENING AND GRAMMAR
this, that, these, those

a ▶ **3.5** Sue and Mike are at a market stall. Listen to their conversation and answer the questions.

1 Who likes the picture and the chairs?
2 Who likes old objects, Sue or Mike?
3 How much is the radio?
4 Does Mike think it's a good price?

b ▶ **3.6** Listen to Sue. Complete the sentences with *this*, *that*, *these* or *those*.

1 'I like _____ picture. What do you think?'
2 'Or _____ chairs. They're really nice.'
3 'Oh, look. _____ books are interesting.'
4 'Look at _____ radio. That's so cool.'

c Complete the table with the words in 2b.

Singular	this	
Plural		

Which words mean … ?

1 here, near me   2 there, not near me

d **Sound and spelling** *this*, *that*, *these* and *those*

1 ▶ **3.7** Listen to *this*, *that*, *these* and *those*. Which words … ?
 • have a short vowel sound
 • have a long vowel sound
 • end in a /s/ sound
 • end in a /z/ sound

2 💬 Practise saying the words.

e ▶ Now go to Grammar Focus 7A on p.122

f 💬 You and your partner are in the shop below. Talk about the objects in the box with *this*, *that*, *these* or *those*.

bags plates guitar picture chair books lamp

Look at those bags.
They're really nice.

I like this chair –
it's a great colour!

3 VOCABULARY Prices

a ▶ **3.9** Listen to the prices. Tick (✓) the phrase you hear.

1 £3.80
 a ☐ three pound eighty
 b ☐ three pounds eighty
 c ☐ three pound and eighty

2 €25
 a ☐ twenty-five euro
 b ☐ twenty-five euros
 c ☐ twenty-five of euros

b ▶ **3.10** Practise saying the prices below. Listen and check.

1 £5.99   3 €4.50
2 $16.50   4 $100

c ▶ **3.11** Read and listen to the conversation. Then complete the gaps.

A Excuse me. ¹_____ _____ is that **clock**?
B ²_____ €13.50.
A Hmm. And ³_____ _____ are these **cups**?
B ⁴_____ €5 each.

d 💬 Practise the conversation in 3c with a partner. Change the **marked** words and the prices.

e 💬 How much are these things in your country?
 • a cup of coffee in a café   • a kilo of apples
 • a phone   • a bottle of water

4 SPEAKING

▶ **Communication 7A**
Student A go to p.106.
Student B go to p.111.

THEY MAKE COLOURFUL CLOTHES, BUT DO THEY WEAR THEM?

Fashion designers often make very different and interesting clothes for people, but they sometimes wear boring clothes. They often wear the same clothes and the same colours.

Tom Ford makes beautiful clothes, for men and for women, but he often wears a white shirt and a black or dark grey jacket.

1 VOCABULARY Clothes

a Look at the pictures of the models and the fashion designers. Which clothes do you like?

b 3.12 Match the words in the box with a–g in the pictures. Listen and check.

> jacket   coat   shirt   skirt   trousers   T-shirt   dress

c Which clothes do you often wear together?

d **Sound and spelling** /ʃ/ and /dʒ/
1 3.13 Listen and practise these sounds.
  1 /ʃ/ **sh**irt   2 /dʒ/ **j**acket
2 3.14 What sound do the **marked** letters have in the words in the box? Listen and add the words to the sound groups below.

> **G**erman   interna**ti**onal   fa**sh**ion   lar**ge**   langua**ge**   villa**ge**   **s**ugar

Sound 1 /ʃ/	Sound 2 /dʒ/
shirt	jacket

3 Practise saying the words.

e ▶ Communication 7B Student A go to p.104. Student B go to p.110.

2 READING

a Read about the fashion designers. What is the same about them?

b Read the text again. Are the sentences true or false? Correct the false sentences.
1 Fashion designers sometimes wear boring clothes.
2 Tom Ford never wears a black jacket.
3 Carolina Herrera often wears a white skirt.
4 Alexander Wang usually wears a jacket.

c Is it a good idea for fashion designers to wear their clothes? Why / Why not?

3 VOCABULARY Colours

a Look at the picture of Tom Ford. Complete the sentence about him with colours in the box.

> black ● grey ● white ○

Tom Ford often wears a _____ shirt and a _____ or dark _____ jacket.

Carolina Herrera makes clothes with lots of different colours, but she usually wears a black skirt and a white shirt.

Alexander Wang is a young designer with unusual ideas, but he usually wears a white T-shirt, black jeans and a black jacket.

Language Plus *dark / light*

■ **dark** *blue*	□ **light** *blue*
■ **dark** *green*	□ **light** *green*

b ▶ Now go to Vocabulary Focus 7B on p.152

c 💬 Work with a partner.
Student A: choose a picture in 1a. Don't tell your partner! Talk about the colours and the clothes.
Student B: guess the picture your partner talks about.

Then swap roles.

4 LISTENING

a ▶3.17 Listen to Kate and Giuseppe Costa. Tick (✓) the clothes you hear.

☐ T-shirt   ☐ skirt   ☐ shoes
☐ jeans   ☐ trousers   ☐ shirt

b ▶3.17 Listen again and complete the information.

who?	what clothes?	why?
Greg	_____	*doesn't wear / doesn't like*
Sara	_____	*doesn't wear / doesn't like*
Giuseppe	_____	*doesn't wear / doesn't like*

5 GRAMMAR Possessive 's; Revision of adverbs

a ▶3.18 Complete the sentences with a name from 4b. Listen and check.

1 **GIUSEPPE** Is this my old T-shirt?
  KATE No, it's _____'s T-shirt. (= It's **his** T-shirt.)
2 **GIUSEPPE** Are these your jeans?
  KATE No, they're _____'s jeans. (= They're **her** jeans.)

b ▶ Now go to Grammar Focus 7B on p.122

c 💬 Look at the picture of Greg, Sara, Giuseppe and Kate. Ask and answer questions about the Costa family.

> Who's Giuseppe?
> He's Kate's husband.

d ▶3.20 Kate talks about the people in her office. Put the word in brackets in the correct place in the sentences. Listen and check.

Everyone wears different clothes at work. [1]My boss wears a blouse and trousers (always). [2]She wears a skirt (never) – she doesn't like them. [3]Johnnie wears jeans and a white shirt (usually), [4]but he wears black trousers (sometimes). [5]And Fran wears a dress (often), [6]but on Fridays she wears jeans (usually).

e 💬 Think of people you work or study with. What do they usually wear? Tell a partner.

6 SPEAKING

a Put the words and phrases in the correct order to make questions. Write another question with your own idea.

1 wear / at work (*or* school) / do you / what ?
2 wear / do you / what colour clothes ?
3 your brother's (*or* sister's, father's, mother's) clothes / do you / wear ?
4 in your home / do you / wear shoes ?

b 💬 Ask and answer the questions in 6a. Add extra information to your answers.

> What do you wear at work?
> I usually wear a blue or black dress and dark shoes. I like dark colours.

The Costa family

7C Everyday English
Can I help you?

1 LISTENING

a Number the things you can buy from 1 to 4.
1 = I like going shopping for this / these very much.
4 = I really don't like going shopping for this / these.

☐ food   ☐ clothes   ☐ things for the home   ☐ IT things

b 💬 Talk with a partner about your ideas in 1a. Do you like shopping for the same things?

c ▶3.21 Watch or listen to Part 1. Answer the questions.

1 Who sees some nice cups?   2 Who buys something?

d ▶3.21 Watch or listen to Part 1 again. Complete the information about the cups with a number.

1 Price: £ _____   3 Sophia needs: _____
2 Number in the shop: _____   4 Megan wants: _____

2 USEFUL LANGUAGE
Going shopping 1

a ▶3.22 Who says each expression – the customer (C) or the shop assistant (S)? Listen and check.

1 How much are these cups?
2 I'd like two of these cups, please.
3 They're three pounds each.
4 Certainly.
5 Can I look around?
6 Can I help you?
7 Of course.

b ▶3.23 Put the conversation in the correct order. Listen and check.

☐ It's fifteen pounds.
☐ Certainly.
☐ It's ten pounds for the small one.
☐1 Can I help you?
☐ And how much is the small bowl?
☐ OK, then I'd like the large bowl, please.
☐ Yes, you can. How much is this large bowl?

c 💬 Practise the conversation in 2b with a partner.

d 💬 Practise the conversation in 2b again, but ask about glasses. Change the prices.

3 PRONUNCIATION Joining words

a ▶3.24 Listen and notice the extra sounds in these sentences.

1 We /j/ only have three.
2 I'd like two /w/ of these cups.

💬 Practise saying the sentences.

b Complete the rules with the sounds in the box.

/w/   /j/

We add a _____ sound between words ending with /iː/ and words starting with a vowel.
We add a _____ sound between words ending with /uː/ and words starting with a vowel.

c ▶3.25 Listen to these sentences. Which extra /j/ or /w/ sound can you hear? Listen again and repeat.

1 Would you like two or three?
2 These are for me and you.
3 Would you like three or four?
4 Are they for you or me?

d 💬 Practise the sentences in 3c with a partner.

4 LISTENING AND USEFUL LANGUAGE
Going shopping 2

a ⓟ 3.26 Watch or listen to Part 2. Are the sentences true or false?

1 Megan pays five pounds.
2 She uses a card to pay.
3 Sophia doesn't buy anything.

b ⓟ 3.27 Complete the sentences with words in the box. Listen and check.

your	that's	here's	you	no

S OK, _____ two pounds, please.
C Here _____ are.
S Enter _____ PIN, please.
C OK, _____ problem.
S _____ your receipt.

c ⓟ 3.28 Complete a conversation between a shop assistant and customer. Use phrases in 4b. Listen and check.

C How much … ? (*shoes*)
S Twenty pounds.
C Here …
S Enter …
C OK …
S And … receipt

d 💬 Practise the conversation in 4c with a partner. Change the things you buy and the price.

5 SPEAKING

▶ Communication 7C
Student A go to p.105.
Student B go to p.112.

6 WRITING

a Sophia saw an online advertisement.

For sale

Chairs, lamps, small tables, a big bed – all in good condition. Not expensive!
Email me for more information:
jack@icemail.com

Read her email. What information does she want to know?

Dear Jack,

You have an online ad for things you want to sell. I need a chair, a bed and a lamp. How old are these things? How much are they? Can I pay online by credit card?

Thank you!

Sophia

b ▶ Now go to Writing Plus 7C on p.157 for Commas, exclamation marks and question marks.

c You see these online advertisements.

For sale
CDs – lots of different music – old and new: pop, techno, jazz, classical and more. Cheap prices!
Email me for more information:
harry@antiques.co.uk

For sale
Books for learning English – dictionaries, grammar books, coursebooks. All in good condition.
Email me for more information:
melissa@mymail.com

Write an email to ask about one of the advertisements. Here are some ideas:

You have a / an / some …
I need …
How old … ?

How much … ?
Can I pay … ?

d Read a partner's email. What objects does your partner ask about? Do you ask about the same things?

 Unit Progress Test

CHECK YOUR PROGRESS

You can now do the Unit Progress Test.

UNIT 7
Review

1 GRAMMAR

a Complete the sentences with the phrases in the box.

these   this   those   that's

1 _____ is my dad's car.

2 I love _____ flowers.

3 _____ an expensive car.

4 _____ flowers in the windows are nice!

b Underline the correct answers to complete the conversation.

JO   Hi Lee. Do you know Kate? ¹*This / That / These* are ²*Kate's / Kates / Kates'* daughters, Amy and Anna.

LEE   Hello! Nice to meet you, girls. Who's who?

JO   This ³*is / are* Amy.

ANNA   And I'm Anna.

LEE   I like your bag, Anna.

ANNA   Oh, thanks. It's my ⁴*dads / dads' / dad's*. Amy and I have a swimming lesson today.

JO   Yes, the ⁵*girl's / girls / girls'* lesson starts at nine.

ANNA   And then we go to the café!

c 🗨 Practise the conversation in 1b in groups of three.

2 VOCABULARY

a Complete the names of these common objects.

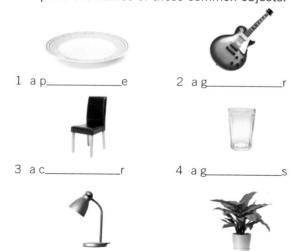

1 a p_____e

2 a g_____r

3 a c_____r

4 a g_____s

5 a l_____p

6 a p_____t

---

b Complete the descriptions using the colours and clothes.

white   light blue   light brown   red   green   dark blue

shirt   coat   skirt   jeans   shoes

1 a _____ dress
2 _____ trousers and black _____
3 a grey _____ and a _____ jacket
4 a light green _____ and a _____ hat
5 a _____ blouse and a red _____
6 dark blue _____ and a _____ T-shirt

c 🗨 How many hats / coats / jackets / shoes do you have? What colour are they? Tell a partner.

3 SOUND AND SPELLING

a ▶3.29 Answer the questions. Practise saying the words.

1 Which words have the /k/ sound? Underline them.

suitcase   clock   place   chair   cup   jacket   coat   dark

2 Which words have the /b/ sound? Underline them.

blue   black   brown   blouse   bed   bowl

3 Which words have the /p/ sound? Underline them.

pink   lamp   photograph   picture   pillow   plate   plant

4 Which words have the /g/ sound? Underline them.

magazine   bag   light   grey   green   thing

b ▶3.30 Complete the table with the words in the box. Practise saying the words.

dress   ~~shoes~~   sugar   Spain   international   jeans
large   fashion   T-shirt   jacket   Germany   this   skirt

/ʃ/	/s/	/dʒ/
shoes		

CAN DO OBJECTIVES

- Talk about past events
- Describe events in the past
- Make and respond to suggestions

UNIT 8
Past events

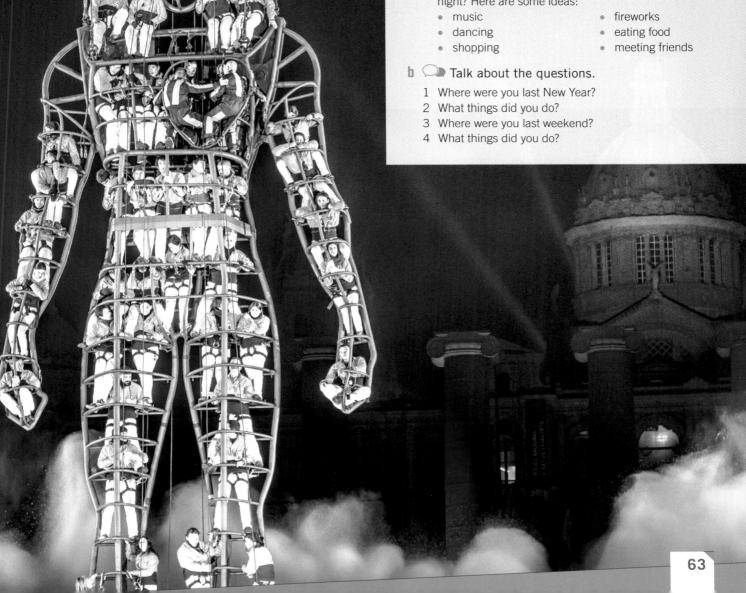

GETTING STARTED

▶ 3.31

a 💬 Look at the picture of a New Year show and talk about the questions.

1 Would you like to be there? Why / Why not?
2 What other things do you think happened here that night? Here are some ideas:
- music
- dancing
- shopping
- fireworks
- eating food
- meeting friends

b 💬 Talk about the questions.

1 Where were you last New Year?
2 What things did you do?
3 Where were you last weekend?
4 What things did you do?

8A I was on tour with my band

1 READING

a 💬 Look at the events in pictures a–d. Choose one you like and one you don't like. Tell a partner. Say why.

a party

a concert

a sports game

a meeting

b Read about Cara, Antonio and Ava. Which events in 1a do they talk about?

c Read the texts again. Which cities does each person talk about?

d 💬 Talk about Cara, Antonio and Ava's lives with a partner. Who would you like to meet? Why?

Hi Jenny,
Thanks for your email. I'm sorry my reply is late! I was in New York three days ago for work and then I was in Dublin yesterday at a meeting about newspaper photography. Life's busy at the moment!
Cara

'Yesterday I was in Dublin.'

The people in OUR TEAM ...

My name's Antonio Marotto. I'm the doctor for our team. It's a great job – I really like helping our players. I often go away with the team. We were in Newcastle two weeks ago for a game and we were in Bristol last week. It's fun to travel with the team.

'At a game in Madrid. It was the World Cup!'

'In this photo we were in Milan.'

Ava on THE ROAD ...

Hi everyone, it's Ava. Last week I was on tour with my band in Europe: three cities in five days. We were in Munich on Wednesday and then we were in Vienna on Thursday. But Saturday was the best night. We were in Milan and about 1,000 people were at our concert.

2 GRAMMAR Past simple: *be* positive

a Complete the table. Find examples of the past simple of *be* in the texts about Cara, Antonio and Ava.

+	
I ¹_____	we ³_____
you were	you were
he / she / it ²_____	they were

b ▶3.32 **Pronunciation** Listen to sentences 1–4. Are *was* and *were* stressed? Practise saying the sentences.

1 We were in Munich. 3 We were in Newcastle.
2 I was in Madrid. 4 I was in New York.

c ▶ Now go to Grammar Focus 8A Part 1 on p.124

d Write sentences about where you were:
   • this morning • last night • yesterday afternoon

e 💬 Compare your sentences in 2d with a partner. Were you in the same places?

> Boris and I were at the supermarket yesterday.

3 VOCABULARY Past time expressions

a Today is Friday of week 3. Put the number of sentences 1–4 in the correct place on the timeline.

week 1	week 2	week 3
		Monday Tuesday Wednesday Thursday (Friday)

1 We were in Munich on <u>Wednesday</u>.
2 We were in Newcastle two <u>weeks</u> ago.
3 … we were in Bristol last <u>week</u>.
4 I was in Dublin <u>yesterday</u>.

b Look at the <u>underlined</u> words in 3a. Change them with words in the box.

> months   this morning   Saturday   year

c ▶ Now go to Vocabulary Focus 8A on p.144

d 💬 Work in pairs.
Student A: say a past time expression.
Student B: say where a person you know was.

Then swap roles.

> last weekend
> My parents were in Izmir last weekend.
> two years ago
> My friend Marco was in Russia two years ago.

4 LISTENING AND GRAMMAR Past simple: *be* negative and questions

a ▶3.37 Listen to Cara, Antonio and Ava talking to friends. Write the correct name in each conversation.
Conversation 1 _____
Conversation 2 _____
Conversation 3 _____

b ▶3.37 Match events 1–3 with adjectives a–c. Listen again and check.
1 the meeting   a exciting
2 the concert   b interesting
3 the game   c fun

c ▶3.38 Listen to Conversation 1 again. Complete the conversation with the words in the box.

> was (x2)   were (x2)   wasn't

LARRY   _____ you at work yesterday?
CARA   Yes, I _____, but I _____ here in the office.
LARRY   Where _____ you?
CARA   I was at a meeting in Dublin.
LARRY   Oh, _____ it interesting?
CARA   Yes, it was really interesting.

d ▶ Now go to Grammar Focus 8A Part 2 on p.124

e ▶3.42 Complete the conversation with *was*, *were*, *wasn't* or *weren't*. Listen and check.
A You _____ at work yesterday.
B No, it _____ a holiday for me.
A Nice. _____ you at home all day?
B No, I _____. I _____ in town in the morning and then I _____ at a party last night.
A _____ the party good?
B Yes, it _____ a lot of fun.

f 💬 Practise the conversation in 4e with a partner. Change some of the information.

> I was at a football game in the morning and then at the cinema last night.
> Was the film good?

5 SPEAKING

▶ Communication 8A Student A go to p.106.
Student B go to p.111. Student C go to p.113.

8B Who killed Lady Grey?

Learn to describe events in the past

G Past simple: positive
V Free time activities

1 READING AND LISTENING

a 💬 Look at picture a and answer the questions with a partner.

1 Do you think this is … ?   a breakfast   b lunch   c dinner
2 Are the people … ?   a rich   b poor

b Read *Who killed Lady Grey?* and <u>underline</u> the correct answers.

1 Lady Grey's diamonds were in the *bedroom / living room*.
2 The guests were there until *3:00 / 4:00*.
3 Someone killed Lady Grey with *a bag / a knife*.
4 At 3:15 the diamonds *were / weren't* in the bag.

c ▶3.43 Read and listen to the police interviews. Which people are A, B and C on the plan?

d 💬 Who do you think killed Lady Grey? Why?

Who killed Lady Grey?

Lord and Lady Grey live in a big house in London. Lady Grey has some very expensive diamonds. They are always in a bag under her bed.

One weekend, Lord and Lady Grey had guests at their house for lunch. After lunch, Lady Grey was tired, so she went to her bedroom to sleep. Lord Grey stayed with the guests until 3:00 and then they went home. At 3:15 he went to the bedroom with some tea for his wife. Lady Grey was on the floor. She was dead. There was a knife next to her and a bag … but no diamonds.

The police interviews

James Green 'After lunch, I went with Lord Grey to the living room and we had coffee. We saw Jane White through the window. She was in the garden with a book. At 3:00 I went home with Sue Black. She lives near me, so we went in my car.'

Jane White 'After lunch, I went into the garden. Sue Black was with me. She said 'Oh, my phone is on the table!' and she went back into the house. I stayed in the garden and read a book. At 3:00, I went home and watched TV. '

Sue Black 'After lunch, I went into the garden. I saw Jane White in the garden and we went for a walk together until 3:00. Then we all went home. James Green lives near me, so I went with him in his car.'

Lord Grey 'We had lunch until 2:00, then I stayed in the living room with James Green. We had coffee together and we talked about business. At 3:00 the guests went home.'

2 GRAMMAR Past simple: positive

a Read the police interviews again and find the past simple forms of the verbs in the table.

A		B	
Verb	Past form	Verb	Past form
kill	killed	go	went
talk		have	
stay		see	
watch		read	

b Answer the questions about the table in 2a.

1 What do we add to the verbs in A to make the past form?
2 Do the verbs in B all change in the same way or in different ways?

c Sound and spelling /t/ and /d/

1 ▶ **3.44** Listen and practise these sounds.
   1 /t/ talk**ed**   2 /d/ kill**ed**

2 ▶ **3.45** Listen to the past forms in the box. Which -*ed* endings sound … ?
   • more like /t/   • more like /d/

stayed   watched   finished   worked   played

3 💬 Practise saying the words.

d 💬 Cover the table in 2a. Test a partner.
Student A: say a verb.
Student B: say the past form.

Then swap roles.

e ▶ Now go to Grammar Focus 8B on p.124

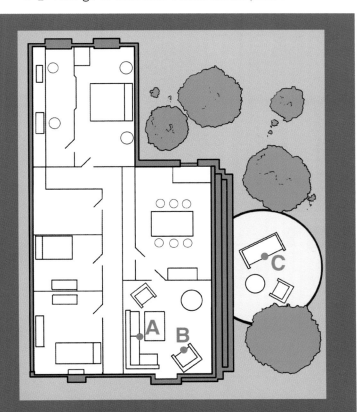

3 LISTENING AND VOCABULARY Free time activities

a ▶ **3.48** Complete the sentences with the correct past simple verbs. Listen and check.

JAMES   I ¹w_____ home with Sue Black.
SUE   We ²w_____ for a walk.
JANE   I ³r_____ a book in the garden. At home I ⁴w_____ TV.
LORD GREY   We ⁵h_____ coffee together. We ⁶t_____ about business.

b Match verbs 1–6 with a word or phrase in the box to make more past simple phrases.

a drink   to a café   at home   breakfast   a film shopping   to my friends   the newspaper

1 went _____, _____
2 read _____
3 stayed _____

4 had _____, _____
5 watched _____
6 talked _____

c ▶ **3.49** Listen to Jane White talk about what she did before she went to Lord and Lady Grey's house for lunch. Put pictures a–e in the correct order.

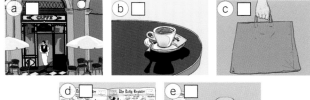

d ▶ **3.49** Complete what Jane White says with phrases in 3b. Then listen again and check.

'I ¹_____ at about 9:00. After that I ²_____. Then I went into town and I ³_____. After that I ⁴_____ near Lord and Lady Grey's house. A few of my friends were there. I talked to my friends and we ⁵_____ together.'

e ▶ Now go to Vocabulary Focus 8B on p.138

f Complete the sentences about free time activities.

1 When I was a child, I _____.
2 After work / university, I often _____.
3 At weekends I like to _____.
4 (your idea)

g 💬 Tell other students your sentences in 3f. What free time activities were / are popular … ?

a when everyone was a child
b after work / university
c at weekends

4 SPEAKING

▶ **Communication 8B** Student A go to p.106. Student B go to p.111.

Learn to make and respond to suggestions
P Main stress and tone
W Thank you note

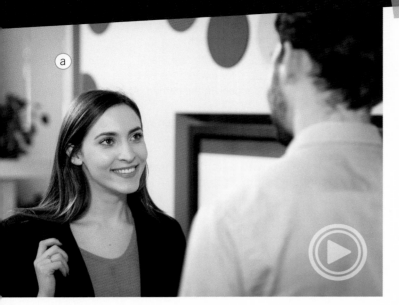

a

1 LISTENING

a 💬 Ask and answer the questions.

1 On the first day at work / university / school after the weekend, how do you feel?
2 What do you talk to your friends about on this day?

b Sophia arrives at work. Choose the answer you think is correct.

1 Sophia asks David about:
   a London and work
   b his home town and family
2 Sophia and Megan talk about:
   a shopping
   b a party

c ▶️ 3.52 Watch or listen to Part 1. Are your answers in 1b correct?

d ▶️ 3.52 Watch or listen to Part 1 again. Tick (✓) the correct sentence.

1 a ☐ Sophia helped Megan on Saturday.
  b ☐ Sophia doesn't like shopping.
  c ☐ Sophia and Megan both enjoyed shopping.

2 a ☐ Sophia wants to go shopping again.
  b ☐ Megan wants to go shopping this afternoon.
  c ☐ Sophia wants to go to a café and then go shopping.

e ▶️ 3.53 Watch or listen to Part 2. Who went to a party? Who watched TV?

f ▶️ 3.53 Watch or listen to Part 2 again and answer the questions.

1 What was the problem with the party?
2 What's difficult for Sophia?
3 What's Megan's idea for next weekend?
4 Does Sophia feel happy or sad at the end of the conversation? Why?

g 💬 Talk about the questions.

1 Is it difficult to meet new people in your town / city? Why / Why not?
2 What are good ways to meet new people?

b

2 USEFUL LANGUAGE Making and responding to suggestions

a ▶ **3.54** Listen to the conversations. <u>Underline</u> the word you hear. Are both options possible?

1 **MEGAN** We *can* / *could* go shopping again some time.
  SOPHIA Yes, OK. *Good* / *Great* idea.

2 **MEGAN** So, *shall we* / *let's* go there for the day next Saturday?
  SOPHIA OK, that's a *nice* / *lovely* idea.

b ▶ **3.55** Complete the conversation with the words in the box. Listen and check.

> we   idea   go   sorry

A Let's _____ for dinner on Saturday.
B Saturday? I'm _____, I can't. I'm away on Saturday.
A Shall _____ go on Sunday?
B Yes, that's a lovely _____.

c 💬 Practise the conversation in 2b with a partner.

d Complete the conversation with words or expressions in 2a and 2b. There is sometimes more than one answer.

A _____ go to the cinema tonight.
B _____, I'm not free. I have a dinner with my family.
A _____ go tomorrow night.
B OK, _____.

e 💬 Practise the conversation in 2d with a partner. Take turns to be A and B.

3 PRONUNCIATION Main stress and tone

a ▶ **3.56** Listen to the expressions. Notice the main stress.

1 Yes, that's a <u>great</u> idea.   2 Yes, that's a <u>lovely</u> idea.

b ▶ **3.56** Listen to the expressions in 3a again. Does the tone rise ↗ or fall ↘ after the main stress?

c 💬 Work with a partner.

Student A: say sentences 1 and 2.
Student B: answer with phrases in 3a.

1 Let's have a cup of coffee.
2 Shall we go for a walk?

Then swap roles.

4 SPEAKING

a Work in pairs. Read the ideas below and think about what you want to say.

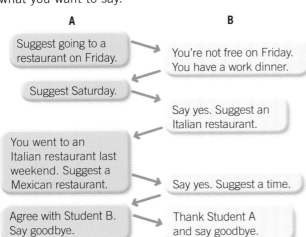

A
Suggest going to a restaurant on Friday.
Suggest Saturday.
You went to an Italian restaurant last weekend. Suggest a Mexican restaurant.
Agree with Student B. Say goodbye.

B
You're not free on Friday. You have a work dinner.
Say yes. Suggest an Italian restaurant.
Say yes. Suggest a time.
Thank Student A and say goodbye.

b 💬 Have a phone conversation with your partner. Then swap roles.

> Shall we go to a restaurant on Friday?

> I'm sorry, I'm not free. I have a work dinner.

5 WRITING

a Read Sophia's note to Megan. Why did Sophia write it?

> Dear Megan,
>
> This is a card to say thank you for your help on Saturday. It was fun to go shopping with you and you helped me find some good shops. I hope we can go shopping again some time soon.
>
> Best wishes,
> Sophia

b ▶ Now go to Writing Plus 8C on p.157 for Writing short emails, letters and notes.

c Write a note to a friend to thank them for something. Here are some ideas:

Here are some flowers / chocolates to say thank you for …
It was …   I hope …

d Read another student's note. What do they say thank you for?

⟳ Unit Progress Test

CHECK YOUR PROGRESS

You can now do the Unit Progress Test.

UNIT 8
Review

1 GRAMMAR

a Write past simple sentences and questions with *be* and the words and phrases.

> (?) where / you yesterday
> *Where were you yesterday?*
1 (+) I / in a meeting.
2 (?) / you OK
3 (–) James / at work this morning.
4 (?) where / he
5 (+) Yasmin and Adele / in New York two weeks ago.
6 (–) we / in Paris six years ago

b Complete the text with the past simple form of the verb in brackets.

Last week my family and I ¹_____ (be) in Dublin. We ²_____ (arrive) on Wednesday morning. First, we ³_____ (visit) my dad's family. My dad and his brothers ⁴_____ (talk) for a long time. Then we ⁵_____ (go) to a big museum in the city centre. We ⁶_____ (see) lots of interesting things there. In the evening we ⁷_____ (watch) a film at the cinema. We ⁸_____ (stay) at the Dylan Hotel. The rooms ⁹_____ (not / be) very big but I ¹⁰_____ (like) the bathroom and the food ¹¹_____ (be) great! Every morning I ¹²_____ (have) toast, eggs, fruit, coffee and cake for breakfast.

2 VOCABULARY

a Tick (✓) the correct answer.

Today is WEDNESDAY 14 OCTOBER 2015. It's 7:30 pm.

1 Wednesday 30 September 2015
   a ☐ two weeks ago
   b ☐ yesterday
2 2:30 pm Wednesday 14 October 2015
   a ☐ last night
   b ☐ this afternoon
3 October 2005
   a ☐ ten years ago
   b ☐ last month
4 Tuesday 13 October 2015
   a ☐ yesterday
   b ☐ a few days ago
5 Saturday 10 October 2015
   a ☐ this morning
   b ☐ last Saturday
6 Sunday 11 October 2015
   a ☐ six months ago
   b ☐ on Sunday

b 💬 Ask and answer questions with *Where were you ... ?* and a past time expression.

c Complete the table with the words and phrases in the box.

a computer game   a football match   a magazine   a pizza   the radio

have	a drink, a coffee, ¹_____, a shower
listen to	music, ²_____
watch	³_____, a film
read	a book, ⁴_____, the newspaper
play	the guitar, ⁵_____, football
go to	the cinema, a party, ⁶_____, a café

d Correct the sentences.

1 I was in Manchester before two weeks ago.
2 We were in Rome at weekend.
3 I had coffee with Lily at Friday.
4 We went a party yesterday.
5 I listened music last night.
6 We played the football this morning.

3 SOUND AND SPELLING

a ▶ 3.57 Look at the words in the box. Is the final sound /t/ or /d/? Complete the table. Practise saying the words.

~~killed~~   talked   stayed   watched
listened   played   helped

/t/	/d/
	killed

b ▶ 3.58 Look at the information in the table.

/eɪ/	/aɪ/
play, stay, day game, paper, radio great, grey	white, knife, wife night, right

c ▶ 3.59 Are the **marked** sounds the same (S) or different (D)? Practise saying the words.

1 white – n**igh**t
2 gr**ea**t – g**a**me
3 r**igh**t – d**ay**
4 st**ay** – gr**ey**
5 p**a**per – kn**i**fe
6 r**a**dio – pl**ay**

CAN DO OBJECTIVES

- Talk about travel and holiday experiences
- Talk about past holidays
- Make and respond to requests

UNIT 9
Holidays

GETTING STARTED

▶ 3.60

a 💬 Look at the picture and answer the questions.

1 What country do you think it is?
2 What transport can you see?
3 What time of year is it?
4 What is the weather in this place?

b 💬 Talk about the questions.

1 Where did you go on your last holiday?
2 What weather do you like on holiday? Why?

c 💬 Ask your partner one question about their last holiday.

71

Garden camping

How does it work?

Do you want a cheap holiday in a beautiful place? Why not camp in someone's garden? It's cheap and you can make new friends. We have more than 1,000 gardens in 70 countries and you can camp in them all!

Old house with a big garden. 20 minutes from the centre of Cambridge.

COST: $15 a night

HOW TO GET THERE: Go to Cambridge by bus from London. Then walk to the house from the bus station (5 minutes).

LAURENCE'S PLACE, CAMBRIDGE, ENGLAND

42 big tents with beds and showers inside. 40 minutes from the city of Marrakesh.

COST: $30 a night

HOW TO GET THERE: Fly to Marrakesh and then get a taxi or drive a car.

YOUSSEF'S PLACE, MARRAKESH, MOROCCO

1 READING

a Where do you usually stay on holiday? Here are some ideas:

- at a hotel
- at a hostel
- at a campsite
- with friends or family

b Read *How does it work?* on the *Garden camping* website. What do you think of the idea?

> It's a great idea!

> Hmm, interesting.

> No, thanks!

c Read about three gardens on the *Garden camping* website. Which answers (a–d) are incorrect? Correct the wrong answers.

1 Laurence's place:
   a old house   c in the centre
   b big garden   d near the bus station
2 Youssef's place:
   a small tents   c not in Marrakesh
   b showers   d not very cheap
3 Guadalupe's place:
   a big garden   c near some restaurants
   b pool   d expensive

2 VOCABULARY Transport

a ▶3.61 Find words on the *Garden camping* website to match pictures 1–5. Listen and check.

b Complete the tables.

| go _____ | bus |
| | plane |

| _____ | a bus |
| | a taxi |

c Find verbs in the texts that mean:
a go by car   b go by plane

d ▶ Now go to Vocabulary Focus 9A on p.153

e How do you … ?

1 go to work or university
2 go to a big town or city nearby
3 go home late at night
4 go to a party
5 go on holiday

> I usually go to work by bike.

Garden camping

HOME | **FIND A GARDEN** | REVIEWS | CONTACT US

House with a big garden and swimming pool. Free bikes. Near to restaurants, a river and a zoo.

COST: $4 a night

HOW TO GET THERE: Go to Villavicencio by plane or bus. Then get a taxi or another bus to our house.

GUADALUPE'S PLACE, CUMARAL, COLOMBIA

Alessandro

WEEK 3

Through the country by bus

We didn't go to big cities. We went by bus and we stayed in small places in the country. In one place we stayed with a family. We didn't stay in their house – we camped in their garden. We bought food in the town and we cooked meals in the house. And we went swimming every morning in their pool. It was very cheap and the family were very friendly. We stayed for four days!

3 GRAMMAR AND LISTENING
   Past simple: negative

a Read Alessandro's travel blog. Which place from the *Garden camping* website does he write about?

b Read the blog again. Tick (✓) the correct sentences.
   1 a They went to small places.   b They didn't go to small places.
   2 a They had a car.   b They didn't have a car.
   3 a They stayed in the house.   b They didn't stay in the house.
   4 a They used the kitchen.   b They didn't use the kitchen.

c Look at the b sentences in 3b. Complete the rule.

   Past simple negative (–):
   I / you / he / she / it / we / they + _____ + verb

d ▶ Now go to Grammar Focus 9A on p.126

e ▶3.68 Pronunciation Listen to the sentences. Is *didn't* stressed or unstressed?
   1 We didn't stay in their house.
   2 We didn't have a car.

f ▶3.69 Listen to Alessandro. He says more things about his trip. What does he say about … ?
   • emails   • money   • bikes   • photos

g 💬 What do you like about Alessandro's holiday? What don't you like?

h Think about your last holiday. Which sentences are true? If they aren't true, make them negative. Then write a true positive sentence.
   1 I stayed in a hotel.   5 I went to bed early.
   2 I visited museums.   6 I cooked my own food.
   3 I bought a lot of clothes.   7 I watched TV.
   4 I had my computer with   8 I read lots of books.
     me.

   1 I didn't stay in a hotel. I stayed in a hostel.

i 💬 Tell a partner your sentences in 3h.

> I didn't visit museums. I went to the zoo.

4 SPEAKING

▶ Communication 9A Student A go to p.107. Student B go to p.110.

Language Plus *go*

go to the cinema

go to work NOT ~~to the work~~

go home NOT ~~to home~~

go on holiday

f **Sound and spelling** the letter *a*
   1 ▶3.64 The letter *a* can have different sounds. Listen and practise the words.
     1 /æ/ t**a**xi 2 /ɑː/ c**a**r 3 /eɪ/ pl**a**ne 4 /ɒ/ w**a**tch
   2 ▶3.65 Listen to these words. Are the **marked** letters Sound 1, 2, 3 or 4?

wh**a**t	fl**a**t	tr**ai**n	f**a**ther

   3 ▶3.66 Listen to these words. Which one in each group has a different *a* sound?
     1 b**a**nk   w**a**nt   m**a**n
     2 h**a**ve   c**a**ke   Sp**ai**n
     3 p**a**rty   b**a**g   g**a**rden
     4 pl**a**nt   gl**a**ss   w**a**nt
   4 💬 Practise saying the words.

9B How did you get there?

1 VOCABULARY The seasons

a ▶3.70 Match the words in the box with pictures a–d. Listen and check.

> winter summer spring autumn

b 💬 Ask and answer the questions.

1 Do you have four seasons in your country?
2 Which seasons do you like? Which seasons don't you like?

2 READING

a Read about the Duncan family's holiday. What was different about this New Year for them?

b Complete Michael's notes with the words in the box.

> party shopping beach hot

Thursday: ¹_____ with family in Chapel Street
New Year's Eve: ²_____ in a park – great fireworks!
Friday: ³_____ and sunny weather; everyone went to the ⁴_____.

New Year down under

The Duncan family, from Edinburgh, went to Melbourne, Australia, for New Year. Read Michael Duncan's diary ...

Thursday 31 December
We went shopping in Chapel Street – it has lots of interesting shops, restaurants and cafés. The weather changes all the time here. It's hot and sunny one minute and then it's cold and rainy. We went to a big New Year's Eve party in a park in the evening. The children loved the fireworks.

Friday 1 January
Australia is 11 hours ahead of Scotland. New Year arrived early this year! It's also summer time here and it's very different to have New Year in the sun. I like the snowy, cold weather in Scotland at New Year, but in Melbourne it was very hot today and it didn't feel like New Year. Everyone went to the beach!

3 VOCABULARY The weather

a ▶ 3.71 What does Duncan say about the weather in Melbourne? Complete the sentences with *hot* or *cold*. Listen and check.

1 It's _____ and sunny and then it's _____ and rainy.

2 I like the snowy, _____ weather in Scotland at New Year.

Language Plus *like*

*I **like** sunny weather.* = I think sunny weather is good.
*What's the weather **like**?* = How's the weather?

b ▶ Now go to Vocabulary Focus 9B on p.145

c **Sound and spelling** the letter *o*

1 ▶ 3.74 The letter *o* can have different sounds. Listen and repeat the words.

1 /əʊ/ sn**ow**   2 /aʊ/ cl**ou**dy   3 /ɒ/ h**o**t

2 ▶ 3.75 Listen to these words. Are the **marked** letters Sound 1, 2 or 3?

h**o**liday   t**ow**n   c**o**ld

3 ▶ 3.76 Listen to these words. Which one in each group has a different *o* sound? Listen again and repeat.

1 g**o**t   j**o**b   g**o**
2 kn**ow**   n**o**t   sl**ow**
3 ph**o**ne   n**ow**   d**ow**n

d ▶ **Communication 9B** Student A go to p.107. Student B go to p.112.

4 LISTENING AND GRAMMAR
Past simple: questions

a ▶ 3.77 Listen to Kiril and Angie talk about summer holidays. Tick (✓) the correct sentence.

1 ☐ They're on holiday now.
2 ☐ They talk about past and future holidays.
3 ☐ They only talk about past holidays.

b ▶ 3.77 Listen again. Match 1–3 with a–c.

1 Kiril last year   a Greece
2 Angie last year   b the south of France
3 Angie two years ago   c Moscow

c ▶ 3.78 Listen to the questions from the conversation. Choose one word from the box to complete the three questions.

do   does   did

1 Where _____ you go on your summer holiday last year?
2 How _____ you get there?
3 _____ you enjoy it there?

d ▶ Now go to Grammar Focus 9B on p.126

e ▶ 3.81 Complete the two conversations about last weekend. Listen and check your answers.

Conversation 1
A go / cinema last weekend?
B Yes, I did.
A What / see?
B The new James Bond film.

Conversation 2
C go / restaurant last night?
D Yes, I did.
C Where / go?
D A new Thai restaurant.

f 💬 Tell a partner about last weekend. Use the conversations in 4e and your own ideas.

Did you see your friends last weekend?

Yes, I did.

Who did you see?

I saw Daniele.

g 💬 Work in new pairs. Tell your new partner about your first partner.

Matteo saw his friend Daniele last weekend.

5 SPEAKING

a Think about a past holiday. Make notes about the:
• place
• weather
• food
• things you did

b Write questions to ask about your partner's holiday.

1 When … the holiday? *When was the holiday?*
2 Where … go?
3 What … the weather like?
4 What … eat?
5 What … do?
6 (your idea for a question)

c 💬 Ask and answer the questions in 5b about your holiday.

When was the holiday?

It was last spring.

Where did you go?

We went to Lombok, in Indonesia.

What was the weather like?

It was hot and sunny.

75

9C Everyday English
Can you do something for me?

1 LISTENING

a 💬 Talk about a place near your town or city with a partner. Ask and answer the questions.

1 Where's a nice place to visit for a day? Why?
2 What can you see and do there?
3 Do you go there often?

b ▶3.82 Look at pictures a and b and talk about the questions. Watch or listen to Part 1 and check your answers.

1 Do you think Sophia and Megan like Henley?
2 What do they see in the shop?

c ▶3.82 Watch or listen to Part 1 again. Are the sentences true or false?

1 They decide to go to the museum before lunch.
2 Megan decides to go in the shop.
3 The clock is difficult to carry.

d 💬 What do you buy when you visit another place?

2 PRONUNCIATION Syllables and spelling

a ▶3.83 Listen to the **marked** word in the sentence. Do you hear all the letters?

It's very **different** from Toronto.

▶3.83 Listen again and repeat the **marked** word.

b ▶3.84 Listen to these words. Underline the letters you don't hear.

restaurant interesting favourite
every family vegetable camera

c 💬 Practise saying the words in 2c.

3 LISTENING

a ▶3.85 Look at picture c and answer the questions. Watch or listen to Part 2 and check your answers.

1 Who does Megan call? 2 What does she want?

b ▶3.85 Watch or listen to Part 2 again. Underline the correct answer.

1 Sophia and Megan *take the train / drive* home.
2 Megan says the problem is the *clock / weather*.
3 James *can / can't* meet Megan and Sophia at the station.

c 💬 Who do you usually ask for help – a friend or someone in your family? Why?

4 USEFUL LANGUAGE Making and responding to requests

a ▶3.86 Listen to the questions. Underline the word you hear. Then answer the question below.

1 *Can / Could* you take it for a minute?
2 *Can / Could* you do something for me?
3 *Can / Could* you pick us up from the station later, please?
4 *Can / Could* you meet us at the station, please?

Is it OK to use *can* and *could* in all the sentences?

b ▶3.87 Put the possible replies to the questions in 4a into the table. Listen and check your answers.

Of course.   No, I can't.   Yes, certainly.
I'm sorry, I can't.   Sure, no problem.

Yes	No

c ▶3.88 Complete mini-conversations 1 and 2 with the phrases in the box. Listen and check.

Oh, OK, I'll do it then.
Thanks, that's really kind of you.

1 **A** Could you help me with the shopping?
  B Sure, no problem.
  A _____.
2 **C** Can you get the children from school?
  D I'm sorry, I can't. I have a lot of work to finish.
  C _____.

d Work in pairs. Take turns to make requests and reply. Use the ideas below and *can / could*.

1 help me with my work   3 meet me after class
2 give me your book   4 phone me this evening

Could you meet me after class?

I'm sorry, I can't. I'm busy.

5 SPEAKING

a Work in pairs. You talk on the phone. Look at the ideas below and think about what you want to say.

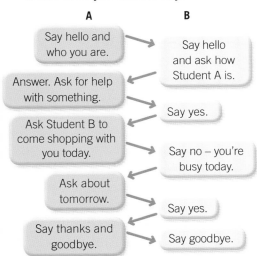

A
Say hello and who you are.
Answer. Ask for help with something.
Ask Student B to come shopping with you today.
Ask about tomorrow.
Say thanks and goodbye.

B
Say hello and ask how Student A is.
Say yes.
Say no – you're busy today.
Say yes.
Say goodbye.

b Have a phone conversation with your partner. Then swap roles.

6 WRITING

a Read about Sophia's weekend. What information about the clock is new?

Last weekend I went to Henley with my new friend, Megan. First, we went for a walk by the river. It was beautiful. Next, we went to a small museum and had lunch. Then, we went shopping and I saw a lovely clock. It was quite expensive (£150!), but I bought it and we took it back to London. It was really heavy! Henley is a nice town – it's very different from Toronto.

b Now go to Writing Plus 9C on p.158 for Making the order clear.

c Write an online post about a trip to another place. Here are some ideas:

Last weekend, / month, / summer, I went to … with …
First, we …   It was …   Next, we …   Then, we …
… is a nice / beautiful / lovely city / town / place.

d Read another student's online post. Do you like the activities he / she did?

 Unit Progress Test

CHECK YOUR PROGRESS

You can now do the Unit Progress Test.

UNIT 9
Review

1 GRAMMAR

a <u>Underline</u> the correct answers.

1 We didn't *stay / stayed* in a hotel last year.
2 I didn't *take / took* any photos this morning.
3 She *doesn't / didn't* buy a book yesterday.
4 They didn't *have / had* fish for dinner last night.
5 We *don't watched / didn't watch* a film last week.
6 He *didn't got / didn't get* a taxi to the airport.

b Look at the answers and complete the questions.

> ' *Did it rain* yesterday?' 'Yes, it did. It rained in the morning.'
1 '_____ football last week?' 'No, I didn't – but I played tennis!'
2 'What time _____ yesterday?' 'I got up at six o'clock.'
3 '_____ any photos at New Year?' 'Yes, I did. I took some photos at the party.'
4 'Where _____ yesterday?' 'I went to the park.'
5 '_____ your phone yesterday? 'Yes, of course! I use my phone every day!'
6 'What _____ for breakfast today?' 'I had cereal and coffee.'

c 💬 Work in pairs. Ask and answer the questions in 1b.

d Correct the past simple sentences.

> Where they did stay? *Where did they stay?*
1 Do you arrived last night?
2 Yes, I arrived.
3 No, I not.
4 What did you bought?
5 I didn't watched TV.
6 What you cooked?
7 We don't visit Pedro yesterday.
8 Saw you the garden?

2 VOCABULARY

a Write the words.

 ① ② ③

 ④ ⑤ ⑥

1 r i t a n _____
2 a t i x _____
3 r u n g e d u n d r o _____
4 m a r t _____
5 e l n a p _____
6 p i s h _____

b <u>Underline</u> the correct answers.

A Was it ¹*cold / wet / warm*?
B Yes! It was –10°C! There was lots of ²*snow / snowy*.
A Wow! It never ³*snows / snowy* in my country.
C Do I need an umbrella?
D I don't know. It's ⁴*rainy / rain* – but it's very ⁵*wind / windy* too!
E Was it ⁶*wet / hot*?
F Yes, very! It was about 35°C! But it was ⁷*cloud / cloudy* all the time. We didn't see the sun.

3 SOUND AND SPELLING

a ▶ 3.89 Which of the **marked** letters in each group has a different sound? <u>Underline</u> the word. Practise saying the words.

1 tr**ai**n c**ar** pl**a**ne r**ai**n
2 c**a**mp wh**a**t h**o**t n**o**t
3 g**o** b**oa**t sn**o**w w**i**nd
4 fl**a**t c**a**mp t**a**ke tr**a**m
5 cl**ou**d h**o**me c**o**ld n**o**
6 b**u**s s**u**n dr**o**ve l**o**vely

b ▶ 3.90 Complete the table with words in the box.

cinema beautiful different expensive
interesting camera lovely difficult
restaurant business favourite museum

We always say all the letters	We don't always say all the letters
cinema	different

🔄 REVIEW YOUR PROGRESS

How well did you do in this unit? Write 3, 2, or 1 for each objective.
3 = very well   2 = well   1 = not so well

I CAN ...

talk about travel and holiday experiences	☐
talk about past holidays	☐
make and respond to requests	☐

CAN DO OBJECTIVES

- Talk about your home
- Ask where people are and what they're doing
- Ask for travel information

UNIT 10
Here and now

GETTING STARTED

▶ 4.2

a 💬 Look at the picture and answer the questions.

1 What room are the people in?
2 What are they doing?
3 How often do you think they do this?
4 Who is the man at the computer talking to? What do you think he's saying?
5 How do the other people feel? Why?

b 💬 Talk about the questions.

1 Do you have a computer at home? Where do you use it?
2 Do you speak to family and friends on the Internet? How often? Who do you speak to?
3 What programmes do you use to speak to people on the Internet?
4 What are the good things and bad things about speaking to people on the Internet and not on the phone?

10A I'm sitting in my flat

Learn to talk about your home
G Present continuous: positive
V The home

1 VOCABULARY The home

a ▶4.3 Match the words in the box with pictures a–f. Listen and check.

| bedroom   garden   living room |
| dining room   kitchen   bathroom |

b ▶ Now go to Vocabulary Focus 10A on p.150

c **Sound and spelling** /ʧ/ and /θ/
1 ▶4.5 Listen and practise these sounds.
  1 /ʧ/ ki**tch**en   2 /θ/ ba**th**room
2 ▶4.6 What sound do you hear in the words in the box, Sound 1 or Sound 2? Listen and add the words to the sound groups below.

| cheese   month   birthday   thanks   chips |
| both   March   question   three   watch |

Sound 1 /ʧ/	Sound 2 /θ/
ki**tch**en	ba**th**room

3 Which letters usually spell /ʧ/ and which spell /θ/?
4 💬 Practise saying the words.

d 💬 Ask and answer the questions with a partner.
1 How many bedrooms are there in your home?
2 Where do you eat your dinner?
3 Is there a TV in your home? Where?
4 Do you have a garden? If yes, is it big or small?
5 Which room do you like best in your home?

2 LISTENING AND SPEAKING

a ▶4.7 Listen to Mimi talk about her flat. Put pictures 1–3 on page 81 in the order Mimi talks about them.

b ▶4.7 Listen again. Are the sentences true or false?
1 Mimi's flat isn't big.
2 The light in her flat is good.
3 There are three chairs in the living room.
4 There's a dining room in her flat.
5 She uses her computer in her living room.

c 💬 Do you like Mimi's flat? Why / Why not?

Language Plus *in / on*

in + room
There's a desk **in** my bedroom.
Put the cake **in** the kitchen.

on + floor, wall
The books are **on** the floor.
There are pictures **on** the wall.

d 💬 Think about your home and the rooms it has. Tell a partner about your home.

In my home there are four bedrooms and a big bathroom.

e 💬 Choose a room in your home and write the names of some objects in that room. Then tell your partner about them.

In my bedroom there's a bed, a chair and a small desk.

3 READING

a Read the messages. Are they for people who are near or far away?

> 1 Come in here! We're watching the game. It's Germany and Brazil.
> **SEND**

> 2 Mum, I'm studying really hard for my exam. Can I have a cup of coffee, please? 🙂
> **SEND**

> 3 Steve's talking too much – I can't hear the TV. Tell him to be quiet!
> **SEND**

> 4 I'm sitting in the car outside the house. Can you come and help me with my suitcase? It's really heavy! Thanks! 🙂
> **SEND**

> 5 I'm cooking your dinner and there's no butter – can you stop watching TV and go to the supermarket for me?
> **SEND**

① ☐

② ☐

b Read the messages again. Where are the writers?

c 💬 Do you sometimes send a message to someone when you're in the same place? Why / Why not?

4 GRAMMAR
Present continuous: positive

a Look at the sentence from message 1. Does it mean *now* or *usually*?

We're watching the game.

b Complete the rule with *-ing* and *be*.

Present continuous positive (+):
I / you / he / she / it / we / they + _____ + verb + _____

c ▶4.8 **Pronunciation** Listen to the sentence in 4a. Underline the stressed words.

d Underline four more examples of the present continuous in messages 2–5 in 3a.

e ▶ Now go to Grammar Focus 10A on p.126

f It's 2 pm on Sunday. What are you doing? Write a message to a friend.

Hi Jules,
I'm having lunch at a new restaurant in the centre of town with my sister. It's really good! We're eating lots of food.
Doug

g 💬 Read your message to the class. Listen to the other students. Is anyone doing the same thing?

5 SPEAKING

▶ **Communication 10A** Student A go to p.107. Student B go to p.112.

③ ☐

10B Are you working?

Learn to ask where people are and what they're doing
G Present continuous: negative and questions
V Place phrases with prepositions

IS YOUR PHONE ON OFF
ALWAYS ON?

Some people always have their phone on and they use it all the time – in a café, in the car, even in bed! Is this a good idea? Tell us what you think! And is *your* phone always on?

KEVIN
My phone's always on, day and night. You never know – maybe someone needs to call you at night.

SAM
My phone is usually on, but not at the cinema of course, and not on a plane. I have it on at night.

YASMIN
I never have my phone with me when I'm with people in a restaurant. I don't want to talk on the phone when I'm eating. And I always turn it off at night.

JENNY
My phone is always off! I use it when I speak to a friend, or maybe at the airport or on a train – sometimes I need to tell my mum that the train's late. But then I turn it off. I don't like talking on the phone.

BRANKO
My phone's always on in the day – when I'm at home and when I'm at work, but I turn it off at night. I want to sleep!

1 READING

a Match the phrases in the box with pictures a–e.

| at the cinema   in bed   in the car |
| in a restaurant   on a mountain |

b 💬 Look at pictures a–e again. Answer the questions.
1 What object is in all the pictures?
2 Which are … ?
   • a good idea   • quite normal   • a bad idea

c Read the comments on the website and answer the questions.
1 You phone the five people from the website. They're in a restaurant. Who will answer?
2 You phone the five people at 3 am. Who will answer?

d 💬 Which person do you think … ?
a has good ideas
b has a problem

e Write a comment about you and your phone for the website.

f 💬 Read your comment to your partner. Are you the same?

2 VOCABULARY Place phrases with prepositions

a Find phrases on the website with *in*, *on* or *at* and the nouns in the box. Add them to the table.

| ~~café~~   airport   car   work   bed   plane |
| cinema   train   restaurant   home |

in	on	at
in a café _____	_____	_____ _____
_____ _____	_____	_____ _____

b 💬 You're in a place in 2a and your partner calls you. Tell your partner what you're doing. Your partner guesses the place.

> I'm going to work.

> Are you in the car?

c ▶ Now go to Vocabulary Focus 10B on p.149

d Sound and spelling /ə/
1 ▶ 4.11 Listen to the sound /ə/ in these words. Is it a long or a short sound? Is it stressed or unstressed?
   teach**er**   stud**e**nt   cin**e**ma   stat**io**n
2 ▶ 4.12 Listen to these words. Underline the /ə/ sound in each word.

| dinner   England   garden   television |
| waiter   breakfast   listen   driver |

3 💬 Practise saying the words.

c ▶ 4.14 Complete the table. Listen and check.

+	−
I'm working.	I'm _____ _____.
I'm having dinner.	I'm _____ _____ dinner.

d ▶ 4.15 Complete Dan's questions. Listen and check.

1 **DAN** What _____ _____ doing?
  LOU I'm at the bus stop. I'm going home.
2 **DAN** _____ _____ working?
  LOU No, I'm not working.
3 **LOU** I'm watching a film.
  DAN Oh, what _____ _____ watching?

e ▶ 4.16 **Pronunciation** Listen to the questions in 3d again. Which word has the main stress?

f ▶ Now go to Grammar Focus 10B on p.128

g ▶ **Communication 10B** Student A go to p.107. Student B go to p.112.

3 LISTENING AND GRAMMAR Present continuous: negative and questions

a ▶ 4.13 Listen and match conversations 1–5 with pictures a–e.

b 💬 Do you think … ?

1 Dan likes Lou
2 Lou likes Dan

How do you know?

4 SPEAKING

a You and a partner are in different places. You want to meet. Before you speak on the phone, make notes. Think about these questions:

- Where are you? (Choose a place from Vocabulary Focus 10B on page 149.)
- What are you doing? (Think of two or more activities.)
- When do you want to meet? (Think of a day, a time and a place.)

b 💬 Phone your partner and have a conversation.

- Ask where your partner is and what he / she is doing.
- Plan when and where to meet your partner.

> Hi, Tom.
> What are you doing?

> I'm at work.

> Are you free this evening? Do you want to go to Café Cabana?

10C Everyday English
What time's the next train to London?

Learn to ask for travel information

P Sound and spelling: /ɪə/ and /eə/
W A message asking for information

1 LISTENING

a 💬 Look at picture a and talk about the questions.

1 How does Sophia feel?
2 What does Megan offer to do?

b ▶️4.20 Watch or listen to Part 1. Check your ideas in 1a.

c ▶️4.20 Watch or listen to Part 1 again. Answer the questions.

1 What does Megan say about James?
2 Do they know what time the train leaves?

2 PRONUNCIATION Sound and spelling: /ɪə/ and /eə/

a ▶️4.21 Listen to these words. Which word has a different sound?

h**ere**   y**eah**   r**ea**lly

b ▶️4.22 Listen and complete the table with the words in the box.

chair   care   hear   real   hair
near   there   clear   pair   meal

Sound 1 /ɪə/	Sound 2 /eə/
here	yeah

c ▶️4.22 Listen again and repeat.

3 LISTENING

a 💬 Look at picture b. What questions do Megan and Sophia ask the station official?

b ▶️4.23 Watch or listen to Part 2. Check your ideas in 3a.

c ▶️4.23 Watch or listen to Part 2 again. Complete the information.

1 Time of next train: _____
2 Time now: _____
3 Platform: _____

d 💬 In your country, what is an easy way to travel – train, bus, car?

4 USEFUL LANGUAGE Asking for travel information

a Who says these expressions – a passenger (P) or the station official (SO)?

1 The next train is at 4:35.
2 Which platform is it?
3 Excuse me.
4 The train leaves in three minutes.
5 No, you change at Reading.
6 Yes? How can I help?
7 What time's the next train to London?
8 Is it a direct train?
9 It's Platform 3.

b ▶ 4.24 Listen and check your answers in 4a. Then listen again and repeat.

c ▶ 4.25 Complete the sentences with *at* or *in*. Listen and check.

1 The next train leaves _____ half an hour.
2 The next train leaves _____ five o'clock.

d ▶ 4.26 Put the conversation in the correct order. Then listen and check.

A

☐ So, at 5:15. And is it a direct bus?
☐ Great! Thanks for your help.
☐ What time's the next bus to Cambridge?
☐ 1 Excuse me.
☐ OK, and which bus stop is it?

B

☐ The next bus leaves in 20 minutes.
☐ It's stop 7, near the ticket office.
☐ No problem.
☐ Yes? How can I help?
☐ No, you change at Birmingham.

e 💬 Practise the conversation in 4d with a partner. Take turns to be the station official and the passenger. Change the times, kind of transport and the platforms / bus stops.

5 SPEAKING

▶ Communication 10C
Student A go to p.106.
Student B go to p.111.

6 WRITING

a Megan helped her friend Amelia plan a holiday in Paris. Amelia sends Megan a message. Read it and answer the questions.

1 Where's Amelia now?
2 Which two questions does she ask?

> **TODAY**
>
> Hi, Megan. I'm travelling to Paris right now on the train. Sorry, I can't remember two things. First, where do I find a taxi at the station? And how much is it from the station to the hotel? I don't have a lot of euros with me! Thanks!

b ▶ Now go to Writing Plus 10C on p.158 for Word order in questions.

c Write a message to a friend. Ask two questions in your message. Here are some ideas:

Hi …
I'm going / doing / having …
Sorry, I can't remember …
Where / How / When … ?
Thanks …

d 💬 Read another student's message. Try to answer the questions.

⟳ **Unit Progress Test**

CHECK YOUR PROGRESS

You can now do the Unit Progress Test.

UNIT 10
Review

1 GRAMMAR

a Correct the present continuous sentences.

> Carmen be wearing a yellow T-shirt.
> *Carmen's wearing a yellow T-shirt.*

1 You wearing my shoes!
2 They're geting a taxi.
3 I'm writeing to Mimi.
4 The lesson starting.
5 She's haveing lunch.
6 We waiting.

b Write present continuous questions with the words and phrases.

1 where / you / sit ?
2 you / wear / black shoes ?
3 it / rain ?
4 you / use / a computer ?
5 why / you / study / English ?
6 what / your friends / do ?

c 💬 Ask and answer the questions in 1b.

d Complete the phone conversation with the verbs in brackets.

CATHY Hi, it's me.
MATT Oh, hi. What ¹_____ (you / do)?
CATHY I'm on the train.
MATT Oh, of course. Well, I ²_____ (cook) dinner. So, ³_____ (you / listen to) music?
CATHY Mm, no. I ⁴_____ (talk) to you, of course.
MATT Oh, very funny. What's the weather like there?
CATHY Not good. It ⁵_____ (rain) outside.
MATT Well, it ⁶_____ (not / rain) here – it ⁷_____ (snow)! But Gwen and Carla are in the garden.
CATHY The garden? Why? What ⁸_____ (they / do)?
MATT They ⁹_____ (make) a snowman!

2 VOCABULARY

a Write the rooms.

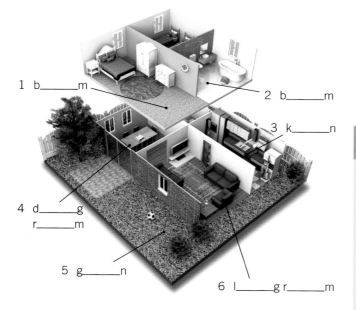

1 b____m
2 b____m
3 k____n
4 d____g r____m
5 g____n
6 l____g r____m

b Complete the questions with *in*, *on* or *at*.

1 Do you listen to music _____ the car?
2 Do you sleep _____ trains / buses / planes?
3 Do you read _____ bed?
4 Do you eat _____ the cinema?
5 Were you _____ home yesterday lunchtime?
6 Did you play football _____ school?
7 What's _____ the floor in this room?
8 Are there any pictures _____ the walls?

c 💬 Ask and answer the questions in 2b.

3 SOUND AND SPELLING

a Notice the three sounds and the marked letters.

1 /tʃ/ **ch**oose
2 /θ/ **th**ree
3 /ð/ **th**ey're

b ▶4.27 Complete the table with the words in the box. Practise saying the words.

bathroom   birthday   **ch**ange   ~~**ch**oose~~   kit**ch**en   mo**th**er
ques**t**ion   **th**anks   ~~**th**e~~   ~~**th**ree~~   ~~**th**ey're~~   wea**th**er

/tʃ/	/θ/	/ð/
choose	three	they're

c ▶4.28 Are the two **marked** sounds in each sentence the same (S) or different (D)? Practise saying the sentences.

1 W**e're** h**e**re.
2 W**ear** a p**air** of shoes.
3 Th**eir** house is n**ear**.
4 It's r**eal** h**air**.
5 Y**eah**, it's th**ere**.
6 Wh**ere**'s the ch**air**?

⟳ **CAN DO OBJECTIVES**

- Talk about people's lives
- Talk about things you know how to do
- Talk about opinions

UNIT 11
Achievers

GETTING STARTED

▶ 4.29

a 💬 Look at the picture and answer the questions.

1 What did this man do before he went into his tent? What are his plans tomorrow?

2 Tick (✓) the things the man can do in his tent tonight. Why can't he do some things?

- [ ] listen to music
- [ ] read a magazine
- [ ] have a coffee
- [ ] play the guitar
- [ ] cook dinner
- [ ] do yoga
- [ ] sleep well

3 What do you think he is writing in his book?

4 What questions do you want to ask him? Write down three.

b 💬 Would you like to be where this man is? Why / Why not?

1 READING

a 💬 Think of two famous people from your country (present or past). Ask and answer the questions with a partner.

1 Why are / were they famous?
2 What do you know about them?
3 Do you think people from other countries know about them? Why / Why not?

b Read *They were the first!*. Who … ?

1 died over 50 years ago
2 had new ideas for machines
3 lived in a village as a child
4 came from a poor family
5 had one child
6 lived in France

c 💬 Read *They were the first!* again. Choose one thing about each person you think is interesting and say why.

THEY WERE THE FIRST!

… BUT THEY WEREN'T WORLD FAMOUS.

#1 THE FIRST WOMAN IN SPACE
Valentina Tereshkova (born 1937)

Who is she?
A Russian cosmonaut

What did she do?
In 1963 she flew in *Vostok 6*. She went round the Earth 48 times and she was in space for almost 3 days.

Her life
She was born in 1937 in a small village in Russia. Her father was a tractor driver and her mother worked in a factory.

She finished school at 16 and started work in a factory. In her free time she studied and she also went parachute jumping.

In 1963 she got married and the next year she had a daughter, Elena. After that, Valentina never flew into space again.

2 VOCABULARY Life events

a ▶4.30 Look at these events in a person's life. Match events 1–6 with pictures a–f. Listen and check.

1 die

2 grow up

3 finish university

4 get married

5 go to school

6 be born

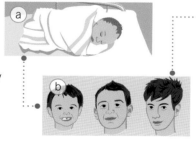

b Write the events in three lists.

1 everyone does this
2 most people do this
3 only some people do this

c 💬 Compare your lists with other students. Are they the same?

d Read *They were the first!* again. Write past simple sentences about the years below.

Valentina Tereshkova
• 1937 • 1953 • 1963 • 1964

Leonardo Torres y Quevedo
• 1852 • 1868 • 1914 • 1936

1937 – Valentina was born.

Language Plus Years

To say a year, we say the numbers in pairs:
1937 ➔ 19 37   *nineteen thirty-seven*   2016 ➔ 20 16   *twenty sixteen*
Note: 1900 = *nineteen hundred*   2000 = *two thousand*
         2005 = *two thousand and five*

#2 HE MADE THE FIRST COMPUTER GAME ... IN 1914!

Leonardo Torres y Quevedo (1852–1936)

Who was he?
A Spanish engineer

What did he do?
In 1914 he made a machine called 'The Chess Player'. You could play chess against it and it was the first computer game in the world.

His life
He was born in 1852 and grew up in the city of Bilbao, in Spain. When he was 16 he went to live in Paris and two years later he went to university in Madrid. After he finished university he travelled around Europe and studied new ideas.

Leonardo got married in 1885 and had eight children. His family was very rich, so he had lots of time to have ideas for new machines – like 'The Chess Player'.

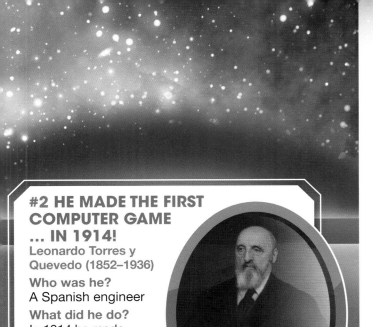

e Sound and spelling /ɜː/

1 ▶ **4.31** Listen to the words.

| university   worked   thirty |

Are the **marked** letters ... ?
a all the same sound
b two different sounds
c three different sounds

2 ▶ **4.32** Underline the letters in these words that have the sound /ɜː/. Listen and check.

| Thursday   first   world   shirt   early   weren't   girl |

3 💬 Practise saying the words.

f ▶ Now go to Vocabulary Focus 11A on p.139

---

3 LISTENING AND GRAMMAR
Object pronouns

a ▶ **4.35** Listen to two friends talking about Valentina Tereshkova. Tick (✓) the questions you can answer after listening to their conversation.

1 ☐ Where did she go to school?
2 ☐ Why did she get the job?
3 ☐ How did she meet her husband?
4 ☐ Where does she live now?
5 ☐ What does she want to do in the future?

b ▶ **4.35** Listen again and answer the questions you ticked in 3a.

c ▶ **4.36** Complete the sentences from the conversation with the words in the box. Listen and check.

| he   him   she   her |

1 _____'s a Russian cosmonaut. Do you know about _____?
2 She married a cosmonaut. She met _____ in 1963. _____ was on the same space programme.

d Underline the correct words to complete the rules.

1 We use **he** and **she** before / after a verb.
2 We use **him** and **her** before / after a verb or preposition.

e ▶ Now go to Grammar Focus 11A on p.128

4 SPEAKING

a Write four or five events in your life and the years.
1997–2011 – I lived in Budapest.
2011 – I started university.

b 💬 Work in pairs. Read your partner's sentences and ask some questions.

Where did you ...?
When did you ...?
Why did you ...?

c 💬 Tell the class two things about your partner's life.

1 READING

a 💬 Look at 1–3 below. What's difficult for you to do? Why / Why not?

1 be cold for a long time
2 swim underwater
3 pull or carry big objects

b Read *Real life X-Men*. Does it talk more about X-Men or about real people?

c Read *Real life X-Men* again. Answer the questions.

1 How long can Wim Hof stay in a cold bath?
2 How long can the Bajau Laut people stay underwater?
3 How does Seema Bhadoria pull things?

d 💬 Which real person / people in *Real life X-Men* can do something useful?

2 GRAMMAR

can: positive and negative

a Underline the correct answer in the table.

+	I / You / He / She /	can / can't	swim.
–	We / They	can / can't	fly.

b Underline examples of *can / can't* in *Real life X-Men*. What is after *can / can't*, a noun or a verb?

c ▶ Now go to Grammar Focus 11B Part 1 on p.130

REAL LIFE X-MEN

The X-Men films are about 'superhumans'. They can do amazing things, for example, Iceman can make ice and Firestar can make fire and fly. Of course, X-Men aren't real, and people in the real world can't do the same things. But a few people can also do some amazing things!

THE FISHMEN
The Bajau Laut people in Southeast Asia can swim underwater for a long time. Sometimes they can go underwater for more than five minutes. They can also see very well in the water – it helps them to see the fish!

THE ICEMAN
Wim Hof is from the Netherlands and he's often called 'The Iceman'. He can't make ice, but he can sit in a bath of ice for one hour, 52 minutes and two seconds. He doesn't feel cold. In 2009, he ran more than 40 kilometres in -20°C wearing only shorts!

THE STRONG WOMAN
Seema Bhadoria is an amazing young woman from India – she can pull really big objects with only her teeth. When she was only 18 years old she pulled a plane with her teeth! She can also pull a ship and a big truck.

3 VOCABULARY Abilities

a Match the verbs in the box with pictures a–d.

| cook sing swim paint |

b ▶ Now go to Vocabulary Focus 11B on p.140

Language Plus (*very / quite*) *well*

I can swim **very well**. = I'm very good.
I can swim **well**. = I'm good.
I can swim **quite well**. = I'm OK.
I can't swim **at all**. = It's impossible for me.

c 💬 Talk about people you know and what they can or can't do.

> My brother can't dance very well.

4 LISTENING

a Read the job advertisement. Does the school want someone who can do one thing or lots of things?

Job alert   CLOSE

We need people to work at our summer school in West Lynn.

We want people who can do lots of different things – sing, dance, play the guitar, draw, ride a horse, but we also want good teachers!

If you're interested, please send us an email or give us a call …

b ▶4.41 Listen to Celia, the head teacher at the school, talk to Andy. Is he a good person for the job?

c ▶4.41 Listen again. What can Andy do? Complete sentences 1–4 with the words and phrases in the box.

| teach   ride a horse   play the guitar   sing   dance |

1 He can _____ and _____ quite well.
2 He can _____ very well.
3 He can't _____ very well.
4 He can't _____ at all.

5 GRAMMAR *can*: questions

a ▶4.42 Complete the conversations. Listen and check your answers.

1 **CELIA** And _____ _____ sing?
  ANDY Yes, _____ _____.
2 **CELIA** _____ _____ dance well?
  ANDY No, _____ _____.

b ▶ Now go to Grammar Focus 11B Part 2 on p.130

c ▶4.44 **Pronunciation** Listen to the sentences. Tick (✓) when *can / can't* is stressed.

1 ☐ I can sing quite well.   3 ☐ Can you sing?
2 ☐ I can't dance very well.   4 ☐ Yes, I can.

d 💬 Practise saying the sentences. Underline the correct words to complete the rules.

> **Can** *is / isn't* stressed in positive sentences and questions.
> **Can** *is / isn't* stressed in negative sentences and short answers.

e ▶4.45 Complete the conversation with the correct form of *can*. Listen and check.

A _____ Andy play the guitar?
B Yes, he _____.
A And _____ he ride a horse?
B Yes, he _____ ride a horse very well.
A _____ he teach?
B No, he _____ teach at all.

f 💬 Practise the conversation in 5e with a partner.

6 SPEAKING

a 💬 Work in pairs. Write one question with *can* for each topic.

- sport   *Can you play tennis?*
- food   *Can you make a cake?*
- language
- music / art

b 💬 Work with a new partner. Ask and answer your questions in 6a.

> Can you play tennis?

> No, I can't play tennis at all.

c 💬 Work with your first partner again. Tell them about your second partner.

> Olga can speak German quite well, but she can't speak Spanish.

11C Everyday English
What do you think?

P Consonant groups
W An email to a friend

1 LISTENING

a 💬 Ask and answer the questions.

1 What's your favourite room in your house?
2 What things have you got there?

b 💬 Look at pictures a–c. Which is the best description of the story, 1 or 2?

1 Sophia, Megan and James arrive home. They tell James about the fun things they did in Henley. Sophia knows where she wants to put the clock.
2 Sophia, Megan and James arrive home. Megan and James talk about places to visit in London. They like different places. Sophia can't choose a good place for the clock.

c ▶4.46 Watch or listen. Check your answer in 1b.

d ▶4.46 Watch or listen again and answer the questions.

1 What does James think of the clock?
2 What did Sophia think of Henley?
3 Why doesn't Megan like London Zoo?
4 Why doesn't James like the Tower of London?
5 Why does James think a clock in the bedroom is a bad idea?
6 Where does Sophia choose to put the clock?

e 💬 Are there any interesting places to visit in / near your town or city?

2 USEFUL LANGUAGE Talking about opinions

a Look at the expressions. Do we use them to ... ?

a ask an opinion
b give an opinion
c have the same opinion
d have a different opinion

1 Did you like Henley?
2 I don't think so.
3 Maybe you're right.
4 I don't think the bedroom is a good idea.
5 I think London Zoo is very nice.
6 What about the Tower of London?
7 I think you're right.
8 What do you think?

▶4.47 Listen and check your answers.

b ▶4.47 Pronunciation Listen to sentences 1–8 in 2a again. Underline the main stress. Listen again and repeat.

c ▶4.48 Look at expressions 1–4. Are they in group a, b, c or d in 2a? Listen and check.

1 Yes, I agree.
2 Do you like this clock?
3 What do you think of London?
4 I'm not so sure.

d ▶4.49 Put the words in the correct order to make expressions. Listen and check.

1 very interesting / museum is / I think the .
2 you think / what do / new restaurant / of the ?
3 you're / I think / right .
4 so / think / I don't .
5 the colour blue / I don't think / is a good idea .

e Complete the conversation with your ideas.

A What do you think of English?
YOU _____
A Yes, maybe you're right. What about the grammar?
YOU _____
A Really? I don't think so. I think your language is very difficult.
YOU _____
A Well, all languages are a bit difficult.
YOU _____

f 💬 Practise the conversation in 2e with a partner. Take turns to be A.

5 WRITING

a Read Sophia's email to a friend in Canada. What does she like about her life in London?

Hi Lisa,

Thanks for your email – it was nice to hear from you.

Things in London are going well. It's a big city and there are lots of things I can do. I'm making some new friends here. I work in an office with a girl called Megan. She's from London and she's very friendly. She helped me a lot when I arrived. I also know her cousin James. He's very kind. I often see them at the weekend.

My flat is quite big. It's comfortable and I like it a lot. It's near my office, so I can walk to work every day. I like that!

I miss my family at home and I miss my friends, too! Write again soon.

Love,

Sophia

b ▶ Now go to Writing Plus 11C on p.159 for Pronouns.

c Write an email to a friend. Tell them about your life now. Here are some ideas:
- Say hi and thank the person for his / her email. (*Hi … Thanks … *)
- Write about your life – your job or studies. (*I'm working / studying … *)
- Write about family and / or friends. (*My parents are well … I see my friend Luisa every … *)
- Say goodbye and ask the person to write to you. (*Goodbye for now … Love / Best wishes … *)

d Read another student's email. What's interesting about their life?

3 PRONUNCIATION Consonant groups

a ▶4.50 Listen to the words. Notice how the **marked** letters are pronounced. Listen again and repeat.

1 /t/ ri**ght**   2 /ŋk/ thi**nk**   3 /st/ touri**st**

b ▶4.51 Listen and match the **marked** letters in 1–6 with a–f.

1 a**sk**	3 fi**nd**	5 restaura**nt**
2 da**nce**	4 difficu**lt**	6 si**x**

a /nt/   c /sk/   e /nd/
b /lt/   d /ks/   f /ns/

c 💬 Practise saying the words.

4 SPEAKING

▶ **Communication 11C**
Student A go to p.106.
Student B go to p.113.

 Unit Progress Test

CHECK YOUR PROGRESS

You can now do the Unit Progress Test.

UNIT 11
Review

1 GRAMMAR

a Complete the sentences with the correct pronoun.

1 I like Rob, but I don't think he likes _____.
2 Those shoes are beautiful. Can I buy _____, please?
3 Sarah's a good friend. I met _____ at university.
4 My husband and I live in the city, but my parents live in a small village. They sometimes visit _____ at the weekend.
5 They had a baby boy and they called _____ Antonio.
6 Happy birthday! I got _____ a present!
7 Your car is dirty. You need to clean _____.

b Look at the table. Then complete the conversation with the words and phrases in the box.

	dance	play tennis	ride a horse
Igor	✗	✓✓	✓
Melanie	✓	✗	✓✓

can (x4)   can't   can she   can you
he can't   I can   she can

A ¹_____ Igor dance?
B No, ²_____. But he ³_____ play tennis very well and he ⁴_____ ride a horse.
A What about Melanie? ⁵_____ ride a horse?
B Yes, ⁶_____. She can ride a horse and she ⁷_____ dance, but she ⁸_____ play tennis.
A What about you? ⁹_____ play tennis?
B Yes, ¹⁰_____.

c 💬 Ask a partner about the activities in 1b. Use *Can you ... ?*

2 VOCABULARY

a Complete the text with the correct form of the verb phrases in the box.

have a baby boy   finish school   go to school   be born
go to university   die   grow up   get married

My parents met in London and I ¹_____ in England, but my family came here to New Zealand when I was three. I ²_____ here and I don't remember anything about England. I ³_____ when I was sixteen. I got a job in a factory, but it wasn't very interesting. So I ⁴_____ and studied for two more years.
Then I ⁵_____ in Australia. I studied engineering and I met Barbara – she's now my wife!
Barbara and I ⁶_____ five years ago. We both got good jobs in Australia, but then my father ⁷_____, so we came back here to New Zealand to be with my mum.
We ⁸_____ last year. Life is good!

b Complete the verb phrases with the words in the box.

dinner   basketball   a motorbike   songs   to work   walls

play	cards, ¹_____, volleyball
sing	²_____
paint	a picture, ³_____
ride	a horse, ⁴_____, a bike
drive	a car, ⁵_____
cook	⁶_____

c 💬 Which of the things in 2b do you do every day? Which do you sometimes do? Which do you never do?

3 SOUND AND SPELLING

a ▶4.52 Tick (✓) the words with an /ɜː/ sound. Practise saying the words.

- ☐ thirteen
- ☐ born
- ☐ university
- ☐ rode
- ☐ sand
- ☐ weren't
- ☐ cooked
- ☐ swam
- ☐ thirty
- ☐ worked
- ☐ married

b ▶4.53 Are the **marked** sounds the same (S) or different (D)? Practise saying the words.

1 si**x** – than**ks**
2 **d**ance – an**s**wer
3 **r**ight – **wh**ite
4 touri**st** – dan**ced**
5 a**s**k – **s**chool
6 si**ng** – sa**ng**

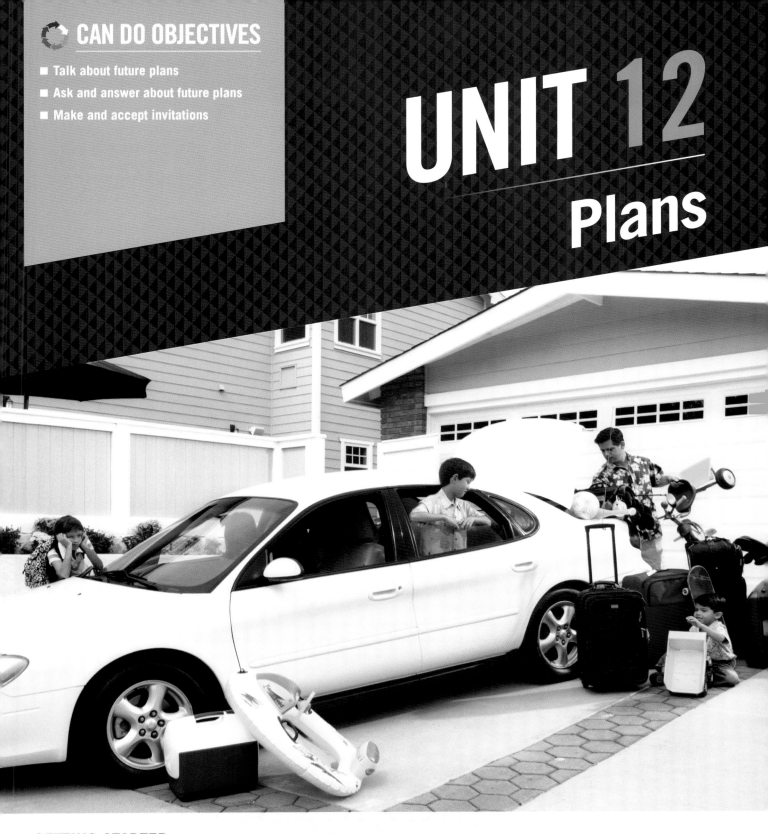

CAN DO OBJECTIVES

- Talk about future plans
- Ask and answer about future plans
- Make and accept invitations

UNIT 12
Plans

GETTING STARTED

▶ 4.54

a 💬 Look at the picture and answer the questions.

1 Do you think this family are going to go … ?
- on a long or short holiday
- somewhere near or far
- somewhere hot or cold
- to stay with family or in a hotel
- all the way by car or drive to the airport

Why?

2 What did this man do … ?
- the day before the holiday
- the morning of the holiday
- a month before the holiday
3 What do you think this family are going to do on holiday? Why?
4 How does the girl on the far left of the picture feel? Why?

b 💬 Talk about the questions.

1 When you go on holiday, do you pack too much or not enough?
2 What do you sometimes forget to take when you go on holiday?

12A I'm going to have a long hot bath

Learn to talk about future plans
G *going to*: positive and negative
V Months and future time expressions; Ordinal numbers

1 READING

a 💬 Talk about everyday objects and activities that are important to you. Think about:
- food and drink (*my morning coffee …*)
- your things (*my sofa …*)
- things you do (*listen to music …*)

> Every day I play video games – I really like them.

b Read about *Outside the comfort zone*. Is it about … ?
1 a fun holiday   2 a dangerous competition

c Read about the programme again. Answer the questions.
1 Where do people on the programme go?
2 Do they have an easy time? Why / Why not?
3 What do the two best people get?

d 💬 Read the people's ideas for after the programme. Which is the best idea? Tell a partner.

2 GRAMMAR *going to*: positive

a ▶4.55 Complete Mick's sentences with the words in the box. Listen and check.

> to   are   going

1 I'm _____ to sleep for a long time.
2 Melissa's going _____ have a long hot bath.
3 Joel and Shelley _____ going to have their favourite food and drink.

b Underline the correct answer in the rule.

> We use *be + going to* to talk about *now / the future.*

c ▶4.55 **Pronunciation** Listen to the sentences in 2a again. Notice the sentence stress and the pronunciation of *going to*. Answer the questions.
1 Do we stress *going*, the main verb or both?
2 Can we hear the words *going to* clearly?

> 💬 Practise saying the sentences.

d ▶ Now go to Grammar Focus 12A Part 1 on p.130

e Write three sentences about something you're going to do after class.

> After class I'm going to meet my friend, Diego.

f 💬 Tell other students your sentences in 2e.

> I'm going to study in the Learning Centre. What about you?

> I'm going to have a coffee.

Outside the COMFORT ZONE

In this exciting new TV programme, ten people go and live in the mountains for ten days. Every day they do something difficult and sometimes dangerous. It's usually cold and wet and they don't have a lot of food. They need to stay safe and comfortable (if possible!), but it's not easy. The two people who do the best win a prize of £25,000!

It starts on Channel Six next Tuesday at 8:30 pm.

It's Day 5 on *Outside the comfort zone* and everyone is thinking about the first thing they're going to do after the programme finishes.

> I'm going to eat a big meal of steak and chips. JOEL

> I'm going to have a long hot bath. MELISSA

> I'm going to sleep for a long time. MICK

> I'm going to have a big cup of coffee. SHELLEY

3 VOCABULARY Months and future time expressions; Ordinal numbers

a It's Monday morning. Put time expressions 1–6 in the correct place on the timeline.

1 this evening   2 tomorrow   3 this Wednesday   4 on Friday   5 at the weekend   6 next Monday

Language Plus The date

*What's the date today? It's **the fifth of August**.*
*When's your birthday? It's **on the twentieth of March**.*
Note: With dates we use ordinal numbers:
    first, second, third, fourth …

b ▶ Now go to Vocabulary Focus 12A on p.147

c 💬 Ask and answer the questions with a partner. Use time expressions in your answers.

1 When's your next English lesson?
2 When's your next English test?
3 When's your birthday?

> It's on the fifteenth of November.

4 LISTENING

a ▶4.60 Listen to Paola (P), Yaz (Y) and Nikita (N) talk about their holiday plans this summer. Match them with pictures a–c.

b ▶4.60 Listen again. Are the sentences true or false?

1 Paola often goes to a cooking school for her holiday.
2 The trip to Norway is a different kind of holiday for Yaz.
3 Nikita doesn't want to make money on the farm.

c 💬 Which holiday plan do you like? Which don't you like? Why?

5 GRAMMAR *going* to: negative

a ▶4.61 Listen and complete the sentences.

1 **PAOLA** I_____ going _____ have a normal holiday.
2 **YAZ** We _____ going _____ do that this year.

b ▶ Now go to Grammar Focus 12A Part 2 on p.130

c ▶4.63 Complete the conversations. Listen and check.

1 **A** After class, I'_____ not _____ to do my homework.
  B Why not?
  A I'm tired. I'm going _____ do it tomorrow.
2 **C** After class, I'_____ not _____ to go home.
  D Why not?
  C I'm going _____ meet friends in a café.

d 💬 Practise the conversations in 5c. Use your ideas to have similar conversations.

6 SPEAKING

a Write two things you're going to do on your next holiday. Think about:

• places   • activities   • places to stay
• things to buy   • sports   • people

b Write two things from your everyday life you aren't going to do on your holiday.

• things you do at school / work
• things you do at home

c 💬 Talk to other students about your ideas in 6a and 6b. Do you all have the same ideas?

> I'm going to go to the beach.

> I'm not going to read work emails.

ONLY **4,000 WEEKENDS** IN YOUR LIFE!
SO, WHAT ARE **YOU** GOING TO DO WITH THEM?

HOME | BOOKS | WRITING

What's your answer to this question? Perhaps it's 'I don't know' or 'Not a lot'?
In her new book, *What the most successful people do on the weekend*, Laura Vanderkam says these are bad answers. She says the weekend is a time to relax, but also a time to do interesting things. With only 4,000 weekends in our life, each one is important. So don't just sit on the sofa and watch TV. It's a good idea to plan the weekend – then you can use the time well. Here are some of her ideas:

1 Plan three to five activities to do at the weekend and write them down. Be sure you do these things.
2 Plan to read a book. Buy a book for the weekend and then plan a time to read it.
3 Write a list of 100 'big' things you'd like to do in your life. Choose one to do this weekend.
4 Get up early. Between 6:00 and 8:00 in the morning is the best time to do things. Plan to wake up early and do something before breakfast!
5 Turn off your phone and don't use your computer. You can read your emails on Monday. On Sunday evening, go for a run, play some music or do yoga, so you relax and don't think about work.
6 Don't clean your house or flat at the weekend. It's a time to do things you like!

1 READING

a 💬 Talk about sentences 1–3 in small groups. Which are true for you?

1 Weekends are too short and we don't have many of them.
2 It's not a good idea to do a lot at the weekend.
3 It's important to use the time well at the weekend.

b Read about Laura Vanderkam's new book. Which sentence in 1a is her main idea?

c 💬 Look at pictures a–e. Which does Laura say are good things to do at the weekend? Which aren't good?

d Look at Wendy, Dermot and Rini's plans for the weekend. Match them with ideas 1–3 in the text.

e 💬 What do you think of Laura's ideas? Which do you like? Which don't you like? Why / Why not?

> Great ideas! I'd like to try them.

> Interesting ideas, but …

> That's not my idea of a good weekend.

Wendy's big ideas

I'd like to …
- make a cheesecake
- (visit Paris)
- paint my room
- learn Chinese
- read a book by Stephen King
- start a blog
- go parachuting

DERMOT'S DIARY
SUNDAY

10:00	
11:00	
12:00	Sit in the park and read my new book.
1:00	
2:00	

Rini's weekend to-do list

This weekend I'm going to:
1 go for a long run (10 km or more!).
2 invite some friends for dinner.
3 have my first tennis lesson.

2 VOCABULARY Common verbs and collocations

a ▶4.64 Match the verbs in the box with the words and phrases in 1–8. Listen and check.

| paint | clean | use | make | invite | visit | go | do |

1 _____ sport / your homework
2 _____ friends / someone to a party
3 _____ a friend / a museum
4 _____ a list / lunch
5 _____ a picture / a wall
6 _____ your flat / windows
7 _____ your phone / the Internet
8 _____ for a walk / shopping

b Find examples of each verb on page 98. Add them to 1–8 in 2a.

c 💬 Tell a partner which activities in 2a and 2b you do at the weekend.

I always … I often … I sometimes … I never …

d ▶ Now go to Vocabulary Focus 12B on p.141

e Sound and spelling /v/ and /w/
1 ▶4.66 Listen and practise these sounds.
  1 /v/ **v**isit   2 /w/ **w**eekend
2 ▶4.67 Listen to these words and practise saying them.

| in**v**ite | **v**erb | **w**atch | **w**ith | e**v**ening | **w**ell | ne**v**er |

3 LISTENING AND GRAMMAR *going to*: questions

a ▶4.68 Listen to Lee and Marcus talk to a friend about their weekend plans. Write their names on the line.

NO PLAN ⟵⟶ CLEAR PLAN

b ▶4.68 Listen again. Tick (✓) the things you know after listening to the conversations.
1 ☐ the name of the film Lee's going to see
2 ☐ Lee's plans for Sunday
3 ☐ Marcus's shopping plans
4 ☐ the name of the restaurant Marcus's going to go to
5 ☐ Marcus's plans for Sunday

c ▶4.69 Tick (✓) the correct questions in 1–2. Listen and check.
1 a ☐ What are you going to do on Saturday?
  b ☐ What you are going to do on Saturday?
2 a ☐ You going to go shopping?
  b ☐ Are you going to go shopping?

d ▶ Now go to Grammar Focus 12B on p.130

e ▶4.72 Put the words in the correct order to make questions. Listen and check.
1 what / you / this weekend / do / going to / are ?
2 go out / you / are / going to ?
3 what / going to / film / see / are / you ?
4 you / are / buy / going to / what ?
5 go / going to / where / you / are ?

f 💬 Have two conversations with a partner.
1 Student A: you're Lee.
   Student B: ask questions 1, 2 and 3 in 3e.
2 Student B: you're Marcus.
   Student A: ask questions 1, 4 and 5 in 3e.

4 SPEAKING

a Write questions to ask your partner about their plans. Use the ideas below and *going to*.
• this evening   • the weekend
• on your next birthday

b 💬 Ask your partner your questions in 4a. Listen to the answers and write your partner's name on the line in 3a.

c 💬 Compare your line with other students. Who has clear plans for the future?

a

1 LISTENING

a You invite friends for a meal. Which of these things do you do? Write *Yes*, *No* or *Sometimes*.

- make special food
- wear your best clothes
- eat at a fixed time
- use the best plates
- play music when you eat
- cook with your friends

b 💬 Talk about your ideas in 1a with a partner.

c Look at pictures a and b. Why do you think James calls Sophia?

d ▶4.73 Watch or listen to Part 1. Check your answer in 1c.

e ▶4.73 Watch or listen to Part 1 again. Underline the correct answer.

1 Sophia's plates are *new / old*.
2 Sophia wants to *help James / thank James*.
3 James *is / isn't* happy about the invitation.

2 USEFUL LANGUAGE Making and accepting invitations

a Look at the expressions. Do we use them to … ?

a make an invitation
b accept an invitation
c say no to an invitation

1 Would you like to come for dinner?
2 I'd love to, but …
3 I'd love to come. Thank you.
4 Are you free on Friday?
5 Sorry, I'm busy then.
6 Saturday's OK.

▶4.74 Listen and check your answers.

b ▶4.75 Complete the conversation with the words in the box. Listen and check.

---
sorry thank love like OK free busy

A Would you ¹_____ to come to the cinema?
B Yes, I'd ²_____ to come. ³_____ you.
A Are you ⁴_____ on Saturday?
B No, ⁵_____, I'm ⁶_____ on Saturday. But Sunday's ⁷_____.
A OK, we can go on Sunday.

c 💬 Practise the conversation in 2b with a partner.

b

3 LISTENING

a 💬 Look at picture c and talk about the questions.

1 Where is James going?
2 Why did he buy flowers?

b ▶4.76 Watch or listen to Part 2. Check your answers in 3a.

c ▶4.76 Watch or listen to Part 2 again. What is Sophia's news? Tick (✓) the correct answer.

1 ☐ She's going to leave her job.
2 ☐ She's going to go back to Canada.
3 ☐ She's going to stay in London.

d Match 1–4 with a–d.

1 James is surprised	because	a James and Megan helped her.
2 Sophia wants to say thank you		b Megan is there too.
3 Sophia wasn't happy in London		c she has new friends.
4 Now she wants to stay		d she missed her friends in Canada.

4 PRONUNCIATION Sound and spelling: oo

a ▶4.77 Listen to these sentences. When is *oo* an /uː/ sound? When is it an /ʊ/ sound?

1 G**oo**d – now you're both here.
2 I'll bring the f**oo**d.

b ▶4.78 Listen to these words. Put them in the correct place in the table.

cool	cook	spoon	look
book	soon	football	

Sound 1 /ʊ/	Sound 2 /uː/
good	*food*

c 💬 Practise saying the words in 2b with a partner.

5 SPEAKING

▶ **Communication 12C**
Student A go to p.108.
Student B go to p.113.

6 WRITING

a James and Megan wrote invitations to friends. Read the invitations and the replies. Do Jon and Emma say yes or no? Why?

> Hi Jon,
> It's my birthday on Saturday. Would you like to come to my party? It's at my flat and it starts at 9:00.
> See you then, I hope.
> James

> Hi James,
> Thanks, I'd love to come, but I'm not in London. I'm in Sheffield and I'm staying here till Sunday.
> Hope you have a great time! See you next week.
> Jon

> Hi Emma,
> I'm in town this afternoon. Would you like to meet for coffee?
> We could go to Café Roma. It's just near your office. I'm free at 4:00. Is that OK for you?
> Megan

> Hi Megan,
> Sorry, I'm working till 6:30.
> Café Roma's a great idea. Maybe we could meet there tomorrow for lunch. Are you in town then?
> Emma

b ▶ Now go to Writing Plus 12C on p.159 for Paragraphs.

c You want to meet a friend. Think of a place and time. Write an invitation. Here are some ideas:

Would you like to … ?   We could …
I'm free at …   Is that OK for you?
See you …

d Read another student's invitation. Write a reply.

◑ Unit Progress Test

CHECK YOUR PROGRESS

You can now do the Unit Progress Test.

UNIT 12
Review

1 GRAMMAR

a Complete Emily's email with *be going to* and the verbs in brackets.

Busy week!

Hi Minna,

I have so many plans for this week! This afternoon I ¹_____ (study) and then I ²_____ (work) from Tuesday to Thursday. On Wednesday evening I ³_____ (cook) for my parents and then on Thursday evening Marco ⁴_____ (cook) dinner for me!

I ⁵_____ (not / work) on Friday morning because you ⁶_____ (arrive) at lunchtime! Jay ⁷_____ (have) a party on Friday evening. Do you want to go? He ⁸_____ (not / invite) a lot of people.

It's a busy week for me! So I ⁹_____ (not / do) any work or housework at the weekend and we ¹⁰_____ (not / go) to lots of different places! I hope that's OK.

See you on Friday!

Emily

---

b Correct the sentences.

> 'Is your friend going to have lunch with us?' 'No, she not.'
> No, she isn't.

1 'You are going to watch TV this evening?' 'No, I'm not.'
2 Are your mum going to cook your dinner this evening?
3 'Are you going to clean your bedroom?' 'Yes, I'm going.'
4 What do you going to wear tomorrow?
5 'Are your friends going to visit you today?' 'Yes, they're.'
6 What you going to do next summer?

c 💬 Ask and answer the questions in 1b. Use *be going to*.

2 VOCABULARY

a ~~Cross out~~ the answers which are NOT possible.

1 *tomorrow / on tomorrow*
2 *this / in / next / on* Friday
3 *at / in* the weekend
4 *on / this / in / next* June
5 *next / at* weekend
6 *on / in* Sunday
7 *in / on* three weeks
8 *this / at* afternoon

b Complete the ordinal numbers.

> 6th   s i x t h
1 2nd   s _ _ _ _ d
2 30th   t _ _ _ _ _ _ _ h
3 21st   t _ _ _ _ _ y-f _ _ _ t
4 3rd   t _ _ _ d
5 15th   f _ _ _ _ _ _ _ h
6 9th   n _ _ _ h

c Complete the questions with the words in the box.

---
clean   do   invite   make   use   visit
---

1 Do you often _____ museums?
2 Are you going to _____ a cake at the weekend?
3 Did you _____ any sport yesterday?
4 Are you going to _____ your bedroom today?
5 Do you _____ the Internet every day?
6 Are you going to _____ someone for a meal next week?

d 💬 Ask and answer the questions in 2c.

3 SOUND AND SPELLING

a ▶4.79 Circle the /v/ sounds in the phrases and underline the /w/ sounds. Practise saying the phrases.

1 visit in the evening
2 we never invite Wendy
3 I love weekends in winter
4 win video games every week
5 watch TV with Vicky and William
6 on Wednesday the twelfth of November

b ▶4.80 Complete the table with the words in the box. Are the *oo* sounds short (/ʊ/) or long (/uː/)? Practise saying the words.

---
good   book   football   boots
cool   look   school   soon

/ʊ/	/uː/
cooking	spoon

🔄 REVIEW YOUR PROGRESS

How well did you do in this unit? Write 3, 2, or 1 for each objective.
3 = very well   2 = well   1 = not so well

I CAN ...

talk about future plans	☐
ask and answer about future plans	☐
make and accept invitations	☐

1A Student A

a You're Yoshi from Japan. You're a student. Complete the conversation.

A Hello, I'm _____.
B Hi, I'm Bella. Nice to meet you.
A Are you from _____?
B No, I'm not. I'm from the USA. And you?
A I'm from _____.
B Are you a teacher?
A No, I'm a _____. And you?
B I'm a teacher.

b Have a conversation with Student B.

c Choose a name and a country and have another conversation.

2A Student A

a Read the information about Kate.

Name: Kate
Town / city: Ely – small city near Cambridge, in England
Home: beautiful, old house

b Tell Students B and C about Kate.

> Her name's …
>
> She's from …
>
> Her home is …

c Listen to Students B and C talk about two people. What information is the same about all three people?

3B Student A

a Ask Student B the time in these cities:

- Paris
- Rio de Janeiro
- Moscow
- Istanbul

b Answer Student B's questions about the time in these cities.

Tokyo   New York   Mexico City   Berlin

c ▶ Now go back to p.27

1B Student A

Denis
Jenna
Sandra and Pietro

Jenna = British   Denis = Russian   Sandra and Pietro = Italian

a Look at the picture and the information box. Then cover the box.

b Tell Student B the names of the people and answer Student B's questions.

> This is …

c Listen to Student B talk about the people in the picture. Then ask Student B about the nationalities of the people.

> Are they British?

> No, they aren't. They're American.

4B Student A

a Read the information about Omar on your card.

'I'm a student. I'm 19 and I study English at Cairo University, in Egypt. I live at home with my parents. My mother is a teacher and my father works at the Bank of Cairo. He's a bank manager. I have one brother. He's married and he lives in Dubai. He works at Dubai Airport.'

b Tell Student B about Omar.

> He's a student. He studies English …

c Listen to Student B talk about Monica. Find six things that are the same about Omar and Monica.

1 They're both students.

d ▶ Now go back to p.35

2B Student A

a Look at the picture. Student B has a similar picture. Ask and answer questions to find seven differences.

> Do you have a phone in your picture?

> I have two phones.

b ▶ Now go back to p.19

4A Student A

a Read the information.

- You live in Paris in France, but you work three days a week in London, in the UK.
- You work two days a week at home.
- You study French and you go to lessons on Friday.

b Start a conversation with Student B about their life. Use the questions below to help you.

> Where do you live?

> Do you work in …?

> Do you speak …?

c Listen to Student B and reply.

> I live in …

> I speak a little …

2C Student A

a Ask Student B about his / her:
- surname
- address
- phone number
- email address

> What's your surname?

b Read the information on your card. Answer Student B's questions.

Surname: Ramirez
Address: 5 High Street
Phone number: 0124 364592
Email address: toniramirez@powermail.com

c ▶ Now go back to p.20

7B Student A

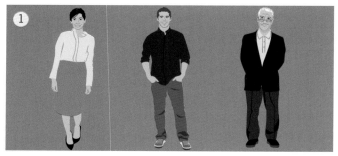

May   Frank   Celia

a Look at picture 1. Make notes about their clothes.

b Tell Student B about the clothes the people in picture 1 are wearing. Find out their names and write them under each picture.

> This person has a blouse and a skirt. What's this person's name?

c Listen to Student B talk about the clothes in picture 2. Tell him / her the people's names.

d ▶ Now go back to p.58

5B Student A

a Read the information about a hostel on your card.

HARRY'S HOSTEL

- big rooms with no shower
- small rooms with a shower
- free wi-fi
- a small café

Note: There isn't a swimming pool or a car park.

b Student B has information about a hotel. Ask and answer questions to find what things are the same and what things are different in the hotel and the hostel.

> Is there a swimming pool in the hotel?

> Yes, there is.

6A Student A

a Look at the information about Rosa and Franco. Make positive (+) and negative (–) sentences.

+ work very hard   – have a lot of free time
+ work at a hospital – sit very much
→ a doctor

Rosa

+ work long hours   – sit down a lot
+ like his job   – work in summer
→ a teacher

Franco

b Tell Student B about Rosa and Franco. Don't say their jobs.

> Rosa works very hard.

c Ask Student B about Lidia and Hassan. Say: *Tell me about ... .* Can you guess their jobs?

Lidia

Hassan

7C Student A

a **Conversation 1.** You're a shop assistant. Student B is your customer. You have six glasses and they are £2.00 each. Your customer can pay by card. Start a conversation with *Hello, can I help you?*

b **Conversation 2.** You're a customer in a shop. Student B is a shop assistant. You want to buy four plates. Ask how much they are.

c ▶ Now go back to p.61

4C Student A

a Look at the pictures. The two people are your friends. You want to show the pictures to Student B. Think about what you want to say.

Rob, teacher, interesting

Carla, hotel manager, happy

b Cover the information under the pictures. Show them to Student B and talk about your friends.

> These are my friends, Rob and Carla.

c Ask Student B about his / her two friends.

> Do you have photos of your friends?

d ▶ Now go back to p.37

6B Student A

a Gamal and Peter live in the same flat. Read about Gamal's daily routine.

Gamal is a student. He usually gets up at 9:00 and has breakfast. Then he goes to university at 10:00. In the afternoon he studies in the library and he gets home at 5:00. In the evening he works in a café near their flat. He starts work at 7:00 and finishes at 11:00. He goes to bed at 12:00.

b Ask Student B questions about Peter. Then write the answers.

When does he get up?

What does he do then?

- When / wake up? *6:30*
- When / get up?
- What / do then?
- When / start work?

- When / finish work?
- When / get home?
- What / do in the evening?
- When / go to bed?

c Answer Student B's questions about Gamal.

d When does Gamal see Peter?

7A Student A

a You have a market stall. You sell the objects in the box.

cups   glasses   plates   bags   knives

Write a price for each object.

b Try to sell things to Student B.

> It's only £5 – it's very cheap.

> They're £3 each. They're very beautiful.

c At Student B's stall you see three things you like:
- a beautiful old picture
- a lamp
- some interesting old books

> Try to buy them for a good price.

> It's very expensive. Is £10 OK?

8A Student A

a Ask Student B about Hanan.

> Where was she a year ago?

> Where was she last weekend?

> Was she at work on Monday?

b Listen to Students B and C talk about Marcella.

c Answer Student C's questions about Henri.

1 year ago	last weekend	on Monday
in Chile	at a party in Paris	at work in Germany

Henri

d What is the same for all three people?

11C Student A

a You and Student B live in the same city. Talk about good places for tourists to visit. This is what you think of the four main places to visit:

the Museum – very interesting
Central Park – OK, nice
the Old Town – a bit boring
the Mega Department Store – very expensive

> What do you think of Central Park?

> I think Central Park is OK.

> Really? I don't think so.

b ▶ Now go back to p.93

8B Student A

a Look at the pictures of Leo's day yesterday. Make notes about what he did.

morning

afternoon

evening

b Tell Student B what Leo did yesterday.

c Listen to Student B talk about what Nina did yesterday. What activities are the same?

10C Student A

a **Conversation 1.** Read your first card. Think about what you want to say. Then start the conversation with Student B with *Excuse me*.

> You want to go to Manchester.
> - Time now: 11:15 am.
> - Ask about the next train.
> - Ask about the platform.
> - You have a big suitcase – it's difficult to run.

b **Conversation 2.** Now read your second card. Think about what you want to say. Listen to Student B and reply.

> You're an official at a bus station.
> - Time now: 2:45 pm.
>
> | | Time | Bus stop | Price |
> |---|---|---|---|
> | Oxford | 3:00 pm | 4 | £16 |
> | Oxford | 4:00 pm | 3 | £11 |

c ▶ Now go back to p.85

10A Student A

a You are in picture 2. Tell Student B:
   • where you are (*I'm sitting in …*)
   • what's in the next room (*There's a … next door.*)
   • what you're doing (*I'm …*)

b Listen to Student B. Are they talking about picture 4, 5 or 6?

c Choose picture 4 or 5. Describe it to Student B.

d Listen to Student B again. Which picture are they talking about now?

10B Student A

a Look at the picture. What are the people doing? Make notes.

b Student B has a similar picture. Ask and answer questions to find five differences. You start. Ask about Ali.

Is Ali in the kitchen?

Yes, he is.

Is he eating?

No, he isn't. He's …

c ▶ Now go back to p.83

9A Student A

a Read notes about your trip to Seville, in Spain. Make sentences from the notes. Use the past simple.
   • Seville – south of Spain
   • plane to Madrid …
   • … then train to Seville
   • small hotel – city centre
   • lots of photos
   • shopping – didn't buy anything
   • restaurants – very good food
   • a concert – you liked it!

b Tell Student B about your trip.

c Listen to Student B talk about a trip to Dubai. Find four things you both did on your trips.

9B Student A

a Read the information about the weather in Mumbai, in India. Listen to Student B and reply.

Weather in Mumbai	
Yesterday	hot, sunny
Today	cloudy, warm
Summer	a lot of rain, hot

b Ask Student B these questions about the weather in Berlin, in Germany.

What was the weather like yesterday?

What's the weather like today?

What's the weather like in winter?

c ▶ Now go back to p.75

12C Student A

a You want to invite Student B to:
1 go for a walk at the weekend.
2 meet for coffee in town.

Think about what you want to say. Start the conversation with Student B. Try to find times when you're both free.

> Would you like to go for a walk at the weekend?

YOUR DIARY

MON	work 8:00–6:00	FRI	work 8:00–6:00 yoga 7:00–8:30
TUES	work 8:00–6:00	SAT	concert 7:00 pm
WED		SUN	visiting parents 12:00–5:00
THURS	work 8:00–6:00		

b ▶ Now go back to p.101

1A Student B

a You're Bella from the USA. You're a teacher. Complete the conversation.

A Hello, I'm Yoshi.
B Hi, I'm _____. Nice to meet you.
A Are you from England?
B No, I'm not. I'm from _____. And you?
A I'm from Japan.
B Are you a _____?
A No, I'm a student. And you?
B I'm a _____.

b Have a conversation with Student A.

c Choose a name and a country and have another conversation.

3B Student B

a Answer Student A's questions about the time in these cities.

Paris   Rio de Janeiro   Moscow   Istanbul

b Ask Student A the time in these cities:
- Tokyo
- New York
- Mexico City
- Berlin

c ▶ Now go back to p.27

1B Student B

Tony

Sara

Marta and Luiza

Sara = Spanish   Tony = American   Marta and Luiza = Brazilian

a Look at the picture and the information in the box. Then cover the box.

b Listen to Student A talk about the people in the picture. Then ask Student A about the nationalities of the people.

> Is he British?

> No, he isn't. He's American.

c Tell Student A the names of the people and answer Student A's questions.

> This is …

2B Student B

a Look at the picture. Student A has a similar picture. Ask and answer questions to find seven differences.

THE NEWS

> Do you have keys in your picture?

> I have one key.

b ▶ Now go back to p.19

2A Student B

a Read the information about Carla.

Name: Carla
Town / city: Hamilton – small city near Toronto, in Canada
Home: nice, new flat

b Listen to Student A.

c Tell Students A and C about Carla.

Her name's …

She's from …

Her home is …

d Listen to Student C talk. What information is the same about all three people?

2C Student B

a Read the information on your card. Answer Student A's questions.

> **Surname:** Adams
> **Address:** 8 Park Road
> **Phone number:** 0124 732816
> **Email address:** alexadams@powermail.com

b Ask Student A about his / her:

- surname
- address
- phone number
- email address

What's your surname?

c ▶ Now go back to p.20

4B Student B

a Read the information about Monica on your card.

'I'm Spanish. I'm 20. I live in Madrid and I study English at university. I live at home with my parents. I have a brother and two sisters. My brother works at Madrid Airport. He's married and he has two children.'

b Listen to Student A talk about Omar.

c Tell Student A about Monica. Find six things that are the same about Omar and Monica.

She's a student. She studies English …

1 They're both students.

d ▶ Now go back to p.35

4A Student B

a Read the information.
- You live in Monterrey, in Mexico, but you work four days a week in Austin, Texas, in the USA.
- You work one day a week at home.
- You study Spanish and you go to lessons on Saturday.

b Listen to Student A and reply.

I live in …

I speak a little …

c Start a conversation with Student A about their life. Use the questions below to help you.

Where do you live?

Do you work in …?

Do you speak …?

4C Student B

a Look at the pictures. The two people are your friends. You want to show the pictures to Student A. Think about what you want to say.

Mia, student, kind

Fred, bank manager, funny

b Ask Student A about his / her two friends.

Do you have photos of your friends?

c Cover the information under the pictures. Show them to Student A and talk about your friends.

These are my friends, Mia and Fred.

d ▶ Now go back to p.37

5B Student B

a Read the information about a hotel on your card.

Hotel Helena

- rooms with showers and TVs
- restaurant
- swimming pool
- car park

Note: There isn't free wi-fi in the hotel. You pay for it.

b Student A has information about a hostel. Ask and answer questions to find what things are the same and what things are different in the hotel and the hostel.

> Is there free wi-fi in the hostel?

> Yes, there is.

6A Student B

a Look at the information about Lidia and Hassan. Make positive (+) and negative (–) sentences.

+ meet a lot of people	– work in the morning
+ work in a restaurant	– sit very much
→ a waitress	

Lidia

+ meet a lot of people	– work in the day
+ like his job	– work very hard
→ a taxi driver	

Hassan

b Ask Student A about Rosa and Franco. Say: *Tell me about ... .* Can you guess their jobs?

Rosa **Franco**

c Tell Student A about Lidia and Hassan. Don't say their jobs.

> Lidia meets lots of people.

7B Student B

① Sue Mark Harry

②

a Look at picture 2. Make notes about their clothes.

b Listen to Student A talk about the clothes in picture 1. Tell him / her the people's names.

c Tell Student A about the clothes the people in picture 2 are wearing. Find out their names and write them under each picture.

> This person has a coat and trousers. What's the person's name?

d ▶ Now go back to p.58

9A Student B

a Read notes about your trip to Dubai, in the UAE. Make sentences from the notes. Use the past simple.

- Dubai – north of the UAE
- plane to Dubai ...
- didn't stay in a hotel ...
- ... my brother's apartment (he lives in Dubai)
- ... then taxi around the city
- lots of photos
- shopping – lots of clothes
- restaurants – very good food

b Listen to Student A talk about a trip to Seville.

c Tell Student A about your trip. Find four things you both did on your trips.

5C Student B

a **Conversation 1.** You're on a street you know. Use the information to answer Student A's questions.

a hotel: not near here – near the station
cafés: Black Cat café in this street

b **Conversation 2.** Now you're on a street you don't know. Ask Student A about:
  • a bank • shops

c ▶ Now go back to p.45

7A Student B

a You have a market stall. You sell the objects in the box.

| pictures   clocks   lamps   chairs   old books |

Write a price for each object.

b At Student A's stall you see three things you like:
  • some beautiful plates • an interesting shopping bag
  • a good knife for your kitchen

Try to buy them for a good price.

> **They're expensive. Is £2 OK?**

c Try to sell things to Student A.

> **They're £10 each.**
> **They're very old.**

> **It's only £5 –**
> **it's very cheap.**

8A Student B

a Answer Student A's questions about Hanan.

1 year ago	**last weekend**	**on Monday**
in Germany	at a party at her home	at university

Hanan

b Ask Student C about Marcella.

> **Where was she**
> **a year ago?**

> **Where was she last**
> **weekend?**

> **Was she at work on Monday?**

c Listen to Students A and C talk about Henri.

d What is the same for all three people?

8B Student B

a Look at the pictures of Nina's day yesterday. Make notes about what she did.

morning

afternoon

evening

b Listen to Student A talk about what Leo did yesterday.

c Tell Student A what Nina did yesterday. What activities are the same?

10C Student B

a **Conversation 1.** Read your first card. Think about what you want to say. Listen to Student A and reply.

 You're an official at a train station.
  • Time now: 11:15 am.
  • Platform 6 is two minutes' walk away.

	Time	Platform
Manchester	11:17 am	6
Manchester	11:35 am	6

b **Conversation 2.** Now read your second card. Think about what you want to say. Then start the conversation with Student A with *Excuse me.*

 You want to go to Oxford.
  • Time now: 2:45 pm.
  • Ask about the next bus.
  • Ask about the bus stop.
  • Ask about the price. (You only have £15 with you.)

c ▶ Now go back to p.85

10A Student B

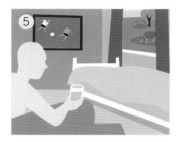 

a Listen to Student A. Are they talking about picture 1, 2 or 3?

b You are in picture 6. Tell Student A:
  - where you are (*I'm sitting in …*)
  - what's in the next room (*There's a … next door.*)
  - what you're doing (*I'm …*)

c Listen to Student A again. Which picture are they talking about now?

d Choose picture 1 or 3. Describe it to Student A.

10B Student B

a Look at the picture. What are the people doing? Make notes.

b Student A has a similar picture. Ask and answer questions to find five differences. Student A starts.

> Is Ali in the kitchen?

> Yes, he is.

> Is he eating?

> No, he isn't. He's …

c ▶ Now go back to p.83

7C Student B

a **Conversation 1.** You're a customer in a shop. Student A is a shop assistant. You want to buy four glasses. Ask how much they are. You'd like to pay by card.

b **Conversation 2.** You're a shop assistant. Student A is your customer. You have three plates and they are £3.00 each. Your customer can pay by card. Start a conversation with *Hello, can I help you?*

c ▶ Now go back to p.61

9B Student B

a Ask Student A these questions about the weather in Mumbai, in India.

> What was the weather like yesterday?

> What's the weather like today?

> What's the weather like in summer?

b Read the information about the weather in Berlin, in Germany. Listen to Student A and reply.

Weather in Berlin	
Yesterday	wet, windy
Today	sunny, cold
Winter	snows, cold

c ▶ Now go back to p.75

6B Student B

a Peter and Gamal live in the same flat. Read about Peter's daily routine.

Peter works in a bank. He always wakes up at 6:30. He gets up at 7:00, has coffee and goes to work. He starts work at 8:30 and he finishes at 5:30. He gets home at 6:00, has dinner and watches TV. Sometimes he goes out, but he always goes to bed at 10:30.

b Answer Student A's questions about Peter.

c Ask Student A questions about Gamal. Then write the answers.

> When does he go to university?

> What does he do in the afternoon?

- When / get up? *9:00*
- When / go to university?
- What / do in the afternoon?
- When / get home?

- What / do in the evening?
- When / start work?
- When / finish work?
- When / go to bed?

d When does Peter see Gamal?

12C Student B

a You want to invite Student A to:
1 go out for a meal one evening.
2 go shopping for clothes.

Think about what you want to say. Listen to Student A and reply. Try to find times when you're both free.

> Would you like to go out for dinner?

Y O U R D I A R Y	**MON**	work 8:00–6:00 theatre 8:00 pm
	TUES	
	WED	work 8:00–6:00 Spanish class 7:00–8:30
	THURS	on holiday – not here
	FRI	on holiday – not here
	SAT	sport 9:00–2:00
	SUN	

b ▶ Now go back to p.101

11C Student B

a You and Student A live in the same city. Talk about good places for tourists to visit. This is what you think of the four main places to visit:

the Museum – OK
Central Park – boring
the Old Town – lovely
the Mega Department Store – lots of fun

> What do you think of the Museum?

> I think the Museum is OK.

> Really? I don't think so.

b ▶ Now go back to p.93

2A Student C

a Read the information about Dave.
Name: Dave
Town / city: Newcastle – small city near Sydney, in Australia
Home: big, new flat

b Listen to Students A and B talk about two people.

c Tell Students A and B about Dave. What information is the same about all three people?

> His name's …

> He's from …

> His home is …

8A Student C

a Listen to Students A and B talk about Hanan.

b Answer Student B's questions about Marcella.

1 year ago	last weekend	on Monday
in Greece	at a party in Venice	in a meeting at work

Marcella

c Ask Student A about Henri.

> Where was he a year ago?

> Where was he last weekend?

> Was he at work on Monday?

d What is the same for all three people?

Grammar Focus

1A be: I / you / we

Part 1: Positive and questions

▶ 1.6

	Positive (+)
I	*I'm fine.*
you	*You're right.*
we	*We're from the USA.*
you	*You're John and Hannah.*

💬 **Tip**

I am → I'm
You are → You're
We are → We're

▶ 1.8

	Wh- questions (?)
I	*Where **am** I?*
you	*How **are** you?*
we	*Where **are** we?*
you	*Where **are** you?*

▶ 1.7

	Yes/No questions (?)		Short answers	
I	**Am** I	at home?	Yes, I **am**.	No, I'**m not**.
you	**Are** you	OK?	Yes, you **are**.	No, you **aren't**.
we	**Are** we	in London?	Yes, we **are**.	No, we **aren't**.
you	**Are** you	students?	Yes, you **are**.	No, you **aren't**.

Are you from Spain? NOT ~~You are from Spain?~~
Yes, **I am**. NOT ~~Yes, I'm.~~

Part 2: Negative

▶ 1.11

	Negative (–)
I	*I'**m not** from Italy.*
you	*You **aren't** a teacher.*
we	*We **aren't** from the USA.*
you	*You **aren't** teachers.*

💬 **Tip**

I am not → I'm not
You are not → You're not
We are not → We're not

I'm not from Brazil. NOT ~~I amn't from Brazil.~~

1B be: he / she / they

Part 1: Positive

▶ 1.19

	+
he	*He'**s** Japanese.*
she	*She'**s** Russian.*
they	*They'**re** American.*

💬 **Tip**

He **is** Japanese. → He'**s** Japanese.
They **are** American. → They'**re** American.

Part 2: Negative and questions

▶ 1.21

	–
he	*He **isn't** Japanese.*
she	*She **isn't** Russian.*
they	*They **aren't** American.*

💬 **Tip**

She **is not** Russian. → She **isn't** Russian.
They **are not** American. → They **aren't** American.

He's Japanese.   She's Russian.   They're American.

▶ 1.22

	Yes/No questions (?)	Short answers	
he	**Is** he Japanese?	Yes, he **is**.	No, he **isn't**.
she	**Is** she Russian?	Yes, she **is**.	No, she **isn't**.
they	**Are** they American?	Yes, they **are**.	No, they **aren't**.

▶ 1.23

	Wh- questions (?)
he / she	*Where'**s** he / she from?* *Who'**s** he / she?*
they	*Where **are** they from?* *Who **are** they?*

Is he Japanese? NOT ~~Is Japanese?~~ OR ~~He is Japanese?~~
Are they American? NOT ~~Are American?~~ OR ~~They are American?~~
Yes, **he is**. NOT ~~Yes, he's.~~

💬 **Tip**

Where **is** he from? → Where'**s** he from?
Who **is** she? → Who'**s** she?

1A *be*: I / you / we

Part 1: Positive and questions

a Write sentences with *'re* or *'m*.

1 I am from New York.   *I'm from New York.*
2 We are students.
3 You are Roberto.
4 I am fine, thanks.
5 We are from Mexico.

b Put the words in the correct order to make questions.

1 you / are / how ?   *How are you?*
2 are / from / the USA / you ?
3 we / in / Russia / are ?
4 OK / I / am ?
5 name / your / what's ?

c ▶ Now go back to p.8

Part 2: Negative

a Write one positive (+) and one negative (–) sentence for 1–5.

1 We / from Brazil
   We're from Brazil. We aren't from Brazil.
2 You / Rebecca
3 I / a teacher
4 We / in Paris
5 I / OK

b Write short answers.

1 **A** Are you from the USA?
   B No, ___*I'm not*___.
2 **A** Are you Eric?
   B Yes, _____.
3 **A** Are we in Spain?
   B No, _____.
4 **A** Are you students?
   B Yes, _____.

c ▶ Now go back to p.9

1B *be*: he / she / they

Part 1: Positive

a Complete the sentences with *he's*, *she's* or *they're*.

1 _____ Italian.

2 _____ Chinese.

3 _____ Brazilian.

4 _____ Russian.

5 _____ Spanish.

6 _____ American.

b ▶ Now go back to p.11

Part 2: Negative and questions

a Complete the sentences with *isn't* or *aren't*.

1 She _____ Italian. She's Brazilian.
2 They _____ American. They're English.
3 He _____ Chinese. He's American.
4 They _____ Russian. They're English.
5 He _____ Spanish. He's Italian.
6 She _____ Brazilian. She's Japanese.

b Tick (✓) the correct questions. Correct the wrong questions.

1 ☐ He is Russian?
2 ☐ Is she Brazilian?
3 ☐ Are English they?
4 ☐ Are he Italian?
5 ☐ She is Chinese?
6 ☐ Are they Japanese?

c Complete the conversations with *is*, *isn't*, *'s*, *are*, *aren't* or *'re*.

A Who is this?
B He [1]_____ my friend, Lee.
A [2]_____ he Chinese?
B No, he [3]_____. He [4]_____ from the USA.

A Who are they?
B They [5]_____ my friends, Nick and Anna.
A [6]_____ they from England?
B No, they [7]_____. They [8]_____ Russian.

d ▶ Now go back to p.11

2A be: it's / it isn't; Possessive adjectives

Part 1: *it's / it isn't*

it = a place / a thing   *they* = 2+ places / things

> **Tip**
>
> It **is** in Chile. → It**'s** in Chile.
> It **is not** in Italy. → It **isn't** in Italy.

▶ 1.42

	+	–
it	It**'s** an old hotel.	It **isn't** a new hotel.
they	They**'re** old houses.	They **aren't** big houses.

▶ 1.43

	Yes/No questions	Short answers	
it	**Is** it a big hotel?	Yes, it **is**.	No, it **isn't**.
they	**Are** they new houses?	Yes, they **are**.	No, they **aren't**.

Is it in Ireland? NOT ~~Is in Ireland?~~ OR ~~It is in Ireland?~~
Yes, **it is**. NOT ~~Yes, it's.~~

Part 2: Possessive adjectives

Pronoun	Possessive adjective	▶ 1.48
I	**my**	**My** flat is small.
you	**your**	Is this **your** book?
he	**his**	**His** home is old and beautiful.
she	**her**	She's here with **her** friend.
we	**our**	This is **our** home in Moscow.
they	**their**	Is that **their** home?

your bag NOT ~~you're bag~~
their house NOT ~~they're house~~

2B Plural nouns

SPELLING: Plural nouns

most words → add *-s*	book → book**s** boy → boy**s** house → house**s**
consonant + *-y* → *-y* add *-ies*	city → cit**ies** baby → bab**ies**
ends in *-o, -ch, -ss, -s, -sh* and *-x* → add *-es*	watch → watch**es** glass → glass**es**
irregular	knife → kni**ves**

books NOT ~~a books~~

a book   a ticket   an apple

book**s**   two ticket**s**   apple**s**

3A Present simple: *I / you / we / they*

▶ 1.80

	+		–	
I	*I **like***	fish.	*I **don't like***	fish.
you	*You **eat***	meat.	*You **don't eat***	meat.
we	*We **eat***	a lot of vegetables.	*We **don't eat***	a lot of vegetables.
they	*They **like***	eggs.	*They **don't like***	eggs.

*I **don't like** fish.* NOT ~~I not like fish.~~

> **Tip**
>
> I **do not** like rice. → I **don't** like rice.

▶ 1.81

	Yes/No questions	Short answers	
I	**Do** I **like** fish?	Yes, I **do**.	No, I **don't**.
you	**Do** you **eat** meat?	Yes, you **do**.	No, you **don't**.
we	**Do** we **eat** a lot of vegetables?	Yes, we **do**.	No, we **don't**.
they	**Do** they **like** eggs?	Yes, they **do**.	No, they **don't**.

Do you eat meat? NOT ~~You eat meat?~~
Yes, **I do**. NOT ~~Yes, I like.~~
No, **we don't**. NOT ~~No, we don't like.~~

2A *be*: *it's* / *it isn't*; Possessive adjectives

Part 1: *it's* / *it isn't*

a Complete the sentences with *it's* or *they're*.

1 _____ a beautiful town near Barcelona.
2 I'm from Istanbul. _____ in Turkey.
3 São Paulo and Rio de Janeiro are big cities. _____ in Brazil.
4 My flat is small. _____ in a new part of town.
5 Our homes are old. _____ in a nice part of town.
6 His home is in St Petersburg. _____ a big, old flat.
7 The flats are in an old part of town. _____ big and beautiful.
8 They're from a small village in China. _____ near Beijing.

b ▶ Now go back to p.16

Part 2: Possessive adjectives

a Complete the sentences.

1 'Hi, I'm Jack. What's _____ name?' 'I'm Selim.'
2 She's from Brazil and _____ name's Maria.
3 They're from America and _____ names are Sam and Erica.
4 We live in Moscow. _____ flat is in an old part of town.
5 'Is this _____ book?' 'Yes, it is, thank you.'
6 They're from London, but _____ parents are from Mumbai.

b ▶ Now go back to p.17

2B Plural nouns

a Write the plurals.

1 an egg _____
2 a knife _____
3 a girl _____
4 a country _____
5 a town _____
6 a phone _____
7 a village _____
8 a city _____

b Underline the correct words.

1 Moscow is *big city* / *a big city*.
2 Villajoyosa is *a town* / *towns* in Spain.
3 It's *small* / *a small* house.
4 They're new *flat* / *flats*.
5 Two *bottle* / *bottles* of water, please.
6 He's a big *baby* / *babies*.
7 New York and Washington are *cities* / *citys* in the USA.
8 Two *tickets* / *ticketes* to London, please.

c ▶ Now go back to p.19

3A Present simple: *I* / *you* / *we* / *they*

a Complete the sentences with the words in the box.

do (x2)   don't (x3)   eat

1 I like rice, but I _____ like bread.
2 _____ you like fruit?
3 **A** Do they eat meat? **B** Yes, they _____.
4 We _____ fruit every day.
5 I eat rice, but I _____ like it.
6 **A** Do you like fish? **B** No, I _____.

b Look at the information about the Brown family. Write five sentences about them.

meat	✓
fish	✗
vegetables	✓
rice	✓
bread	✗

They eat …   They don't eat …

c Write sentences about things you eat and drink.

I eat rice. I eat vegetables every day. I don't like coffee …

d ▶ Now go back to p.25

3B Adverbs of frequency

We **always** have breakfast at 7:00.

I **usually** have a sandwich for lunch.

We **sometimes** eat fish for dinner.

I **never** eat cake.
NOT ~~I never don't eat cake.~~

> 💬 **Tip**
> Adverbs of frequency go **before** the verb.
> NOT ~~**Always we have** breakfast at 7:00.~~ OR ~~**We have always** breakfast at 7:00.~~

4A Present simple: *Wh-* questions

When **do** they **go** to school?

 2.17

Wh- questions with *be*	
What**'s** your name?	My name**'s** Lucia.
When **are** you at home?	We**'re** at home this evening.
Where **are** they from?	They**'re** from Brazil.

NOT ~~What **your name is**?~~ OR ~~Where **you are** from?~~

> 💬 **Tip**
> Wh- word + *is / are* + person (*you / they*, etc.)?

 2.18

Wh- questions with other verbs	
Where **do** you **live**?	I **live** in Barcelona.
What **do** you **study**?	We **study** Russian.
When **do** they **go** to school?	They **go** to school at 8:00.

NOT ~~Where **you live**?~~ OR ~~Where **live you**?~~

> 💬 **Tip**
> Wh- word + *do* + person (*you / they*, etc.) + verb?

4B Present simple: *he / she / it* positive

2.26

	+	
he	My brother **works** He **lives**	in a hotel. in a small house.
she	Ingrid **lives** She **works**	in Berlin. in an office.
it	My room **has** It **has**	a big window. a big table.

> 💬 **Tip**
> I / you / we / they **work** in a hotel.
> He / She **works** in a hotel.

SPELLING: verb + -s

most verbs → add *-s*	work → work**s** live → live**s**
consonant + *-y* → *-y* add *-ies*	study → stud**ies**
ends in *-o, -ch, -ss, -s,* *-sh* and *-x* → add *-es*	go → go**es** do → do**es** teach → teach**es**
irregular	have → **has**

He **studies** NOT ~~He **studys**~~
She **has** NOT ~~She **haves**~~

3B Adverbs of frequency

a Put the words in the correct order to make sentences.

1 sometimes / at 10:00 / have dinner / we
2 I / in the evening / have coffee / never
3 have a tomato sandwich / I / for lunch / usually
4 we / at home / always / have dinner
5 at lunchtime / always / eat fruit / I
6 usually / in a café / I / have lunch

b Look at Monica's diary. Complete her sentences with adverbs of frequency.

1 'I _____ have coffee in a small café.'
2 'I _____ eat breakfast.'
3 'My friends and I _____ have lunch at work.'
4 'We _____ have dinner at home.'

c ▶ Now go back to p.27

	Monday	Tuesday	Wednesday	Thursday	Friday	Sa
	2	3	4	5	6	
8:00	coffee at Café Blanc		coffee at Café Blanc			
12:30	lunch at work	lunch at work	lunch at work	lunch at work	lunch at work	
7:00	dinner with the family	dinner with the family	dinner with the family	dinner with the family	dinner with the family	
	9	10	11	12	13	

4A Present simple: Wh- questions

a Complete the questions with 's, are or do.

1 Where _____ they work?
2 What _____ you eat for breakfast?
3 Where _____ your home?
4 What _____ the time?
5 Where _____ you study English?
6 Where _____ you from?
7 What time _____ you go to university every day?
8 When _____ he at home?

b Write questions for the sentences. Use the question word in brackets.

1 I work in Madrid. (where)
   Where do you work?
2 We go to work at 7:00 in the morning. (when)
3 I eat a sandwich for lunch. (what)
4 We study at a big language school in Madrid. (where)
5 I study business at university. (what)
6 I go to my lesson at 6:00 in the evening. (when)

c ▶ Now go back to p.33

4B Present simple: he / she / it positive

a Underline the correct words.

1 She always *drink / drinks* tea for breakfast.
2 My son *studies / studys* Spanish at university.
3 He *works / workes* in a supermarket.
4 The car *have / has* new lights.
5 She has breakfast and then she *gos / goes* to school.
6 The dog *live / lives* in the garden.

b Look at the picture. Complete the sentences about Carmen with the verbs in the box.

have   drink   eat   live   study

1 She _____ in Madrid.
2 She _____ English.
3 She _____ bananas.
4 She _____ coffee.
5 She _____ a computer.

c ▶ Now go back to p.35

5A *there is / there are*: positive

On Regent Street …
… **there's** a supermarket.
… **there's** a cinema.
… **there are** two cafés.
… **there are** lots of people.

▶ 2.39

	+	
Singular	**There's**	a café. one café.
Plural	**There are**	cafés. three cafés.

There's = There is
There's a café. NOT ~~There a café.~~
There are three cafés.
NOT ~~There's three~~ cafés.

5B *there is / there are*: negative and questions

▶ 2.53

	−	
Singular	**There isn't**	a shower. a blanket.
Plural	**There aren't**	any pillows. any rooms.

> 💬 **Tip**
>
> There **is not** a hotel. → There **isn't** a hotel.
> There **are not** any cafés. → There **aren't** any cafés.
> Use *any* after *there aren't*.

▶ 2.54

	Yes/No questions		Short answers	
Singular	**Is there**	a café?	Yes, **there is**.	No, **there isn't**.
Plural	**Are there**	any small rooms?	Yes, **there are**.	No, **there aren't**.

NOT ~~There is a café?~~ OR ~~There are small rooms?~~
NOT ~~Yes, there's.~~ OR ~~No, there not.~~

> 💬 **Tip**
>
> Use *any* after *Are there … ?*

Are there any hotels near here?

6A Present simple: *he / she / it* negative

▶ 2.71

	−	
he	He **doesn't work**	on Monday.
she	She **doesn't study**	Spanish.
it	The village **doesn't have**	a school.

He **doesn't work** on Monday. NOT ~~He doesn't works on Monday.~~
OR ~~He don't works on Monday.~~
OR ~~He not works on Monday.~~

> 💬 **Tip**
>
> I **do not work** at night. → I **don't work** at night.
> He **does not work** at night. → He **doesn't work** at night.

5A *there is / there are*: positive

a Write three more sentences about Regent Street on page 120. Use *there's* or *there are* and the words in the box.

> house   car   park

1 _____
2 _____
3 _____

b Look at the picture. Change the sentences to make them true.

1 There's a taxi.
2 There are two restaurants.
3 There's one shop.
4 There are three women.
5 There are three girls.
6 There's a boy.
7 There are two schools.

c ▶ Now go back to p.40

5B *there is / there are*: negative and questions

a Complete the sentences with a negative (–) or question (?) form of *there is* or *there are*.

1 _____ any cafés in my street.
2 _____ a cinema in this part of town.
3 _____ a hotel near the station?
4 _____ any shops near the hotel?
5 _____ any restaurants on High Street.
6 _____ a café near here?
7 _____ a restaurant near the cinema.
8 _____ any supermarkets near the hostel?

b Add *any* to the sentences if possible.

1 There aren't good restaurants in this town.
2 Are there shops near the hotel?
3 Is there a TV in the room?
4 Sorry, there aren't free rooms.
5 There's a café on the first floor.
6 There are two cinemas near here.

c Complete the conversation with the correct form of *there is / there are*.

A Excuse me, _____ _____ any hotels near here?
B No, _____ _____. But _____ one near the station.
A And _____ _____ a restaurant near the hotel?
B Yes, _____ _____. It's a very good one.

d ▶ Now go back to p.43

6A Present simple: *he / she / it* negative

a Complete the sentences with *don't* or *doesn't*.

1 They __don't__ speak French.
2 He _____ like chocolate cake.
3 She _____ eat toast for breakfast.
4 We _____ go to work early.
5 Eva and Marek _____ like their jobs.
6 Blanca and her sister _____ live in Spain.
7 Her brother _____ work in a bank.
8 My sister, Lucia, and I _____ eat fish.

b Make the sentences negative.

1 Pia works in a shop.   *Pia doesn't work in a shop.*
2 My brother works in a car factory.
3 My parents like coffee.
4 We live near the station.
5 He studies Italian.
6 They go to work early.
7 Akira lives in Tokyo.
8 Their son works in a bank.

c ▶ Now go back to p.49

6B Present simple: *he / she / it* questions

▶ 2.79

	Yes/No questions		Short answers	
he	**Does** he	**work** in a bank?	Yes, he **does**.	No, he **doesn't**.
she	**Does** she	**get up** early?	Yes, she **does**.	No, she **doesn't**.
it	**Does** the party	**start** at 9:00?	Yes, it **does**.	No, it **doesn't**.

Does he work in a bank?   NOT ~~Does he works …?~~
Yes, **she does**.   NOT ~~Yes, she works.~~
No, **she doesn't**.   NOT ~~No, she doesn't work.~~

▶ 2.80

	Wh- questions		
he	Where	**does** he	**work**?
she	When	**does** she	**get up**?
it	What time	**does** it	**start**?

Where **does she** work?   NOT ~~Where she does work?~~
                       OR ~~Where she works?~~

Does she get up early?

7A this, that, these, those

▶ 3.8

this, these = here, near me   *that, those* = there, not near me

'My brother wants **this** car.'   'I love **these** flowers.'   'My sister wants **that** car.'   'I love **those** flowers.'

Singular	**this** car	**that** car
Plural	**these** flowers	**those** flowers

this / that / these / those + be
That's my car.
Is this your bag?

this / that / these / those + noun
I like **that car**.
These flowers are beautiful.

7B Possessive 's

▶ 3.19

This is my friend, Millie.

Kristina is my sister.

Kristina's Zane**'s** sister.
Millie's Kristina**'s** friend. → Millie is Kristina**'s** friend.
KRISTINA My brother**'s** jeans are red.
The girls**'** dresses are beautiful.

These are our parents.

Zane and Kristina**'s** parents are Lara and Jim.

My brother's jeans are red. NOT ~~The jeans of my brother are red.~~
The **girls'** dresses are beautiful. (2+ girls) NOT ~~The girl's dresses are beautiful.~~ (1 girl)

6B Present simple: *he / she / it* questions

a Complete the questions.

1 **A** He works in a restaurant.
  B _____ he like it?
2 **A** I'm a taxi driver.
  B _____ you meet interesting people?
3 **A** My brother's in London.
  B _____ he live there?
4 **A** My children go to school at 7:30.
  B What time _____ they get up?
5 **A** She often works in the evenings.
  B When _____ she get home?

b <u>Underline</u> the correct words.

1 **A** Does your daughter like school?
  B Yes, she *likes / does*. She thinks it's great.
2 **A** Do you like ice cream?
  B *Yes / No*, I don't. I never eat it.
3 **A** Does he watch football?
  B No, he *don't / doesn't*. He only likes tennis.
4 **A** Do you start work early?
  B Yes, we *are / do*. We start at 5:00 in the morning!
5 **A** Does your wife work in a restaurant?
  B No, she *doesn't work / doesn't*. She's a hotel receptionist.

c ▶ Now go back to p.51

7A *this, that, these, those*

a <u>Underline</u> the correct words.

1 Excuse me, is *this / these* your coat?
2 Who's *this / that* man in the next room?
3 How much are *those / that* watches?
4 This *is / are* my wife, Susanna.
5 Are *this / these* your glasses?

b Complete the sentences with *this*, *that*, *these* or *those*.

1 'Look at _____ beautiful house.'
2 '_____ are our tickets.'
3 'Who are _____ people?'
4 'Is _____ your phone?'

c ▶ Now go back to p.57

7B Possessive *'s*

a Complete the sentences with the words in brackets.

1 It's _Mara's skirt_. (Mara / skirt)
2 It's _____. (Steven / shirt)
3 It's _____. (Liza / dress)
4 They're _____. (Luke / jeans)
5 They're _____. (Sara / shoes)
6 It's _____. (Tim / jacket)

b Write new sentences. Use the names in brackets.

1 **His** new jeans are dark blue. (Sam)
  Sam's new jeans are dark blue.
2 **His** house is near the station. (Jake)
3 **Her** shoes are brown. (Louise)
4 I like **her** new coat. (my friend)
5 **Their** new car is blue. (Ross and Emma)
6 **Her** new dress is lovely. (Penny)
7 He's **his** best friend. (Ron)
8 **Their** room is on the first floor. (the boys)

c ▶ Now go back to p.59

8A Past simple: *be*

Part 1: Positive

▶ 3.33

	+	
I / you / he / she / it	I **was** You **were** He / She **was** It **was**	in Munich yesterday. in Madrid yesterday. in Rome yesterday. fun.
we / you / they	We **were** You **were** They **were**	in Istanbul last weekend. in Moscow last weekend. in Paris last weekend.

She **was** in Rome yesterday. NOT ~~She **is** in Rome yesterday.~~
OR ~~She **were** in Rome yesterday.~~

> 💬 **Tip**
>
> We often use past forms of *be* with past time expressions like *yesterday, last night, two days ago, on Saturday, this morning.* (See Vocabulary Focus 8A on p.144.)

Part 2: Negative and questions

▶ 3.39

	−	
I / you / he / she / it	I **wasn't** You **weren't** He / She **wasn't** It **wasn't**	in Munich yesterday. in Madrid yesterday. in Rome yesterday. fun.
we / you / they	We **weren't** You **weren't** They **weren't**	in Istanbul last weekend. in Moscow last weekend. in Paris last weekend.

I **wasn't** at home yesterday.   NOT ~~I'm **not** at home yesterday.~~
OR ~~I **not was** home yesterday.~~

> 💬 **Tip**
>
> I **was not** in Munich yesterday. → I **wasn't** in Munich yesterday.
> You **were not** in Madrid yesterday. → You **weren't** in Madrid yesterday.

▶ 3.40

Yes/No questions		Short answers	
Were you	in Madrid yesterday?	Yes, you **were**.	No, you **weren't**.
Was she	in Rome yesterday?	Yes, she **was**.	No, she **wasn't**.
Were they	in Paris yesterday?	Yes, they **were**.	No, they **weren't**.

▶ 3.41

Wh- questions		
Where	**was** she	yesterday?
When	**was**	the meeting?
Where	**were** you	yesterday?
When	**were** they	in Milan?

Where **were you** yesterday? NOT ~~Where **you were** yesterday?~~

8B Past simple: positive

▶ 3.46

Regular verbs	+	
talk	I **talked**	to Sue yesterday.
play	They **played**	tennis on Saturday.
like	He was nice – I **liked**	him.
arrive	They **arrived**	last night.

I **talked** to Sue. NOT ~~I **was talk** to Sue.~~

SPELLING: -*ed* endings

most verbs → add -*ed*	talk → talk**ed** play → play**ed**
verb ends in -*e* → add -*d*	like → like**d**

▶ 3.47

Irregular verbs	+	
go	I **went**	to a party on Friday.
have	We **had**	sandwiches for lunch.
see	I **saw**	Peter yesterday.

I **went** to a party. NOT ~~I **goed** to a party.~~
We **had** sandwiches. NOT ~~We **did** have sandwiches.~~

▶ See Irregular verbs on p.165

> 💬 **Tip**
>
> The past simple form is the same for all persons, e.g. *I played tennis., He played tennis., We played tennis.*, etc.

8A Past simple: *be*

Part 1: Positive

a Complete the sentences with *was* or *were*.

1 I _____ at home yesterday.
2 He _____ in the office in the morning, but not in the afternoon.
3 We _____ at the cinema last night.
4 They _____ in Buenos Aires last month.

5 The film _____ really great.
6 Melissa _____ at school last week.
7 Ahmed and Jamal _____ at the football game on Saturday.
8 The concert _____ very good.

b ▶ Now go back to p.65

Part 2: Negative and questions

a Complete the text with *was*, *were*, *wasn't* or *weren't*.

'It ¹_____ Saturday yesterday, but I ²_____ at work all morning. I ³_____ (not) at my desk – I ⁴_____ in a meeting. It ⁵_____ very boring. In the afternoon I ⁶_____ at home with a book – it ⁷_____ great. In the evening, my friend Masha and I ⁸_____ at the cinema, but the film ⁹_____ (not) very good. We ¹⁰_____ tired so I ¹¹_____ (not) out late.'

b Put the words in the correct order to make questions.

1 last night / were you / at the cinema ?
   Were you at the cinema last night?
2 football game / was / on Saturday / he at the ?
3 were / the supermarket / they at / yesterday ?
4 you three / where were / years ago ?
5 interesting / film / was the ?
6 China / you in / when were ?
7 was the / concert / where ?
8 a boring / was it / meeting ?

c ▶ Now go back to p.65

8B Past simple: positive

a Match verbs 1–6 with the past forms in the box.

arrived	had	watched	saw	stayed	went

1 go _____
2 have _____
3 stay _____
4 see _____
5 watch _____
6 arrive _____

b Underline the correct words.

1 She *goed* / *went* to Spain last week.
2 I *was sees* / *saw* my sister at the weekend.
3 It wasn't a very interesting evening. Everyone *talkd* / *talked* about work.
4 I *staied* / *stayed* in a cheap hotel near the station.
5 We *watch* / *watched* Germany v. Uruguay last night.
6 She *read* / *readed* a magazine in the garden.

c Complete the text with the past form of the verbs in the box.

have (x2)	go (x2)	stay	read	talk	watch	~~get~~

Last Saturday, Mr Jones ¹_____got_____ up late and he ²_____ a big breakfast. Then he ³_____ shopping. He ⁴_____ a pizza for lunch and in the afternoon he ⁵_____ to his mother on the phone for an hour. In the evening he ⁶_____ at home and he ⁷_____ football on TV. He ⁸_____ to bed at 10:30 and ⁹_____ a book until 11:00.

d Complete the sentences about you or your friends. Use the past simple.

1 Last weekend, _____ .
2 Yesterday, _____ .
3 This morning, _____ .
4 Last Monday, _____ .

e ▶ Now go back to p.67

9A Past simple: negative

She **didn't get** a taxi to the airport.

▶ 3.67

	–	
stay	We **didn't stay**	at a hostel.
finish	They **didn't finish**	work early.
see	I **didn't see**	them at the party.
get	She **didn't get**	a taxi to the airport.

I **didn't see** them. NOT ~~I don't saw them.~~
We **didn't stay**. NOT ~~We didn't stayed.~~

> 💬 **Tip**
> In the negative:
> • add *didn't* before the verb
> • the verb doesn't change

9B Past simple: questions

▶ 3.79

Yes/No questions		Short answers	
Did you	**see** the film?	Yes, you **did**.	No, you **didn't**.
Did she	**work** in a café?	Yes, she **did**.	No, she **didn't**.
Did they	**go** to the party?	Yes, they **did**.	No, they **didn't**.

Did you **work** … ?   NOT ~~Did you worked …?~~
Did she **go** … ?   NOT ~~Did she went …?~~
Yes, she **did**.   NOT ~~Yes, she worked.~~
No, she **didn't**.   NOT ~~No, she didn't work.~~

▶ 3.80

Wh- questions		
Where	**did** you	**work**?
Where	**did** she	**go**?
When	**did** they	**arrive**?

Where **did** you **work**?   NOT ~~Where you worked?~~
    OR ~~Where did you worked?~~
Where **did** she **go**?   NOT ~~Where did she went?~~

Did they go to the party?

Yes, they did.

10A Present continuous: positive

We use the present continuous to talk about now.

▶ 4.9

	+
I	I**'m writing** an email.
you	You**'re working** a lot.
he / she	He**'s** / She**'s studying**.
it	It**'s raining**.
we	We**'re watching** TV.
they	They**'re eating** a big dinner.

I**'m working** hard. NOT ~~I working hard.~~ OR ~~I'm work hard.~~
I**'m having** breakfast. NOT ~~I'm haveing breakfast.~~
I**'m sitting** in the car. NOT ~~I'm siting in the car.~~

"It's raining and I'm writing this email ..."

> 💬 **Tip**
> I **am writing** an email. → I**'m writing** an email.
> We **are watching** TV. → We**'re watching** TV.
> He **is studying**. → He**'s studying**.

9A Past simple: negative

a Complete the sentences with the past simple negative form of the verb in brackets.

1 I _didn't play_ football. (play)
2 I _____ early. (get up)
3 I _____ cereal for breakfast. (have)
4 I _____ my phone. (use)
5 I _____ my emails. (read)

6 I _____ a friend. (visit)
7 I _____ shopping. (go)
8 I _____ any photos. (take)
9 I _____ to the radio. (listen)

b Look at the pictures. Complete the sentences with the verbs in the box. Make one positive and one negative sentence.

arrive   play   go (x2)   have   ~~get up~~

1 Last week Jan _didn't get up_ at 6:00. He _got up_ at 7:00.

2 He _____ to work by bus. He _____ to work by train.

3 He _____ at work at 9:00. He _____ at work at 10:00.

4 He _____ a pizza for lunch. He _____ spaghetti.

5 After work, he _____ basketball. He _____ tennis.

6 In the evening, he _____ to the cinema. He _____ to a restaurant.

c ▶ Now go back to p.73

9B Past simple: questions

a Put the words in the correct order to make questions.

1 you go / where did / on holiday ?
2 see / what did / you ?
3 you have / did / a good time ?
4 you / meet / who did ?
5 you / what did / eat ?
6 like it / you / did ?

b Complete the questions with *did* or *do* / *does*.

1 Where _____ you go last night?
2 _____ you see Jim yesterday?
3 What time _____ he go to work every day?
4 _____ they go to the cinema every Saturday?
5 What _____ you do after class last week?
6 What time _____ their lessons usually start?
7 What time _____ she start work yesterday?
8 Who _____ you see at the party last night?

c Complete the answers to the questions.

1 **A** Did you go home early?
   B Yes, __I__ __did__. I left at 4 o'clock.
2 **A** Did they enjoy their holiday?
   B No, _____ _____. It was boring.
3 **A** Did he watch the football game?
   B No, _____ _____. He was at the cinema.
4 **A** Did you go to the supermarket?
   B Yes, _____ _____. We got some bread and cheese.
5 **A** Did your sister work in a restaurant?
   B No, _____ _____. She worked in a café.

d ▶ Now go back to p.75

10A Present continuous: positive

a Write the -ing forms of the verbs.

1 eat _____
2 cook _____
3 talk _____
4 listen _____
5 get _____
6 have _____
7 wear _____
8 go _____

b Complete the sentences with the present continuous form of the verbs in brackets.

1 I (wear) jeans and a T-shirt.
2 We (listen) to Coldplay's new song.
3 Lisa (study) in her bedroom.
4 They (have) dinner at the moment.
5 Lisa and Matt (play) football in the park.
6 He (watch) a film in the living room.
7 Our children (cook) dinner for us.
8 I (write) this email at work.

c ▶ Now go back to p.81

10B Present continuous: negative and questions

▶ 4.17

	—
I	I'*m not waiting* for the bus.
you	You **aren't listening**!
he / she	She **isn't reading** a book.
it	It **isn't raining**.
we	We **aren't staying** in a hostel.
they	They **aren't working**.

She **isn't reading**.   NOT ~~She not reading.~~
OR ~~She isn't read.~~

▶ 4.18

	Yes/No questions		Short answers	
you	**Are** you	**waiting** for the bus?	Yes, you **are**.	No, you **aren't**.
he / she	**Is** she	**reading** a book?	Yes, she **is**.	No, she **isn't**.
it	**Is** it	**raining**?	Yes, it **is**.	No, it **isn't**.
they	**Are** they	**working**?	Yes, they **are**.	No, they **aren't**.

Are you waiting?   NOT ~~You waiting? You are waiting?~~

▶ 4.19

	Wh- questions		
you	What	**are** you	**doing**?
he / she	Where	**is** he	**going**?
it	Why	**is** it	**raining**?
they	What	**are** they	**watching**?

What **are you** doing?   NOT ~~What you are doing?~~

11A Object pronouns

Subject pronouns	Object pronouns	▶ 4.37
I	me	*I talked to Mark last night. He called* **me**.
you	you	**You** *were in town yesterday. I saw* **you**.
he	him	**He**'s a great singer. I like **him**.
she	her	**She** lives nearby. I often visit **her**.
it	it	I live near Henley. **It**'s a nice town. I like **it**.
we	us	**We** were at the party. Did you see **us**?
they	them	These shoes are nice, but **they**'re expensive. I can't buy **them**.

He called **me**. NOT ~~He called I.~~

> 💡 **Tip**
> We use *it* and *them* to talk about things and places.
> **It** *isn't a very interesting book. I don't want to finish* **it**.
> NOT ~~She isn't an interesting book. I don't want to finish her.~~
> **It**'s a nice town. I like **it**.
> NOT ~~He's a nice town. I like him.~~

10B Present continuous: negative and questions

a Complete the sentences using the negative form of the present continuous.

1 She _isn't studying_ (study). She's watching TV.
2 They _____ (have) lunch. They're having breakfast.
3 I _____ (work). I'm at home.
4 He _____ (play) football. He's watching the game.
5 We _____ (stay) in a hotel. We're camping.
6 Are you OK? You _____ (eat).

b Put the words in the correct order to make questions.

1 wearing / a coat / you / why / are ?
2 working / she / is ?
3 you / doing / are / what ?
4 are / where / going / you ?
5 she / is / phoning / who ?
6 a computer game / playing / he / is ?

c Write two questions to ask your partner about now. Use the present continuous. Ask and answer your questions.

d ▶ Now go back to p.83

11A Object pronouns

a <u>Underline</u> the correct words.

1 We're waiting at the station. Please come and meet *we* / *us*.
2 She was in town. We saw *her* / *him* there.
3 My parents live in London. *It* / *They* have a small flat.
4 I bought a pizza. Do you want to have *it* / *her* for dinner?
5 Where are my keys? Do you have *they* / *them* in your bag?
6 Here's a photo of my new boyfriend. I met *it* / *him* last week at a party.

b Complete the text with the words in the box.

> he she it we me him her us

c Write sentences about your favourite things and people. Use pronouns in your sentences.

d ▶ Now go back to p.89

JULIE THOMPSON, ACTOR
MY FAVOURITE THINGS AND PEOPLE ...

1 My car

It's a very old Volkswagen, but I use
[1]_____ every day.

2 My brother

[2]_____ works in Japan so we don't
see [3]_____ very often, but he always
stays with [4]_____ at New Year.

3 The singer, Lana del Rey

I think [5]_____'s a wonderful singer. I
can listen to [6]_____ for hours.

4 My husband, Paul

We got married 30 years ago and
[7]_____'re very happy. He always
listens to [8]_____ when I have
problems.

11B *can* for ability

He **can't** swim very well.

> **Tip**
>
> I **cannot** swim. → I **can't** swim.
> In all persons (*I / you / he / she / it / we / they*) *can / can't* and the verb don't change.

Part 1: Positive and negative

We use *can* to talk about things we know how to do.

▶ 4.38

+	I / You / He / She / It / We / You / They	can	swim.
–		can't	fly.

I **can swim** well.   NOT ~~I can to swim well.~~
She **can swim** well.   NOT ~~She cans swim well.~~
He **can't swim** well.   NOT ~~He not can swim well.~~

Part 2: Questions

▶ 4.43

Yes/No questions	+	–
Can you **swim**?	Yes, you **can**.	No, you **can't**.
Can she **swim**?	Yes, she **can**.	No, she **can't**.
Can they **swim**?	Yes, they **can**.	No, they **can't**.

Can you swim?   NOT ~~You can swim?~~
Yes, **I can**.   NOT ~~Yes, I swim.~~
No, **I can't**.   NOT ~~No, I not swim.~~

12A *going to*: positive and negative

Part 1: Positive

We use *be + going to* to talk about things we plan to do in the future.

▶ 4.56

	+		
I	I**'m**		have a cup of coffee.
you / we / they	You**'re**	**going to**	go shopping.
he / she / it	She**'s**		have chicken tonight.

I**'m going to have** a bath.   NOT ~~I going to have a bath.~~
                              OR ~~I'm going have a bath.~~
                              OR ~~I'm go to have a bath.~~

Part 2: Negative

▶ 4.62

	–		
I	I**'m not**		go on a holiday.
you / we / they	You **aren't**	**going to**	read a book.
he / she / it	She **isn't**		visit her sister.

We **aren't going to have** a bath.
NOT ~~We're going not to have a bath.~~

12B *going to*: questions

▶ 4.70

	Yes/No questions			Short answers	
I	**Am** I		**see** you soon?	Yes, I **am**.	No, I**'m not**.
you / we / they	**Are** you	**going to**	**go** out?	Yes, you **are**.	No, you **aren't**.
he / she / it	**Is** he		**leave** home?	Yes, he **is**.	No, he **isn't**.

Are you going to … ?   NOT ~~You are going to …?~~
Yes, **I am**.   NOT ~~Yes, I'm going.~~

▶ 4.71

	Wh- questions			
I	When	**am** I		**see** you?
you / we / they	What	**are** you	**going to**	**do**?
he / she / it	Where	**is** he		**live**?

What **are you going to** do? NOT ~~What you going to do?~~
                         OR ~~What you are going to do?~~

Am I going to see you soo[n]

Yes, you are.

11B *can* for ability

Part 1: Positive and negative

a Complete the sentences with *can* or *can't*.

1 I studied Spanish at university for three years.
   I _____ speak with Spanish people.
2 Her meals are terrible. She _____ cook!
3 My brother and I don't like the sea or swimming pools.
   We _____ swim.
4 I went to guitar lessons. Now I _____ play some easy songs.
5 I don't have a bicycle, but I _____ ride one.
6 I don't like that band. They _____ sing.

b ▶ Now go back to p.91

Part 2: Questions

a Put the words in the correct order to make questions.

1 you ride / can / a horse ?
2 well / cook / can he ?
3 sing and / can / play the guitar / they ?
4 can / draw pictures / she ?
5 speak / both Japanese / can you / and Mandarin ?
6 he drive / a car and / can / a bus ?

b ▶ Now go back to p.91

12A *going to*: positive and negative

Part 1: Positive

a Complete the sentences with *going to* and the verb in brackets.

1 I'm hungry. I'm _____ (eat) a sandwich.
2 It's very hot. He's _____ (have) a swim.
3 We're bored. We're _____ (watch) a DVD.
4 It's very cold today. I'm _____ (wear) a coat.
5 She's tired. She's _____ (go) to bed.

b ▶ Now go back to p.96

Part 2: Negative

a Put the words in the correct order to make sentences.

1 his homework at / he's going / the weekend / to do
2 visit my parents / aren't / next week / we / going to
3 going to / Friday night / I'm / party on / have a
4 they aren't / to play football / going / on Saturday
5 isn't / cook dinner / she / going to / this evening
6 to meet / tomorrow evening / we're going / some friends

b Complete the conversation with the correct form of *be going to* and the verb in brackets.

A What are your plans for this evening?
B I ¹_____ (stay) home.
A That's not very interesting.
B Maybe not. But I ²_____ (cook) a nice dinner.
A OK, and then maybe watch a DVD?
B No, I ³_____ (not / watch) a DVD. I ⁴_____ (read) a book. And you?
A Well, I ⁵_____ (not / cook) dinner. I ⁶_____ (get) a pizza and then I ⁷_____ (go) to a party. Would you like to come?
B No, thanks. I ⁸_____ (have) a quiet evening.

c ▶ Now go back to p.97

12B *going to*: questions

a Make questions with *be going to*.

1 you / see / a film / tonight?
   Are you going to see a film tonight?
2 what / you / do / this evening?
3 they / go / Italy / next summer?
4 when / you / have / lunch?
5 how / she / get / the airport?
6 when / we / clean / the flat?

b Complete the questions with *be going to* and the words in brackets.

1 **A** _____ at home tonight? (you / stay)
   B No, we aren't. We're going to go out.
2 **A** What _____? (she / buy)
   B A new coat.
3 **A** _____ shopping? (you / go)
   B Yes, I am. Do you want to come with me?
4 **A** Who _____? (they / invite)
   B Oh, just a few friends. They don't want to have a big party.
5 **A** _____ TV? (he / watch)
   B No, he isn't. He's going to work.

c ▶ Now go back to p.99

Vocabulary Focus

1A Countries

a Listen and write the countries on the map.

> the USA   Brazil   the UK / Britain
> Spain   Mexico   Russia   China   Japan

Tip
the USA = the United States of America
the UK = the United Kingdom

b ▶1.14 Listen again and practise saying the countries.

c 🗩 Add the name of your country in English to the list in a. Practise saying it.

d ▶ Now go back to p.9

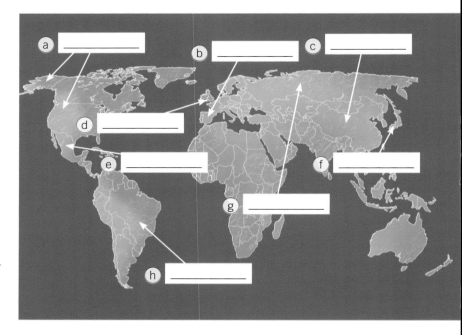

1B Nationalities

a Complete the tables with countries from page 9.

Country	Nationality
	-ian
Australia	Australian
1_____	Brazilian
Canada	Canadian
Italy	Italian
2_____	Russian
	-an
3_____	Mexican
4_____	American

Country	Nationality
	-ish
Poland	Polish
5_____	Spanish
Turkey	Turkish
the UK / 6_____	British
	-ese
7_____	Chinese
8_____	Japanese

b ▶1.17 Listen and repeat the countries and nationalities.

c Write your nationality.
   I'm _____.

d 🗩 Work in pairs.
   Student A: say a country.
   Student B: say the nationality.

   Canada   Canadian

   Then swap roles.

e ▶ Now go back to p.10

2B Common objects 1

a book (books)

a bottle of water
(bottles of water)

a computer (computers)

a key (keys)

a newspaper
(newspapers)

a knife (knives)

a phone (phones)

a ticket (tickets)

a watch (watches)

an umbrella (umbrellas)

a ▶1.50 Listen and repeat the objects.

b Write three objects on three pieces of paper.
Don't show your partner!

a phone   *an umbrella*   *a book*

c 💬 Guess your partner's words.

Is it a watch?   No.

Is it a book?   Yes.

d ▶ Now go back to p.18

7A Common objects 2

a ▶3.3 Listen and repeat the objects.

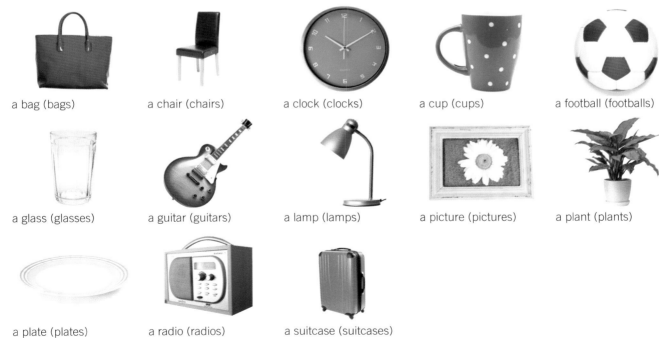

a bag (bags)

a chair (chairs)

a clock (clocks)

a cup (cups)

a football (footballs)

a glass (glasses)

a guitar (guitars)

a lamp (lamps)

a picture (pictures)

a plant (plants)

a plate (plates)

a radio (radios)

a suitcase (suitcases)

b 💬 Work in groups of three. Cover the pictures and
make sentences. Add one more object each time.

At home, I have a guitar.

At home, I have a
guitar and ten plates.

c ▶ Now go back to p.56

At home, I have a guitar, ten plates
and three big plants.

2A Common adjectives

a ▶1.47 Listen and repeat the adjectives.

1 small   big   2 old   new

3 good   bad   4 happy   sad

5 interesting   boring   6 easy   difficult

7 right   wrong   8 beautiful   9 funny

b 💬 Work in pairs.

Student A: say an adjective.
Student B: say the opposite.

happy
    sad

c Complete the sentences with an adjective. There is no correct answer.

1 New York is a _____ city.
2 Harry Potter books are _____.
3 My house is very _____.
4 The English language is _____ for me.
5 My best friend is _____.

💬 Tell a partner your sentences. Are the adjectives the same?

d ▶ Now go back to p.17

4B Family and people

a ▶ 2.21 Listen and repeat the words.

b Look at the words in a. Complete 1–10.

c ▶ 2.22 Listen and repeat the words.

d Complete the sentences with words from a and c.

1 They have three c_____n, a b_____y and two g_____s.
2 I'm Sue and this is Boris. He's my h_____d.
3 That w_____n is my s_____r.
4 They have a new b_____y. It's a g_____l. Her name's Lucia.
5 My yoga class has ten p_____e: nine w_____n and only one m_____n!

e ▶ Now go back to p.34

4A Common verbs

a ▶ 2.14 Listen to the sentences. Repeat the verbs.

1 We **live** in a big house.

2 I **work** in a factory.

¡Hola!

3 I **speak** Spanish.

4 We **study** at school.

5 I **go** to the cinema every weekend.

6 I **teach** young children.

7 We **play** tennis on Saturdays.

8 I **meet** my friends for coffee every day.

b Complete the phrases with verbs in a.

1 _____work_____ in an office / in a bank
2 _____ football / the guitar
3 _____ in a flat / in New York
4 _____, 5 _____ and 6 _____ Italian
7 _____, 8 _____ and 9 _____ at university
10 _____ people / a friend
11 _____ to the gym / home

c Write two sentences about you with phrases in a and b.

I study English. I play football.

💬 Tell a partner your sentences.

d ▶ Now go back to p.32

6B Daily routine

a ▶2.74 Listen to Danny's daily routine and complete the times.

1 Danny **wakes up** at
_____.

2 He **gets up** at
_____.

3 He **has breakfast** at
_____.

4 He **goes to work** at
_____.

5 He **starts work** at
_____.

6 He **has lunch** at
_____.

7 He **finishes work** at
_____.

8 He **gets home** at
_____.

9 He **has dinner** at
_____.

10 He **goes to bed** at
_____.

b ▶2.75 Listen and repeat the verb phrases.

wake get	up	have	a shower breakfast lunch dinner coffee	go	to school to work to bed	start finish	work	get arrive	home

have breakfast / lunch / dinner NOT ~~have the breakfast, have a lunch~~
go to work NOT ~~go to the work~~
go to bed NOT ~~go in the bed~~

c Read about Misha's daily routine. Then complete the sentences about him with words in a and b.

I sleep from 11:00 to 7:00 every night.
In the morning, I get up and have breakfast. I finish at 7:30.
It's 30 minutes by bus to go to work.
I work from 8:30 until 12:30, then I have lunch for half an hour.
Then I work for three hours until I go home.

1 He _____ at 7:00.
2 He _____ at 7:30.
3 He _____ at 8:00.
4 He _____ at 8:30.
5 He _____ at 12:30.
6 He _____ at 4:00.
7 He _____ at 11:00 in the evening.

d ▶ Now go back to p.50

8B Free time activities

a **⏵3.50** Listen to five people talk about free time activities. Put their activities in the correct order.

1 go (**past simple**: *went*)

 ☐ I went to the cinema.
 ☐ I went to a party.
 ☐ I went shopping.
 ☐ I went to a café.

2 have (**past simple**: *had*)

 ☐ I had a pizza.
 ☐ I had a drink.
 ☐ I had a coffee.
 ☐ I had a shower.

3 listen (**past simple**: *listened*); watch (**past simple**: *watched*)

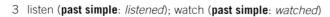
 ☐ I listened to music.
 ☐ I watched a football match.
 ☐ I listened to the radio.
 ☐ I watched a film on TV.

4 read (**past simple**: *read* (/red/)

 ☐ I read a book.
 ☐ I read a magazine.
 ☐ I read the newspaper.

5 play (**past simple**: *played*)

 ☐ I played the guitar.
 ☐ I played a computer game.
 ☐ I played football.

b **⏵3.51** Listen and repeat the present and past verbs in a.

c Complete the sentences with the correct past simple verb.

1 We _____ football on TV last night.
2 He had breakfast and _____ the newspaper.
3 I _____ to a party last night until 2:00.
4 I _____ to music on the bus this morning.
5 We went to a café and _____ a pizza.

d Write two true sentences about a free time activity in a.

On Friday, I went to a party.

e 💬 Read the first part of your sentences in d. Stop at the verb! Your partner guesses the second part of the sentence.

> On Friday, I went …

> … to the cinema … ?

> No, try again!

f ▶ Now go back to p.67

11A Life events

a Put the life events in the order you think is correct.

☐ be born
(**past simple:** *was born*)

☐ finish university
(**past simple:** *finished*)

☐ grow up
(**past simple:** *grew up*)

☐ get married
(**past simple:** *got*)

☐ go to school
(**past simple:** *went*)

☐ have a baby
(**past simple:** *had*)

☐ finish school
(**past simple:** *finished*)

☐ stop working
(**past simple:** *stopped*)

☐ go to university
(**past simple:** *went*)

☐ die
(**past simple:** *died*)

b ▶ 4.33 Listen and repeat the verb phrases in a.

c Complete the sentences with the verbs in brackets.
1 I _____ (go to) university when I was 18 and I _____ (finish) university when I was 24.
2 Nelson Mandela _____ (be born) in 1918 and he _____ (die) in 2013.
3 My father _____ (stop) working when he was 68.
4 She _____ (get married) when she was 21 and she _____ (have) a baby two years later.
5 I _____ (finish) school when I was 16 and I _____ (get) a job in a car factory.
6 Michelle Obama _____ (be born) in 1964 and she _____ (grow up) in Chicago.

d ▶ 4.34 Look at the answers and complete the questions. Listen and check.
1 **Q** _____ go to school? **A** In Valencia.
2 **Q** _____ finish? **A** In 2012.
3 **Q** _____ do after that?
  A I went to Canada.
4 **Q** _____ go there?
  A My brother lives there.
5 **Q** _____ like it? **A** Yes, I had a great time.

e 💬 Ask and answer the questions in d with a partner. Say answers that are true for you.

f ▶ Now go back to p.89

11B Abilities

a ▶ 4.39 Listen and repeat the verbs.

swim
(**past simple:** *swam*)

cook
(**past simple:** *cooked*)

paint
(**past simple:** *painted*)

sing
(**past simple:** *sang*)

dance
(**past simple:** *danced*)

drive a car
(**past simple:** *drove*)

play volleyball

play cards
(**past simple:** *played*)

ride a horse

ride a bike
(**past simple:** *rode*)

run
(**past simple:** *ran*)

b ▶ 4.40 Complete the phrases with verbs in a. Listen and check.

1 _____ a picture

2 _____ a motorbike

3 _____ a song

4 _____ dinner

5 _____ basketball

6 _____ to work

c Write four sentences about what you did:

- yesterday
- last night
- last weekend
- last Monday

Yesterday I drove my car to work.
I danced at a party last weekend.

💬 Tell a partner your sentences.

Last night ...

d ▶ Now go back to p.91

12B Common verbs and collocations

a ▶ **4.65** Listen and repeat the verbs and their past forms.

make (**past simple:** *made*)

make a cake

go (**past simple:** *went*)

go to the beach

clean (**past simple:** *cleaned*)

clean a room / your flat

visit (**past simple:** *visited*)

visit a friend   visit a museum   visit London

invite (**past simple:** *invited*)

invite someone to a party   invite someone for a meal

use (**past simple:** *used*)

use a computer   use the Internet

do (**past simple:** *did*)

do sport   do yoga   do your homework   do the cleaning   do the washing

b <u>Underline</u> the correct words.

1 He's 85 kilos. He eats a lot and he never *does* / *makes* sport.
2 It's my birthday next week. I'm going to *visit* / *invite* some friends to my flat for a meal.
3 She's going to *paint* / *draw* the walls of her room dark green. Don't ask me why!
4 We were in Moscow and we *visited* / *went* Red Square.
5 I'm going to *do* / *make* some coffee.
6 A woman comes on Wednesday. She *does* / *makes* all the cleaning and washing for us.
7 Excuse me, can I *clean* / *use* your phone? I need to call my sister.

c Write three sentences with the phrases in a.

I'm going to clean my bedroom tomorrow.

💬 Tell a partner your sentences.

d ▶ Now go back to p.99

3A Food 1

a ▶1.75 Listen and repeat the words.

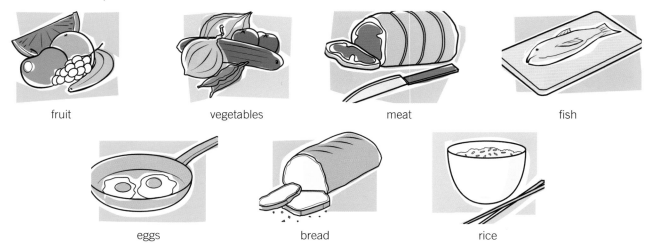

fruit   vegetables   meat   fish

eggs   bread   rice

b 💬 Talk to a partner. What food is in the pictures?

① ② ③

④ ⑤ ⑥

c Match pictures 1–6 with the words in the box.

coffee   cola   fruit juice   milk   tea   water

① ② ③

④ ⑤ ⑥

d ▶1.76 Listen and check your answers in c. Practise saying the words.

e 💬 Talk to your partner. Which drinks are in the pictures?

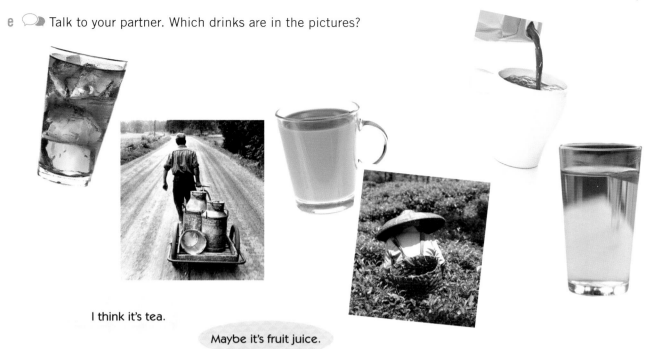

I think it's tea.

Maybe it's fruit juice.

f ▶ Now go back to p.24

3B Food 2

a ⏵1.82 Listen and repeat the words.

breakfast   lunch   dinner

I have breakfast at 7:30. NOT ~~I have a breakfast at 7:30.~~
She has lunch at 12:30. NOT ~~She has a lunch at 12:30.~~
We have dinner at 7:00. NOT ~~We have a dinner at 7:00.~~

b ⏵1.83 Match the words in the box with pictures 1–12. Listen and check your answers.
Then listen and repeat.

orange sandwich butter biscuit banana pizza potato tomato apple ice cream cheese cake

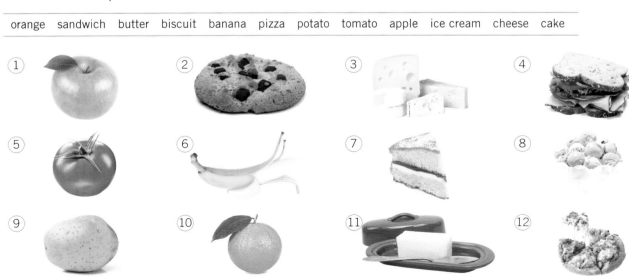

① ② ③ ④

⑤ ⑥ ⑦ ⑧

⑨ ⑩ ⑪ ⑫

c 💬 Which food in b do you eat for … ?
• breakfast • lunch • dinner

d ▶ Now go back to p.27

8A Past time expressions

a (▶)**3.34** Listen and repeat the days of the week.

b Complete the sentences.
1 Today is _____.
2 Yesterday was _____.
3 My favourite day is _____, because
_____.

💬 Tell a partner your answer in 3.

> My favourite day is ...

JUNE

Monday 5	*Back to work* 😞
Tuesday 6	
Wednesday 7	*2 days and it's the weekend!*
Thursday 8	
Friday 9	*Last day at work!*
Saturday 10	
Sunday 11	*Weekend!*

c (▶)**3.35** Listen and repeat the past time expressions.

yesterday

a year ago

at the weekend

two days ago *or* on Monday

last night

this morning

d (▶)**3.36** Complete the table with words in the box. Listen and check.

ago   last   on   this

1 _____	night Sunday month
a week two months ten years	2 _____
3 _____	morning afternoon
4 _____	Monday Friday

two months ago NOT ~~before two months ago~~
on Monday NOT ~~at Monday~~

e Complete the sentences with words from c and d.
1 I was in Warsaw _____ the weekend.
2 They were at the World Cup _____ year ago.
3 Were you at home _____ morning?
4 I was at a meeting two days _____.
5 We were at work _____ Friday.
6 He was at his friend's house _____ night.

f ▶ Now go back to p.65

9B The seasons and the weather

a **▶3.72** Listen and repeat the seasons.

spring   summer   autumn   winter

b 💬 Look at weather pictures 1–5 below. Which season do you think it is in each picture?

c **▶3.73** Complete the sentences with the words in the box. Listen and check.

windy sunny snowy rainy cloudy

1 It often **rains** in England. (verb)
   There's a lot of **rain** in England. (noun)
   It's often _____ in England. (adjective)

2 It often **snows** in Antarctica. (verb)
   There's always **snow** in Antarctica. (noun)
   It's always _____ in Antarctica. (adjective)

3 There's a lot of **wind** in my town. (noun)
   It's often _____ in my town. (adjective)

4 It's very **sunny** and **hot** today. (adjectives)
   It was _____ and **warm** yesterday. (adjectives)

5 There are a lot of **clouds** today. (noun)
   It's _____ and **cold** today. (adjectives)

d Underline the correct words.
   1 Do you like hot and *sun / sunny* weather?
   2 Is the weather *cloudy / cloud* today?
   3 Is winter cold and *snow / snowy* in your country?
   4 Is summer hot and *sunny / sun* in your country?
   5 Does it *rainy / rain* in autumn in your country?

e 💬 Ask and answer the questions in d with a partner.

f ▶ Now go back to p.75

2B Numbers 1

a ▶1.57 Listen and repeat the numbers.

1 one **2** two **3** three **4** four **5** five **6** six **7** seven **8** eight **9** nine **10** ten

11 eleven **12** twelve **13** thirteen **14** fourteen **15** fifteen **16** sixteen **17** seventeen **18** eighteen **19** nineteen

thirteen NOT ~~threeteen~~, *fifteen* NOT ~~fiveteen~~

20 twenty **30** thirty **40** forty **50** fifty **60** sixty **70** seventy **80** eighty **90** ninety

thirty NOT ~~threety~~, *forty* NOT ~~fourty~~, *fifty* NOT ~~fivety~~

b ▶1.58 Listen to a–g. Underline the number you hear.

a 13 / 30   c 15 / 50   e 17 / 70   g 19 / 90
b 14 / 40   d 16 / 60   f 18 / 80

c ▶ Now go back to p.19

3B Time

a ▶1.86 Match the clocks with the times in the box. Listen and check.

two o'clock   twenty past two   (a) quarter past two
half past two   (a) quarter to two   twenty to two

b ▶1.86 Listen again and repeat the times.

c Complete the sentences.
1 My English class is at _____.
2 My favourite TV programme is at _____.
3 My school / job starts at _____.

💬 Tell a partner your sentences.

d ▶ Now go back to p.27

4B Numbers 2

a ▶2.25 Listen and repeat the numbers.

21 twenty-one **34** thirty-four **42** forty-two **57** fifty-seven **63** sixty-three **79** seventy-nine **85** eighty-five **99** ninety-nine **100** a hundred

thirty-four NOT ~~thirty and four~~ OR ~~four and thirty~~

b 💬 Work with a partner.
Student A: say a number in the box.
Student B: say the next two numbers.

52 41 29 68 98 36 82 75 59

fifty-two

fifty-three, fifty-four

c ▶ Now go back to p.35

12A Months and future time expressions

a ▶ **4.57** Listen and repeat the months.

1 December, January, February
2 March, April, May
3 June, July, August
4 September, October, November

b 💬 Which seasons are 1–4 in a in your country?

c ▶ **4.58** Listen and repeat the time expressions.

tomorrow

on Monday

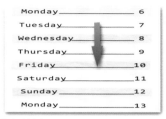
this Friday

at the weekend

next Tuesday

in two weeks

d Complete groups 1–4 with words and phrases in the box. Some of them can go in more than one group.

Thursday   three months   June   winter   year   the winter

1 **on** Monday, Tuesday, Wednesday …
2 **this** afternoon, Monday, week, March, month, summer …
3 **in** March, the summer, two weeks …
4 **next** Monday, week, March, month, summer …

e Complete the sentences with a time expression.

1 I'm going to have (*meal*) _____.
2 I'm going to go on holiday _____.
3 I'm going to visit a friend _____.
4 I'm going to buy a new (*object*) _____.

💬 Tell a partner your sentences.

I'm going to visit a friend tomorrow.

Ordinal numbers

a ▶ **4.59** Listen and repeat the ordinal numbers.

 first
 second
 third
 fourth
 fifth
 sixth
 seventh
 eighth
 ninth

tenth   eleventh   twelfth   thirteenth   fourteenth   twentieth   twenty-first   twenty-second   thirtieth   thirty-first

b 💬 Work with a partner.
Student A: say a number.
Student B: say the ordinal number.

c ▶ Now go back to p.97

fifteen   fifteenth

5A Places in a town

a ▶ 2.41 Listen and repeat the places.

station

supermarket

school

hotel

hospital

cinema

restaurant

bank

shop

café

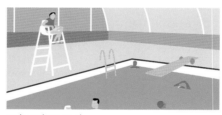
swimming pool

park

museum

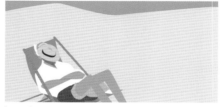
beach

b 💬 Talk to your partner. Where are these signs?

> I think 1 is at a swimming pool, or maybe a beach.

①

②

③

④

⑤

⑥

⑦

⑧

⑨

⑩

c ▶ Now go back to p.41

5B Hotels

a ▶ 2.48 Listen and repeat the words.

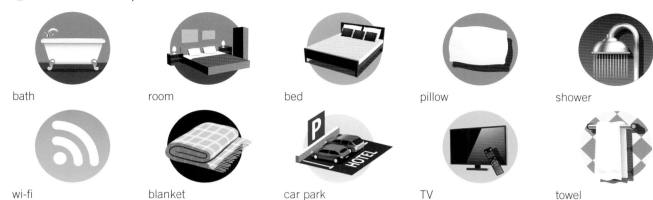

bath   room   bed   pillow   shower

wi-fi   blanket   car park   TV   towel

There's wi-fi in the room. NOT ~~There's a wi-fi in the room.~~ OR ~~There are wi-fi in the room.~~

b 💬 Which word is different in each group? Compare your answers with your partner.

1	shower	pillow	bath
2	TV	wi-fi	room
3	shower	blanket	pillow

4	car park	towel	blanket
5	bed	room	bath

c ▶ Now go back to p.42

10B Place phrases with prepositions

a ▶ 4.10 Listen and repeat the phrases.

in the car   **in** a taxi   **in** a restaurant   **in** a café   **in** a hotel   **in** bed

at the station   **at** the airport   **at** the bus stop   **at** the cinema   **at** a party   **at** home   **at** work   **at** school

on a bus   **on** a train   **on** a plane   **on** holiday

b Correct the phrases with prepositions.

1 It's 10:00, but he's still at the bed.
2 I'm waiting for the plane on the airport.
3 I can't talk now. I'm on the car. I'm driving home.
4 Are you in home or are you at the work?
5 I'm having a coffee on a café.
6 John isn't here. He's still in the holiday.

c 💬 Think about people you know. Where are they now?

I think my sister is on a plane.

My husband is at work.

d ▶ Now go back to p.82

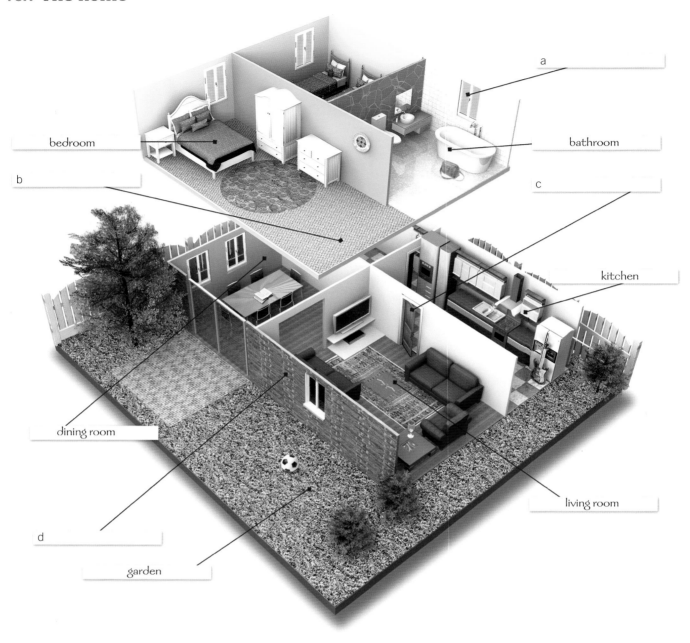

bedroom

bathroom

b

a

c

kitchen

dining room

living room

d

garden

a 💬 Look at the picture. Where are objects 1–6? Ask and answer questions with a partner.

1 the glass   3 the book   5 the guitar
2 the bag   4 the football 6 the plate

Where's the glass?

It's in the living room.

b ▶4.4 Match the words in the box with a–d in the picture. Listen and check.

wall   window   floor   door

c Complete the sentences with the correct words.

1 My family has dinner in the d_____ r_____ every evening.
2 We have a small g_____ behind our house. We often sit there on summer evenings.
3 My bedroom has a large w_____ and I can see the mountains.
4 I don't need a chair – I can sit on the f_____.
5 There are lots of pictures on the w_____ in the dining room.
6 After dinner I like to read in the l_____ r_____.
7 My brother is always in the b_____ – he likes long showers.
8 There are two d_____s in the dining room – one goes to the kitchen, the other to the living room.

d ▶ Now go back to p.80

6A Jobs

a ▶ 2.69 Listen and repeat the jobs.

football player

student

receptionist

waiter / waitress

taxi driver

factory worker

bank worker

shop assistant

businessman / businesswoman

chef

office worker

IT worker

teacher

doctor

b Cover the words and pictures in a. Correct the spelling in each job. Then check your answers.

1 studint
2 waitres
3 factery worker
4 shop asistant
5 taxi drivar
6 fotball player
7 receptonist
8 bank woker
9 ofice worker

c 💬 Do you know people who do the jobs in a? Tell your partner.

My father is a taxi driver.

My friend, Kumiko, is a chef.

d ▶ Now go back to p.49

7B Clothes and colours

a ▶ 3.15 Listen and repeat the clothes.

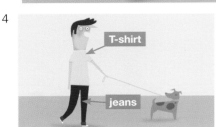

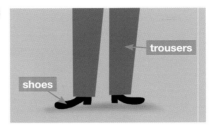

b ▶ 3.16 Listen and repeat the colours.

light blue   dark blue   light brown   dark brown   light green   dark green   light grey   dark grey   red   black   white   yellow

c What do the people usually wear? Write sentences.

Enrico

Sunyin

Ali

1 Enrico usually wears a dark grey jacket and a light blue shirt.

2 _____

3 _____

Carmen

Shinji

Elena

4 _____

5 _____

6 _____

d ▶ Now go back to p.59

9A Transport

a ▶ 3.62 Listen and repeat the words.

 bike
 bus
 train
 car

plane
 boat / ship
 taxi
 tram
 metro / underground

b Cover the transport pictures in a. What do these signs show?

1   2   3   4

5   6   7 8

c 💬 Which kind of transport do you prefer? Why?

d Notice how we use *go by*, *get* and *take* with different kinds of transport.

go by	bus train plane		get take	a bus a train a taxi

go by bus NOT ~~go with bus, go by the bus~~
get a bus NOT ~~get bus~~

e ▶ 3.63 Listen to sentences 1–5. Tick (✓) the sentence you hear. Is it past or present?

1
☐ I **go** to work by train.
☐ I **went** to work by train.

2
☐ He **gets** / **takes** a bus to school.
☐ He **got** / **took** a bus to school.

3
☐ She often **drives** to work.
☐ Yesterday she **drove** to work.

4
☐ She **flies** to Tokyo every month.
☐ She **flew** to Tokyo last month.

5
☐ They always **walk** to school.
☐ They **walked** to school this morning.

f Think of three places you went to in the last year. Write how you went there.

I went to a friend's house by bike yesterday.
I flew to Turkey last summer.

💬 Tell a partner your sentences.

g ▶ Now go back to p.72

Writing Plus

1C Capital letters and full stops

a Look at the sentence. Read the information about capital letters and full stops.

My name's Sophia Taylor.

> **Capital letters**
> We use capital letters (*A, B, C, D* …):
> - for names (**S**ophia **T**aylor, **O**lga **V**asin, **M**aria **G**onzález)
> - names of places (**T**oronto, **C**anada, **H**igh **S**treet)
> - for nationalities (**I**talian, **B**ritish, **C**hinese)
> - at the beginning of a sentence (**M**y name's …)
>
> **Full stops**
> . = full stop
> We usually use full stops at the end of sentences.
> *My name's Sophia Taylor.*

b Write the capital letters.

1	a A	6	h
2	b	7	q
3	d	8	r
4	e	9	t
5	g		

c Add capital letters and full stops to each sentence.

T
they're married.
1 we're from brazil
2 he's a student
3 this is ruben
4 i'm in a class with amy lee
5 my name is sandro
6 their flat is in mexico city it's small

d ▶ Now go back to p.13

2C The alphabet and spelling

Part 1: The alphabet

a ⓟ **1.64** Listen to how we say the letters of the alphabet.

/eɪ/ (*day*)	/iː/ (*we*)	/e/ (*ten*)	/aɪ/ (*hi*)	/əʊ/ (*no*)	/uː/ (*you*)	/ɑː/ (*car*)
Aa /eɪ/	Bb /biː/	Ff /ef/	Ii /aɪ/	Oo /əʊ/	Qq /kjuː/	Rr /ɑː/
Hh /eɪtʃ/	Cc /siː/	Ll /el/	Yy /waɪ/		Uu /juː/	
Jj /dʒeɪ/	Dd /diː/	Mm /em/			Ww /dʌbəljuː/	
Kk /keɪ/	Ee /iː/	Nn /en/			('double u')	
	Gg /dʒiː/	Ss /es/				
	Pp /piː/	Xx /eks/				
	Tt /tiː/	Zz /zed/				
	Vv /viː/					

b Add the letters to the group with similar sounds. Say the letters.

R H Q O Z Y C F

1 (**you**) U, Q, W
2 (**day**) J, __, A, K
3 (**hi**) I, __
4 (**we**) T, __, B, D, E, G, P, V
5 (**ten**) N, L, __, M, S, X
6 (**car**) __
7 (**no**) __

c ▶ Now go back to p.20

Part 2: Spelling

Some words in English have double letters in their written form.
*vi**ll**age*
Other words in English have letters in their written form that might seem different from what you hear.
city /sɪti/

d ⓟ **1.68** Correct the spelling. Listen and check. Then practise spelling the words.

1	adress	5	smal	9	rong
2	vilage	6	dificult	10	nife
3	umbrela	7	intresting		
4	hapy	8	rite		

e ▶ Now go back to p.21

3C Contractions

a Look at the sentences and read about contractions.

I'm in a café with Sophia. **She's** my new friend at work.

I'm (contraction) = *I am*   *She's* (contraction) = *She is*
We use contractions in speaking and writing, usually in informal situations.

be: positive and negative

+		–	
Full form	Contraction	Full form	Contraction
I am	*I'm*	*I am not*	*I'm not*
you are	*you're*	*you are not*	*you aren't*
we are	*we're*	*we are not*	*we aren't*
he is	*he's*	*he is not*	*he isn't*
she is	*she's*	*she is not*	*she isn't*
it is	*it's*	*it is not*	*it isn't*
they are	*they're*	*they are not*	*they aren't*

It is a pizza. → **It's** a pizza.

Present simple: negative

Full form	Contraction
I / you / we do not	*I / you / we don't*

I **do not** eat fish. → I **don't** eat fish.

b Match the contractions in the box with 1–8.

aren't   isn't   don't   I'm   you're   she's   they're   we're

1 you are _____
2 she is _____
3 I am _____
4 do not _____
5 they are _____
6 are not _____
7 we are _____
8 is not _____

c Add the words in brackets to each sentence. Use contractions.

1 _____ from Sweden. (He is)
2 _____ tomatoes. (They are)
3 It _____ five o'clock. (is not)
4 I _____ have a big meal in the evening. (do not)
5 You _____ a teacher. (are not)
6 _____ OK. (I am)
7 We _____ eat meat. (do not)
8 _____ Spanish. (I am not)

d ▶ Now go back to p.29. Try to use contractions in your text message.

4C Word order

a Look at the examples and the word order.

Word order
- **subject + verb**

I work.
You don't work.
- **subject + verb + object**

Clara and Lisa don't have a brother.
They speak French.
- **subject + verb + preposition + noun**

My daughters study at university.
They don't live in a flat.
- **subject + verb + object + preposition + noun**

I don't have a phone in my bag.
I like milk in my coffee.

We can use *here* or *there* after a verb.
*I live **there**.*
*You don't work **here**.*

b Tick (✓) the correct sentences.

1 a ☐ Tennis we play.
   b ☐ We play tennis.
2 a ☐ I don't teach children.
   b ☐ Don't teach children I.
3 a ☐ They there don't study.
   b ☐ They don't study there.
4 a ☐ My sister in Japan lives.
   b ☐ My sister lives in Japan.
5 a ☐ These are my friends.
   b ☐ These my friends are.
6 a ☐ I have a flat in New York.
   b ☐ I in New York have a flat.

c Put the words in the correct order to make sentences. Remember to use capital letters and full stops.

1 don't speak / they / German
2 there / have coffee / you
3 we / in a factory / don't work
4 teaches / at the university / my dad / Italian
5 the computer / I / at the office / don't like
6 have / in New Zealand / a nice house / they

d ▶ Now go back to p.37

5C *and* and *but*

a Look at the sentences and read about *and* and *but*.

The flat is near my office **and** there's a beautiful park in the next street.
There isn't a supermarket near me, **but** there's a shop in the next street.

☺	*and*	☺
It's big	and	it's near my office.

☹	*and*	☹
There isn't a supermarket	and	it isn't near my office.

☹	*but*	☺
There isn't a supermarket	but	there's a shop in the next street.

☺	*but*	☹
There's a shop in the next street,	but	there isn't a supermarket.

b Underline the correct words.

1 I love London, but it's very *expensive / nice*.
2 The hotel has free wi-fi and *there's / it doesn't have* a TV in every room.
3 Ghadames is a very hot city, but *the old houses are always cool / it's sometimes 55°C*.
4 There are lots of expensive hotels, but *there are lots of / there aren't any* cheap hostels.
5 There are lots of good books in the bookshop and *they are very boring / the shop assistants are very friendly*.
6 The Maris Hotel is beautiful and *it's near the sea / the restaurant isn't very good*.

c Add *and* or *but* to each sentence.

1 I live in Spain, _____ I don't speak Spanish.
2 The food is good, _____ it's very expensive!
3 Their house is nice _____ it's near the station.
4 This hotel room is small _____ the shower is cold.
5 The city has a good university _____ I'd like to study there.
6 There isn't a supermarket here, _____ there is a market in the next street.

d ▶ Now go back to p.45. Try to use *and* and *but* in your writing.

6C *because* and *also*

a Look at the sentences and read about *because* and *also*.

I walk to work every day **because** my flat is near the office.
We go out to a café for coffee every day. We **also** have lunch there.

We use *because* and *also* to join ideas.

- *Because* joins two ideas in <u>one</u> sentence. We use *because* to give a reason. It answers the question *Why?*

> Why do you like your job?

> It's interesting.

I like my job **because** it's interesting.
He sleeps in the morning **because** he works at night.

- *Also* joins two ideas in <u>two</u> sentences. It means *and*.
He plays football and tennis. He plays rugby.
He plays football and tennis. He **also** plays rugby. (= He plays football, tennis and rugby.)

- We use *also* before the verb:
He sleeps in the morning. He **also** sleeps in the afternoon.

- We use *also* after *be*:
I'm a doctor. I'm **also** a teacher.

b Underline the correct answers.

1 She plays sport *also she teaches sport. / . She also teaches sport*.
2 I feel good in the morning *because I sleep for seven hours at night. / . Because I sleep for seven hours at night*.
3 I speak English. I also speak Italian because my parents *Italian / are Italian*.
4 Michael works at night. His wife *also works / works also* at night.
5 We always eat at home because *like / we like* cooking.
6 He's a student. He *also is / 's also* a waiter.

c Use *because* and *also* to join the ideas.

I want to go shopping. I need some cups. (because)
I want to go shopping because I need some cups.
She teaches English at the school. She teaches French. (also)
She teaches English at the school. She also teaches French.

1 I don't like my job. It's boring. (because)
2 She doesn't have breakfast. She isn't hungry in the morning. (because)
3 I need to make lunch. I need to go to the supermarket. (also)
4 The children are nice. They're very funny. (also)

d ▶ Now go back to p.53. Try to use *because* and *also* in your writing.

7C Commas, exclamation marks and question marks

a Look at the sentences and read about commas, exclamation marks and question marks.

Chairs, lamps, small tables, a big bed – all in good condition.
Not expensive!
How much are they?

, = comma   ! = exclamation mark   ? = question mark

Commas

- We use commas in lists of nouns (things or people).
  *Books for learning English – **dictionaries, grammar books, coursebooks***
- We often finish a list with *and* + noun. We don't use a comma before *and* in lists.
  *I need a chair, a bed **and a lamp**.*

Exclamation marks

- We use exclamation marks to mean *Look at this* or *This is important*.
  Not expensive!

Question marks

- We use question marks at the end of questions.
  How much are they?

b Add commas to each list.

1 For sale: old books newspapers magazines.
2 I love old cups plates and glasses.
3 She's wearing black trousers a white shirt a grey jacket and black shoes.
4 They sell radios clocks pictures lamps tables chairs …
5 For sale: coats jackets hats shoes shirts dresses …
6 We need bread milk cheese and apples.

c Add a question mark (?) or an exclamation mark (!) to each sentence.

1 How old are these things
2 Thank you
3 Write soon
4 New bookshop
5 Can I pay by credit card
6 How much are they

d ▶ Now go back to p.61. Try to use commas, exclamation marks and question marks in your email.

8C Writing short emails, letters and notes

a Look at the note and read about writing short emails, letters and notes.

> Dear Megan,   ← **start**
>
> This is a card to say thank you for your help on Saturday. It was fun to go shopping with you and you helped me find some good shops. I hope we can go shopping again some time soon.   **the main part**
>
> Best wishes,   ← **finish**
> Sophia

We start emails, letters and notes like this:
- *Dear* (name),
- *Hi* (name),

In the main part, we use phrases like:
- *This is a note to say …*
- *Thanks for your email / letter / note.*
- *Thank you for …*
- *Here is / are …*
- *I was …*
- *It was …*
- *I hope …*

We often use the past simple, e.g *You **helped** me find some good shops. I **stayed** at home. I **went** into town.*

We finish emails, letters and notes like this:
- *Best wishes,*
  (name)
- *See you soon,*
  (name)

b Put a–e in the correct order to make a note.

a The food was great and it was good to talk! I went home and watched a film in the afternoon.

b I hope we can go to the concert on Friday.

c Hi Suzy,

d See you soon,
Matt

e This is a note to say thank you very much for lunch yesterday.

c Complete the email with the words and phrases in the box.

| hope | wishes | sorry | It was | Here are | Dear | talked |

> ¹_____ Allie,
> ²_____ some photos of the party on Saturday night. I'm ³_____ I was late!
> ⁴_____ good to meet your friends. I ⁵_____ to Debbie and Nasim – they're really nice!
> I ⁶_____ we can meet for coffee next week.
> Best ⁷_____,
> Kirsty

d ▶ Now go back to p.69

9C Making the order clear

a Look at part of Sophia's online post and read about making the order clear with *first, next, then*.

> **First**, we went for a walk by the river. It was beautiful.
> **Next**, we went to a small museum and had lunch.
> **Then**, we went shopping and I saw a lovely clock.

When we write about events in the past, it's good to make the order clear. We use phrases like:
- *First, …*
  First, we flew to Berlin.
- *Then, …   Next, …   After that, …*
  After that, we took a bus to Claudia's village.
  Then, we went shopping.

We usually use *Next* for the middle event, not the last event.

First, we went to the zoo. **Next**, *we had lunch. Then, we went shopping.*

b <u>Underline</u> the correct words.

> The weather was very bad! ¹*Then, / First,* it rained. ²*First, / Next,* it was very windy. ³*Then, / After,* it snowed!

> ⁴*First, / Next,* we camped in Anton's garden.
> ⁵*After, / After that,* we stayed in a hotel.

> Last summer I went to the UK with Sasha and Yuri. ⁶*First, / Then,* we went to London. It was great. ⁷*Next, / First,* we went to Scotland for three days. ⁸*After this, / After that,* we stayed with Yuri's family in Cambridge.

c Add the words and phrases in brackets in the correct place to make the order clear.

We visited Emma's family in the country. We went to the city. (*then, first,*)

First, we visited Emma's family in the country. Then, we went to the city.

1 I went to a café. I went to the park. (*first, after that,*)
2 It was sunny and warm. It was sunny and cold. (*then, first,*)
3 We went to a restaurant. We saw a film. We went home. (*next, first, then,*)
4 I finished work. I went for a walk by the river. I met Terry at the station. (*first, after that, next,*)

d ▶ Now go back to p.77. Try to make the order clear in your online post.

10C Word order in questions

a Look at part of Amelia's message to Megan and read about word order in questions.

First, where do I find a taxi at the station? And how much is it from the station to the hotel?

Yes/No questions		
Do	they	have a garden?
Did	Eduardo	visit you?
Can	you	call me, please?
Is	she	working?

Wh- questions			
How many rooms	does	your house	have?
Where	do	I	find a taxi?
When	did	the train	leave?
What	is	Selma	doing?

Questions with *be* are different.

Yes/No questions with *be*	
Is	Mimi's flat big?
Were	you at work today?

Wh- questions with *be*		
Where	was	your phone?
How much	is	it from the station to the hotel?

b <u>Underline</u> the correct words.

1 Where *are you / you are* going?
2 Who *is that / that is*?
3 *Did you use / You did use* your phone on the plane?
4 *You can / Can you* help me?
5 How many taxis *there were / were there*?
6 What film *is your sister watching / is watching your sister*?
7 *There is / Is there* a garden?
8 How *you do often / often do you* watch TV?

c Put the words in the correct order to make questions. Add capital letters and question marks.

there / at the station / a café / is
Is there a café at the station?

1 where / the bus stop / is
2 do / when / start / work / you
3 you / the tickets / buy / did
4 some bread / you / buy / can
5 doing / what / you / are
6 the film / is / what time

d ▶ Now go back to p.85

11C Pronouns

a Look at part of Sophia's email to Lisa and read about subject and object pronouns.

… I work in an office with a girl called Megan. She's from London and she's very friendly. … I also know her cousin James. He's very kind. I often see them at the weekend.

We use subject and object pronouns so that we don't repeat nouns and names.

I work in an office with a girl called Megan. She's from London and she's very friendly.

I also know her cousin James. He's very kind.

I work in an office with a girl called Megan … I also know her cousin James. I often see them at the weekend …

▶ Read more about pronouns in Grammar Focus 11A on p.128

We often use *you* to mean 'people in general / everyone'. *You can study English on the internet.*

b Underline the correct words.

Seema Bhadoria is a young woman from India. People call [1]*she / her* 'The Strong Woman'. [2]*She / Her* can pull a truck with her teeth.
X-Men aren't real. [3]*They / Them* are 'superhumans' in films. Do you know [4]*they / them*?

Leonardo Torres y Quevedo was an engineer. [5] *It / He* lived from 1852 to 1936. In 1914 [6]*it / he* invented a machine called 'The Chess Player'. [7]*It / He* was the first computer game in the world. [8]*It / You* could play chess against [9]*it / them*.

c Swap the underlined words with the subject and object pronouns in the box.

he	her	him	him	it	it	me
us	she	she	~~they~~	they	we	

> I met a doctor and an IT worker. The doctor and the IT worker live in Madrid.
> *They live in Madrid.*

1 Why is my sister eating that sandwich? My sister made that sandwich for me!
2 Do you like this picture of my wife and me? Valerie gave this picture to my wife and me.
3 My friends have a baby boy called Luke. My friends talk about the baby boy called Luke all the time!
4 Neil and Andy are students. Neil, Andy and I met at university.
5 I'm Ivana Marikova. Do you remember Ivana Marikova?
6 That's Sophia and that's James. James likes Sophia but Sophia doesn't like James!

d ▶ Now go back to p.93. Try to use pronouns in your email.

12C Paragraphs

a Look at Megan's email to Emma and read about paragraphs.

Hi Emma,

I'm in town this afternoon. Would you like to meet for coffee? ← **Paragraph 1 = invitation**

We could go to Café Roma. It's just near your office. I'm free at 4:00. Is that OK for you? ← **Paragraph 2 = making plans for the time and place**

Megan

Paragraphs divide writing into groups of ideas. We use them to make our writing clear. In Megan's email she uses two paragraphs – one for the invitation and the other for making plans.
To start a new paragraph, write the next sentence on a new line, like this:

I'm sorry, I can't come this afternoon. I'm working today.

Would you like to meet on Tuesday?

~~I'm sorry, I can't come this afternoon. I'm working today. Would you like to meet on Tuesday?~~

b Match paragraphs a–b with 1–2.

1 _____
We could meet tomorrow. I'm free in the afternoon. What do you think?

There's a new restaurant in town. It looks really good.
2 _____

a
Thanks for the lunch invitation, but I can't come today. I'm busy.

b
Would you like to go there on Saturday?

c Rewrite the emails with two paragraphs.

1 Do you have any plans for the weekend? I'd like to see a film. We could meet at the cinema at 6:30. Is that OK for you?
2 It's my birthday next Friday. I'm going to be 30! ☹ Would you like to come here for a meal on Saturday? I'm going to invite a few friends.

d ▶ Now go back to p.101. Try to use paragraphs in your invitations.

Unit 1

▶ 1.25 **PART 1**

RECEPTIONIST Good morning, Electric Blue Technology?
SOPHIA Hi, my name's Sophia Taylor. It's my first day.
R Sophia? Sophia Taylor? From Canada?
S Yes, that's right.
R Come on in!

▶ 1.27 **PART 2**

DAVID Is this Sophia?
RECEPTIONIST Yes.
D Hello!
SOPHIA Good morning!
D Welcome, Sophia. I'm David.
S Nice to meet you, David.
D Nice to meet you, too. How are you?
S I'm good, thank you. And you?
D I'm fine, thanks. OK, well, come with me, please.
S OK!

▶ 1.31 **PART 3**

DAVID Hi, Megan – Sophia's here.
MEGAN Oh. Already? Great!
D Sophia, this is Megan Jackson.
SOPHIA Nice to meet you, Megan.
M Nice to meet you too, Sophie.
S Mm, Sophia. My name's Sophia, not Sophie.
M Oh! Yes, yes, of course. I'm sorry. Sophia.
S That's OK!
M Nice to meet you, Sophia!
D So, this is your office. Your home for the next year.
M It's not home, David!
D No, OK. Well, you're in here with Megan, and she can help you with …
M Everything!
S Thank you, Megan. That's great.
D Sorry, but I need to …
M Oh, yes, of course.
D See you later, Sophia.
S Sure. Thank you, David.
D Bye!
M OK, so … this is your desk.
S Oh, right. Good!
M So, welcome to your new office, welcome to Electric Blue Technology, and welcome to the UK!
S Thank you, Megan! Thank you very much!

Unit 2

▶ 1.40

Conversation 1

INTERVIEWER Carlo, where are you from?
CARLO I'm from Ravello, in Italy.
I Ravello? Is it a big city?
C No, no. It isn't a city. It's a small village near Naples.

Conversation 2

I Where are you from, Katia?
KATIA I'm from Santiago.
I Santiago? In Chile?
K Yeah.
I It's a big city.
K Yes, it is. It's a very big city.

Conversation 3

I Yuri, where are you from?
YURI I'm from Vyborg, in Russia.
I Is it a city?
Y No, it isn't. It's a big town. It's near St Petersburg.

▶ 1.51

INTERVIEWER What things are OK at an airport?
JOHN Most things are fine. Computers are fine, and phones, and watches of course, all no problem.
I What about umbrellas?
J Yes, they're fine.
I So, what's not OK?
J Well, bottles of water, they're not OK.
I And of course, no knives?
J Er, no!

▶ 1.59 **PART 1**

RACHEL Good morning.
SOPHIA Good morning.
R Can I help you?
S Well … yes … I need a flat near here.
R OK – sure – we can help! Please sit down. OK, so … a flat just for you?
S Yes, just me.
R One bedroom?
S One bedroom is fine, yes.
R One or two questions, if that's OK?
S Of course.
R What's your name?
S Sophia Taylor.
R OK. That's Sophia … S-O-F-I-A?
S No. S-O-P-H-I-A.
R Ah yes, sorry. Sophia – er Taylor. How do you spell that?
S T-A-Y-L-O-R.
R T-A-Y-L-O-R. And what's your address? Do you have an address in London?
S Well yes, but it's a hotel.
R OK.
S It's the Alpha Hotel, A-L-P-H-A.
R Alpha Hotel. Right. And what's your phone number, please?
S Well, it's my mobile number. It's 07832 647893.
R 07832 67489 …
S No, sorry, it's 647893.
R 647893?
S That's right.
R OK, thanks. Well now … we have two nice flats in this part of London. This one. It's an old flat. Very big rooms.
S Hmm.
R And this one. It's quite big, and it's a really nice flat.
S Oh, yes. That is nice.
R It's near here. We can go there now.
S OK, great!

▶ 1.65 **PART 2**

RACHEL So, this is it. One bedroom. And a kitchen, of course. And it's quite big!
SOPHIA Yes, it is. It's beautiful.
R Yes, it's a very good flat for one person … It's a nice street. And near a park.
S Oh, good.
R Take a look.
S Thank you.
S OK, thank you. It's a good flat – it's great. I like it. I really like it.
R OK, great!

Unit 3

▶ 1.89

Conversation 1

INTERVIEWER Are you from China, Julie?
JULIE No, I'm not. My parents are Chinese, but I'm American.
I What time do you have dinner?
J In my family, we usually have dinner at about 7 o'clock.
I And what do you have?
J We usually have rice with meat and vegetables.

Conversation 2

I Where are you from, Misha?
MISHA I'm from Russia.
I And when do you have dinner?
M I always have dinner early.
I What time?
M At 5 o'clock.
I And what do you have?
M Different things, but I like fish for dinner.

Conversation 3

I Are you Spanish or Mexican, Bianca?
BIANCA I'm Spanish.
I What time do you have dinner?
B I usually have dinner between 9 and 10 o'clock.
I You have dinner late.
B Yes. People never have dinner early in Spain.
I What do you have?
B I usually have meat and vegetables, but I sometimes have bread and cheese.

▶ 2.4

MEGAN Hi Sophia. How are you?
SOPHIA I'm well. In fact, I'm very well!
M What's that? A key?
S It sure is!
M Your new flat!
S That's right.
M Great.
S I'm so happy! Come on – time for a coffee!
M Yes, good idea.
S OK – something to drink?
M Yes, I'd like a cup of coffee, please.
S Coffee. OK.
ASSISTANT Hi.
S Hi. So two cups of …
M No … um … I'd like tea. Yes, a cup of tea, please.
S Tea – right. Cake?
M No, thank you.
S OK. Can I have a cup of tea, a cup of coffee and a piece of chocolate cake, please?
A OK … So that's a cup of tea, a cup of coffee and a piece of chocolate cake.
S That's right. Thanks.
M Sorry, but I'd like a piece of chocolate cake too. Sorry!
S Sure – no problem. Can we have two pieces of chocolate cake, please?
A Certainly.
A That's £11.00, please.
S Here you are.
A Thank you.
M So – the flat?
S It's nice. Look – it's quite big and very beautiful.
M Oh yes, lovely.
S And it's quite old. I like that.
M Is it near the office?
S Yes, it is. It's also near a park. It's great.
M Sorry. It's from my cousin, James.
S That's OK.
M Sorry. I can answer later. So, London's now home!
S Yes! London's now home.

Unit 4

▶ 2.15

TOM Where are you from, Miriam?
MIRIAM I'm from Brazil – Rio de Janeiro, but I live here in New Zealand now.
T Where do you live?
M I live in Auckland – it's really nice there.
T And where do you work?
M I work in Wellington.
T Wellington? But that's so far away.
M Yes, I go to work three days a week – I fly.
T Do you work at home?
M Yes, I work two days at home.
T Are you married?
M Yes, my husband's name is Bernardo.
T Is he Brazilian?
M Yes, he is.
T Ah, OK. Do you speak English or Portuguese at home?
M We speak Portuguese, of course!

▶ 2.20

1 e Oh, it's the Hemsworth brothers. They're Australian film actors. It's Liam and his older brother Chris.
2 d This is Shakira, she's a singer from Colombia. And in this photo she's with her parents.
3 f And this one – this is Ronaldo the football player – Cristiano Ronaldo. He's about ten in this photo, and he's with his father and his two sisters.
4 c This is an old photo of Hillary Clinton, and that's her husband Bill Clinton and their daughter Chelsea.
5 b This is a photo of Will Smith with his wife Jada Pinkett-Smith. The three children are Jaden, Willow and Trey Smith.
6 a It's a photo of George Clooney as a boy. I think he's about seven. And he's with his mother and his sister.

▶ 2.27 **PART 1**

MEGAN Good morning!
SOPHIA Hi there.
M So … how's the new flat?
S Oh, it's great. I really like it. You must come and see it.
M I'd love to … Are you OK, Sophia?
S Well, yes and no … It's an email from my sister.
M In Canada?
S That's right.
M Is she OK?
S Oh, she's fine. It's just …
M … she's in Canada.
S And my parents, and my brother.
M And you're here in London.
S It's difficult.

▶ 2.28 **PART 2**

MEGAN Yeah … Do you have photos of your family?
SOPHIA Yes. Yes, I do.
M Oh, can I see them?
S Sure … OK. This is my mother. She's a teacher.
M Oh, yes. Nice picture!
S And this one, this is my father.
M Oh, right. Is he a teacher too?
S No, he's a manager. He works for a big supermarket.
M And who's this?
S This is my sister, Jackie. And her two girls.
M Oh, they're beautiful. How old are they?
S This is Kylie, she's ten, and this is Amanda, she's eight.
M Oh. They're lovely.
S Yes, they are … So, what about you? Do you have photos?
M Yes, I do! Just a minute … Ah, here we are. So … this is Mike.
S Oh right. Who's Mike? … Is he your … husband?
M No, I'm not married! He's my brother.
S Oh! He looks nice.
M He is. He lives in Scotland.

S What's his job?
M He works with computers.
S OK.
M And this is Helen, his wife. She works in a hotel. She's a manager.
S Ah. Nice photo.
M And this is James. He's my cousin. He's really great!
S Oh, yes.
M James lives near you. Maybe we can go and see him?
S Yes … I'd like that. Thank you, Megan.

Unit 5

▶ 2.44

A Excuse me! Where are the shops? Are they near here?
B Yes, there are a few shops in New Street, that's just near here. There's a small food shop and there's also a good bookshop. It's really big and the people there are very nice! Oh, and there's a nice Italian café in New Street, near the station. They have very good cakes, and great coffee.
A What about a bank?
B A bank … Yes, there's a bank in Old Street. It's near the school.
A And restaurants?
B Well, there's a new Chinese restaurant. That's in Old Street. It's near the cinema. But it's expensive.

▶ 2.51

RECEPTIONIST Good afternoon.
BARRY Good afternoon. Do you have a free room tonight?
R Tonight … ? Yes, we have four free rooms. They all have wi-fi.
B Oh good. Is there a car park here?
R No, I'm sorry, we don't have a car park.
B Oh. Is there a restaurant or café?
R No, but there's a kitchen.
B Right. Well, are there any cafés near here?
R Yes, there are two cafés on this street.
B Oh that's good. … And the room … is there a shower in the room?
R No, but there's a shower next to the room.
B So, it's not my shower?
R No, other guests use it too. There are two showers.
B Really?! What kind of hotel is this?
R Well, it's not a hotel. It's a hostel.

▶ 2.55 **PART 1**

MEGAN It's a really nice flat, Sophia.
SOPHIA Yeah, I like it here. But I need to get some things – you know, to make it a home.
M Of course.
S Would you like a cup of tea?
M Oh, yes, please.
S Oh no!
M What's the problem?
S I don't have any tea.
M Oh.
S I need to go shopping!
M Well, is there a supermarket near here?
S I don't know.
M Well, are there any shops near here?
S I don't know!
M Come on. We can look for a shop.
S OK!

▶ 2.59 **PART 2**

MEGAN Umm … there's one in this street. … I think.
SOPHIA I think maybe that's a shop … there.
M No, it's a café!
S Oh dear. Well, maybe we can have tea there!
M James?
JAMES Megan. Hi.
M How are you?
J I'm good, thanks.
S Hi there.

M Oh, sorry. Sophia, this is my cousin, James. And James, this is Sophia – we work together.
S Nice to meet you.
J Yes, nice to meet you too.
M Sophia's from Toronto.
J Really?
S But I live here now.
J In London?
S Yes. Really near here.
M James lives near here too.
S Oh, right. Where's your flat?
J It's in the next street.
M James, do you know? Is there a supermarket near here?
J No, sorry, there isn't.
M Well, are there any shops near here? We need some tea.
J Yes, there's one near my flat … I can show you.
S Well, thank you very much.
J No problem – no problem at all. It's this way.

Unit 6

▶ 2.78

INTERVIEWER Paul, you usually take photos at night. Do you go to bed early?
PAUL No. Usually around 11 o'clock.
I And when do you wake up?
P I always wake up at about 2:00am every night.
I And what do you do then?
P Well, I get up and I go out. I walk in the city at night and I take photos. Then I go home and I sleep until morning.
I What about your wife? Does she wake up?
P No, she never wakes up. She just sleeps!

▶ 2.82 **PART 1**

MEGAN James, hi! You again!
JAMES Yes, me again! Hi, Sophia!
SOPHIA Hi, James.
J They're nice flowers.
M Yes. They're for Sophia – for her flat.
J Yes … Oh yes, your flat's near here.
S That's right. Just there, in fact.
J Oh, right.
M Come with us … Is that OK, Sophia?
S Yes, why not?
J Are you sure?
S Yes!
J Well … yeah, I'd love to. … OK … great!
S Good. Come on.
S They're lovely flowers. Thanks again, Megan.
M No problem.
J I really like your flat, Sophia.
S Yeah, thanks. I like it here. Would you like a cup of coffee?
J Yes, please.
M Yes, thanks.
S Ah, there's just one problem.
J What's that? No coffee? Well, you have tea now, I know that!
S Yes, but there are only two cups. And one glass! Look!
M You need to go shopping!
S I know, I need a lot of things. Cups, glasses …
M Well, I can go with you. I'll help you buy things.
S That's great, thanks.
M What do you need? Cups, glasses, what else?
S Mm, I need plates, and …
M Do you want to go today? We can go this afternoon.
S OK, great. I don't have a lot of things, but I have biscuits! Would you like one, Megan?
M No, it's OK, thanks.
S James?
J Yes, please!

JAMES I'll come with you if you like. I love shopping!
SOPHIA Oh, thank you, James, that's very kind. But I'm sure you have other things to do – it's the weekend.
J Oh, that's OK.
MEGAN Sophia and I are fine, James.
S But nice to see you again. See you soon, maybe. Bye.
M Bye, James. See you later.
J OK … Bye. Thanks for the … biscuit.

Unit 7

▶ 3.5

SUE I like this picture. What do you think? For the kitchen.
MIKE Hmm … it's OK.
S Or these chairs. They're really nice.
M No, I don't really like them. That clock's quite nice.
S But it's new!
M Yeah, well, who wants an old clock?
S Hmm … Oh, look. Those books are interesting. And look at that radio. That's so cool.
M Is it? It's very old!
S I know, but it's beautiful. I love old things …
M Hmm.
S Excuse me.
STALLHOLDER Yes?
S How much is that radio?
ST The radio? £135.
M What?! That's very …
S OK, I'll buy it!

▶ 3.17

KATE Look at all our old clothes! There are a lot! We need to throw some away.
GIUSEPPE Yeah, you're right. … Is this my old T-shirt?
K No, it's Greg's T-shirt. He never wears it.
G Are these your jeans?
K No, they're Sara's jeans.
G But she sometimes wears these.
K But she doesn't like them.
G OK. … Wait just a minute – that's my shirt. I sometimes wear that.
K Really?
G Well, no … not really.
K So … ?
G Fine – out it goes.

▶ 3.21 PART 1

SOPHIA So, where are the cups?
MEGAN OK, let's see. Ah … These cups are nice.
S Yes, they are.
M But there are only three.
FRANK Can I help you?
S Yes, how much are these cups?
F They're five pounds each.
M That's a good price.
S But I need six. Do you have any more?
F No, I'm sorry. We only have three.
S Oh dear.
F These cups are the same price.
S Mm … no … I don't think so. Can I look around?
F Of course.
M Sophia, these cups are really nice.
S Yes, they are. But I need six.
M Yes, I know … but not for you … for me!
S Oh. Do you need some cups too?
M Not really, but I really like them … and they're so cheap. Excuse me … I'd like two of these cups, please.
F Certainly.

FRANK OK, that's ten pounds, please.
MEGAN Here you are.
F Thank you. Enter your PIN, please.
M OK, no problem.
F Thank you. And here's your receipt.
M Thank you. Can you see anything you want?
SOPHIA No, I don't really like anything.
M OK – well, there's another shop near here.
S But now you have some nice new cups!
M Yes, I do!
S Bye.
F Bye. Thank you.

Unit 8

▶ 3.37

Conversation 1

LARRY Were you at work yesterday?
CARA Yes, I was, but I wasn't here in the office.
L Where were you?
C I was at a meeting in Dublin.
L Oh, was it interesting?
C Yes, it was really interesting.

Conversation 2

DENIZ Were you at the game last Saturday?
ANTONIO No, I wasn't – not the game here in Manchester.
D Oh, really? Were you away?
A Yes, I was away with the team in Bristol.
D How was the game there?
A It was good – really exciting.

Conversation 3

VICTOR Were you at home at the weekend?
AVA No, I wasn't. I was away.
V Oh, where were you?
A I was in Milan with my band – there was a concert.
V Great! Was it fun?
A Yes, it was. And Milan is a beautiful city.

▶ 3.52 PART 1

DAVID Hi, Sophia. How was your weekend?
SOPHIA Yeah, it was nice. Yours?
D Well, you know, busy with friends. So, how do you like it here in England?
S Oh, I love it. Well, I like London, but that's not England! Where are you from, David?
D I'm from Bristol. It's in the west of England.
S Oh, right. Do you miss your family?
D Oh, you know, my parents, but I love living in London. Well … I … um
S Oh, of course. See you later.
MEGAN Good morning, Sophia.
S Oh, hi Megan!
M How are you?
S Yeah, OK, thanks. Thank you for Saturday. You really helped a lot.
M Oh, that's all right. I love shopping.
S It was fun.
M Yes, it was. We could go shopping again some time.
S Yes, OK. Good idea.
M Steph, did you get my email?

▶ 3.53 PART 2

MEGAN Thank you.
SOPHIA So, how was your Sunday?
M It was OK. I was at a party in the evening.
S Was it good?
M Yeah … but the food wasn't very nice.
S Oh dear.
M I was tired. I went home early. What about you?
S Me?
M How was your Sunday?
S Oh, it was OK. I went for a walk in the afternoon. And then I stayed at home and watched TV. London's really big. It's difficult to meet people.

M Well, you know me!
S Yes, that's true.
M I find London difficult too, sometimes. I know – let's go somewhere this weekend. So you can see a different town. We could go to Henley.
S Henley? Where's that?
M Oh, it's a small town, it's not far from London. I went to school there.
S Really?
M Yes, it's a beautiful place. Look.
S Oh, yes, it looks nice.
M So, shall we go there for the day next Saturday?
S OK, that's a lovely idea. I'd like to see some different places. Let's go to Henley!

Unit 9

▶ 3.69

MICHAELA So how was your trip to Colombia?
ALESSANDRO Oh it was great. It was very relaxing – I didn't read my emails for three weeks!
M Where were you? In Bogotá?
A No, no, we didn't go to big cities at all. We wanted to see the country, so we went by bus and we stayed in small towns and villages. The best place we stayed was with a family.
M In their house?
A Well, we didn't stay in their house. We camped in their garden. They had a swimming pool. They also had bikes, so we saw lots of nice places nearby. I took some beautiful photos!
M I'd love to see them.
A Of course.
M Was it cheap to camp?
A Yes … $4 a night!
M $4! That's really cheap.
A Yeah, it was good, because we didn't have a lot of money!

▶ 3.77

KIRIL Where did you go on your summer holiday last year, Angie?
ANGIE I went to an island in Greece.
K Great! How was the weather?
A It was hot and sunny. What about you, Kiril?
K I stayed here in Moscow. It rained a lot of the time. I want to go somewhere different this year.
A Well, try Greece. It isn't expensive to fly there.
K Hmm … but, well, I don't like flying.
A Oh, I see. Well, what about the south of France? I went there two years ago. It was beautiful.
K Oh, really? How did you get there?
A By train. And, you know, the weather was really warm.
K Did you enjoy it there?
A Yes, I did. I had a great time. Try to go this year!

▶ 3.82 PART 1

SOPHIA It's beautiful here.
MEGAN I'm so happy you like it.
S Very different from Toronto. So, what's the plan for today?
M Well, first we can go to the museum.
S OK.
M And then maybe some lunch?
S Lovely!
S Well, I'm full. So much food!
M I know!
S Oh wow! I love that clock!
M Oh yes – really nice.
S Let's have a look.
M OK … Are you OK?
S I think so.
M Is it very heavy?
S Yeah, it's really heavy. Can you take it for a minute?
M Of course!
S Thanks! … OK.
M That's OK.
S Thank you.

▶ 3.85 PART 2

MEGAN Why don't you … put it down?
JAMES Megan, hi! How are you?
M Hi, James. I'm OK, thanks.
J Did you go to Henley?
M Yeah, and we're still here!
J Oh, right …
M James, can you do something for me?
J Well … yes … maybe.
M Could you pick us up from the station later, please? In London.
J Mm … OK. From where? Paddington?
M Yes.
J OK. Is there a problem? Can't you take the underground?
M No, it's just we've got this clock.
J Clock?
M Yes, it's very heavy. So … could you meet us at the station, please?
J Why did you buy a clock?
M I didn't. Sophia bought it.
J Sophia?
M Yes, Sophia bought a very big clock.
J Oh, right, I see!
M So, can you help us, please?
J Sure, no problem.
M Oh, thanks, James, that's really kind of you.
J No problem.
M Bye.
J Bye. See you later.

Unit 10

▶ 4.7

MIMI I really love my flat – it's great! But it's very small and I need to think about how I use the space. One really good thing is the windows. I have really big windows, so lots of light comes into the flat. The place doesn't feel very small. Everything is in one big room. The living room area has a TV, a small table and two chairs. There's also a small kitchen area in one corner. I don't have a dining room. I have a table where I eat my meals and I do all my work on my computer. It's next to the kitchen. Then the bedroom has, well, a bed, of course … and a small lamp on a table. So I don't have a big flat, but I live in the city centre – the city is my home!

▶ 4.13

Conversation 1
LOU Hello.
DAN Hi, it's Dan. How are you?
L Fine. Look, Dan, I'm busy. I can't talk now.
D Are you working? I can hear a lot of people there.
L Well, no, I'm not working. I'm in a café. I'm with some people and they're talking. I'll call you later, OK?
D OK.

Conversation 2
L Hi.
D Hi, it's Dan again. What are you doing?
L I'm at the bus stop. I'm going home.
D Oh, OK. Look, do you want to go out this evening?
L I don't know. Look, I can't talk now. My bus is coming.
D Oh. I'll call you later, then.

Conversation 3
L Dan … Hi.
D Hi Lou. Are you at home now?
L Yes. Look, I can't talk now.
D Are you working?
L No, I'm not working. I'm cooking dinner.
D Oh, OK. Look, what about this evening?
L No, sorry, I'm too tired. Let's talk later, OK?

Conversation 4
L Hi Dan.
D Hi, it's me again. Can you talk now? Or are you having dinner?
L No, I'm not having dinner. I'm watching a film.
D Oh, what are you watching? Is it good?
L Yes … it's just a film. I can't talk now. Maybe later … OK?
D OK.

Conversation 5
L Hello. This is Lou. I'm sorry, I'm not here at the moment. Please leave a message.
D Hi, this is Dan. Um, well I guess you're sleeping, so … er, I'll call you tomorrow. Tomorrow morning. OK? Maybe we can go out together. Yeah. Bye.

▶ 4.20 PART 1

SOPHIA Oh, this clock!
TAXI DRIVER Eight pounds fifty, please.
S Mm … OK … just a minute.
MEGAN Hey! Let me.
S No, no!
M Please!
S No! I'll get it. Could you take the clock, please?
M Sure!
S Thanks. Thank you very much.
T Oh, thank you!
M It is really heavy! Shall we carry it together?
S OK! Why did I buy it? I'm so glad James can meet us in London.
M Yeah, James is really kind.
S So, what time's the train?
M I don't know! We need to check.

▶ 4.23 PART 2

SOPHIA Excuse me.
STATION ASSISTANT Yes? How can I help?
S What time's the next train to London?
ST The next train is at … 4:35.
S What time is it now?
ST What time is it now? What time does it say on your clock? 12:30. Well, that's not right. How much did you pay for that clock? Anyway, it's 4:32 now.
MEGAN The train leaves in three minutes! Quick! Let's go!
S Sorry, which platform is it?
ST It's Platform 3. It's across the bridge and down the stairs.
M Thanks!
ST Would you like some help with the clock? I can carry it if you like.
S No thanks, we're fine.

Unit 11

▶ 4.35

A What are you reading?
B Oh, it's about Valentina Tereshkova.
A Who's she?
B She's a Russian cosmonaut. Do you know about her?
A No. What did she do?
B Well, she was the first woman in space. She went into space in 1963. It says here, 400 people wanted the job, but they asked her.
A Why did they ask her?
B Well, she was young, and she was quite small. And she also did a lot of parachute jumping.
A Oh, so she went in planes a lot.
B Yes! And she married a cosmonaut, too. She met him in 1963. He was on the same space programme. And they had a daughter.
A So, did she go into space again?
B No, she only went once. But she said she would like to fly to Mars one day. She said that when she was 70!

▶ 4.41

CELIA Hi, Andy! I'm Celia, nice to meet you!
ANDY Hi, Celia! Nice to meet you, too.
C Well, let's start. First question, what fun things can you do with the students?
A Well, I can play the guitar.
C Great. And can you sing?
A Yes, I can. I can sing and play the guitar quite well. Oh, and I can ride a horse very well. You wanted someone who can ride a horse.
C That's right – great! Now, our students also like parties and they like dancing. Can you dance well?
A No, I can't. I don't really like dancing, so I can't dance very well.
C That's OK. And what about your teaching?
A Teaching?
C Yes, can you teach well?
A What? Sorry. I'm not a teacher. I can't teach at all.
C Really? But … but did you read the advertisement?
A Well … sort of … but not very well. I just read some of the words 'sing, dance, ride a horse …' – you know …
C But we want teachers – English teachers.
A Oh. Sorry!

▶ 4.46

SOPHIA Are you sure you're OK with the clock, James?
JAMES Fine – just fine.
S It isn't too heavy?
J No, no!
S OK.
J It's a great clock.
S I like it.
J Yeah, it looks really good.
S Thanks for meeting us.
MEGAN Yes, thank you, James.
J No problem. Did you like Henley?
S Yes, very much. We had a nice time.
J Oh, that's good.
M We can go somewhere in London next weekend.
J I think London Zoo is very nice.
M London Zoo?
J Yes!
M I don't think the zoo's very interesting.
J Oh? Why not?
M Well, it's more for children.
J I don't think so.
M What about the Tower of London?
J Oh no! I don't think the Tower of London's a good idea.
M Really?
J There are lots of tourists.
S Well … I'm a tourist!
M A kind of tourist.
S Where's a good place for the clock?
J In here?
M What about the bedroom?
J I don't think the bedroom is a good idea.
S Why not?
J You can hear it all the time. It's difficult to sleep.
S Not for me!
J Oh. OK.
S But maybe you're right. It is better here in the living room. Maybe over there.
J OK. Here?
S Maybe. What do you think, Megan?
M Yes, perhaps. Or maybe … No, I think there is good.
S Yes, I think you're right. What do you think, James?
J I think this clock is very heavy!

Unit 12

 4.60

PAOLA This summer, I'm not going to have a normal holiday. I'm going to do something different. I read about a cooking school in the mountains. I'm going to learn how to cook really well. It's a two-week course. I think it's going to be fun!

YAZ Every summer my family normally gets a house near the beach and we spend the holiday there. But we aren't going to do that this year. For a change, we're going to go on a trip to Norway. There's a boat that goes along the coast of Norway. They say it's a very beautiful trip.

NIKITA Most summers I go to another country – last year I went to Munich in Germany. This summer, I'm not going to travel abroad. I'm going to stay in this country. I'm going to stay on a farm and I'm going to work there. They aren't going to pay me, but it's not important for me. I want to do something different and be outside all day.

4.68

Conversation 1

JESSICA What are you going to do this weekend, Lee?
LEE Oh, I don't know. Nothing much.
J Are you going to go out?
L I'm going to see a film.
J What film are you going to see?
L I don't know yet. I don't know what's on.
J What about Sunday?
L Well, I'm going to go out somewhere … maybe. See what the weather's like.

Conversation 2

JESSICA So what are you going to do this weekend, Marcus?
MARCUS Well, on Saturday I'm going to get up early and I'm going to go for a run. Then I'm going to go shopping.
J What are you going to buy?
M Well, I want to buy a new jacket and some shoes. And in the evening I'm going to meet some friends for a meal.
J Where are you going to go?
M There's a new restaurant called *Sandy's*. We're going to go there. And on Sunday, I'm going to go play tennis.

4.73 **PART 1**

SOPHIA Hi, James?
JAMES Hello, Sophia!
S How are you?
J I'm fine. How about you?
S Yes, really good. I bought some more things for my flat today and I'm just putting them away.
J Oh, great. Oh, so, mm, I wanted to ask you … Would you like to come for dinner? You know, at my flat?
S Well, that's really kind of you, James. I'd love to, but …
J Oh, good.
S No, I'd love to, but I just think … you've helped me so much. You know, you met us at the station, the clock …
J Oh, that was nothing.
S No, but I'd like to say thank you. So, would you like to come for dinner at my flat?
J Oh, well, yes. I'd love to come. Thank you.
S Are you free on Friday?
J Oh, no. Sorry, I'm busy then, a work thing, but Saturday's OK.
S Great! Come on Saturday.
J OK.
S See you then.
J See you then.
S Bye.
J Bye.

4.76 **PART 2**

SOPHIA Hi. Is that you, James?
JAMES Yes, it is.
S OK. Come on in!
J These are for you.
S Oh … thank you. They're beautiful.
J Oh, Megan – you're here too. Hi.
MEGAN Hi, James. You look smart!
J Er, yes. Thank you.
S Good – now you're both here.
J Yes, we're both here.
S Well, I just … I wanted to say thank you – to both of you. It was my first month in a new city and you really helped me a lot. And … well … I'm really feeling at home here now.
M Great.
S I wasn't sure about staying in London.
J Oh?
S No. But now I feel like I have new friends here, so … So last week I decided. I'm going to stay.
M Oh, that's wonderful news.
J Yeah, great!
M Oh, that's so nice.
S Yes, yes it is. Now let's have dinner.
J Great …
S OK, sit down, both of you, and I'll bring the food.
M Lovely!
J Thank you, Sophia.

Phonemic symbols

Vowel sounds

Short

/ə/	/æ/	/ʊ/	/ɒ/	/ɪ/	/i/	/e/	/ʌ/
breakf**a**st	m**a**n	p**u**t	g**o**t	ch**i**p	happ**y**	m**e**n	**u**p

Long

/ɜ:/	/ɑ:/	/u:/	/ɔ:/	/i:/
sh**ir**t	p**ar**t	wh**o**	w**al**k	ch**ea**p

Diphthongs (two vowel sounds)

/eə/	/ɪə/	/ʊə/	/ɔɪ/	/aɪ/	/eɪ/	/əʊ/	/aʊ/
h**air**	n**ear**	t**our**	b**oy**	n**i**ne	**ei**ght	wind**ow**	n**ow**

Consonants

/p/	/b/	/f/	/v/	/t/	/d/	/k/	/g/
picnic	**b**ook	**f**ace	**v**ery	**t**ime	**d**og	**c**old	**g**o
/θ/	/ð/	/tʃ/	/dʒ/	/s/	/z/	/ʃ/	/ʒ/
think	**th**e	**ch**air	**j**ob	**s**ea	**z**oo	**sh**oe	televi**si**on
/m/	/n/	/ŋ/	/h/	/l/	/r/	/w/	/y/
me	**n**ow	si**ng**	**h**ot	**l**ate	**r**ed	**w**ent	**y**es

Irregular verbs

Infinitive	Past simple
be	was
begin	began
buy	bought
catch	caught
choose	chose
come	came
do	did
drink	drank
drive	drove
eat	ate
feel	felt
find	found
fly	flew
forget	forgot
get	got
give	gave
go	went
grow up	grew up
have	had
hear	heard
know	knew
learn	learned / learnt
leave	left
lose	lost

Infinitive	Past simple
meet	met
pay	paid
put	put
read	read
ride	rode
run	ran
say	said
see	saw
sell	sold
send	sent
sing	sang
sit	sat
sleep	slept
speak	spoke
spell	spelled / spelt
swim	swam
take	took
teach	taught
tell	told
think	thought
understand	understood
wake up	woke up
wear	wore
write	wrote

START

1 Say four countries and their nationalities.

2 Make and answer the question.
you / are / Spanish ?

3 Think of three other ways to say 'hello'.

4 GO ON FOUR SQUARES

5 Are you from a city, town or village?

6 GO BACK FOUR SQUARES

7 Say the numbers 1–12.

8 Spell your name and country.

9 Say and spell four foods.

10 What time did you get up this morning?

11 Make the question.
chocolate cake / have / I / a piece of / can / please ?

12 GO ON FOUR SQUARES

13 Make and answer the question.
live / you / where / do ?

14 Who lived with you when you were a child?

15 Make and answer the question.
do / have / you / of / photos / friends / your / any ?

16 Say and spell four places in a town.

17 GO BACK FOUR SQUARES

18 Make and answer the question.
hotels / your / in / there / are / any / town ?

19 Say where a supermarket is.

20 GO ON FOUR SQUARES

21 Say and spell four jobs.

22 Make and answer the question.
usually / when / you / get / home / do ?

23 Offer to buy other students a cup of coffee.

24

Say these prices.
£7.99 $15.30 €100

25

GO BACK FOUR SQUARES

26

Say and spell four colours.

27

Make the question.
much / how / these / shoes / are ?

28

GO ON FOUR SQUARES

29

Make and answer the question.
were / you / where / weekend / last ?

30

Say two things you can watch and two things you can play.

31

Invite other students to the cinema tomorrow.

32

Say and spell three kinds of transport.

33

GO BACK FOUR SQUARES

34

Say and spell the four seasons.

35

Ask other students to pick you up at the station.

36

Say and spell four places in a home.

37

Make the question.
doing / you / are / what ?

38

GO ON FOUR SQUARES

39

Make the question.
Edinburgh / time's / the / train / next / what / to ?

40

Say four life events.

41

Say two things you can do well.

42

Say two things you can't do well.

43

Ask other students their opinion about a place you all know.

44

Say two plans you have for next weekend.

45

Say ordinal numbers 1–10.

46

Make and answer the question.
tomorrow / going / do / to / are / what / you ?

FINISH

Acknowledgements

The publishers would like to thank the following teachers and ELT professionals for the invaluable feedback they have provided during the development of the A1 Student's book:

Peggy Alptekin, Turkey and the Gulf; Zahra Bilides, Russia; Cassia Cassinha, Brazil; Maria Higina Almeida, Brazil; Steve Laslett, UK; Julian Oakley, UK; Litany Pires Ribeiro, Brazil; Elena Pro, Spain; Wayne Rimmer, Russia; Rodrigo Rosa, Brazil.

The publishers are grateful to the following contributors:

Gareth Boden: commissioned photography

Leon Chambers: audio recordings

Hilary Luckcock: picture research, commissioned photography

Rob Maidment and Sharp Focus Productions: video recordings

Mike Stone: video stills

The authors and publishers acknowledge the following sources of copyright material and are grateful for the permissions granted. While every effort has been made, it has not always been possible to identify the sources of all the material used, or to trace all copyright holders. If any omissions are brought to our notice, we will be happy to include the appropriate acknowledgements on reprinting.

The publisher has used its best endeavours to ensure that the URLs for external websites referred to in this book are correct and active at the time of going to press. However, the publisher has no responsibility for the websites and can make no guarantee that a site will remain live or that the content is or will remain appropriate.

The publishers are grateful to the following for permission to reproduce copyright photographs and material:

Key: L = left, C = centre, R = right, T = top, B = bottom, b/g = background

p6(a): Shutterstock/EDHAR; p6(b): Shutterstock/Brian A Jackson; p6(c): Shutterstock/ARENA Creative; p6(d): Getty/Photo and Co.; p6(e): Getty/Silvia Jansen; p6(f): Shutterstock/Andrey_Popov; p6(g): Shutterstock/Hero Images Inc; p7: Corbis/Volker Möhrke; p7(background): Corbis/Arctic-Images; p10(a): Getty/Patrick Kovarik; p10(b): Corbis/Thomas Eisenhuth/dpa; p10(c): Getty/Patrick Kovarik; p10(d): Getty/Anadolu Agency; p10(e): Getty/Vanderlei Almeida; p10(f): Corbis/BPI/Robin Parker; p10(g): Getty/Paul Crock/Stringer; p10(h): Getty/Miguel Tovar/STF; p11: Shutterstock/YanLev; p15: Corbis/Louie Psihoyos; p16(a): Shutterstock/Pablo Rogat; p16(b): Shutterstock/kostin77; p16(c): Corbis/Atlantide Travel; p17(TR): Corbis/Atlantide Phototravel; p17(CR): Alamy/Danny Nebraska; p17(BR): Corbis/Andreas von Einsiedel; p18(TR): Getty/quavondo; p23: Alamy/Foodfolio; p24(1): Shutterstock/keko64; p24(2): Shutterstock/Neirfy; p24(3): Shutterstock/Denis Vrublevski; p24(4): Getty/dbvirago; p24(5): Shutterstock/Africa Studio; p24(6): Alamy/Geoffrey Kidd; p24(7): Getty/Elena_Danileiko; p24(BR): Shutterstock/wong sze yuen; p25(TR): Shutterstock/sireonio; p25(CL): Getty/Medioimages/Photodisc; p25(BL): Superstock/Wolfgang Kaehler; p26 L(fruit): Shutterstock/ElenaGaak; p26 L (cereal): Shutterstock/Madlen; p26 L(toast): Getty/Joe Gough; p26 L(eggs): Shutterstock/Thomson D; p26 L(a): Getty/Images Bazaar; p26 L(b): Alamy/MBI; p26 L(c): Corbis/68/Ocean; p27(1): Getty/gofugui; p27(2): Corbis/Johner Images; p27(3): Getty/Rafael Elias; p31: Getty/Michael Cogliantry; pp32/33(B): Shutterstock/Luciano Mortula; p32(a): Getty/John Rensten; p32(b): Alamy/MBI; p32(c): Getty/Jupiterimages/Brand X Pictures; p32(d): Alamy/IndiaPicture; p32(e): Corbis/Image Source; p32(C): Corbis/Roland Weihrauch/epa; p33(TR): Alamy/Blend Images; p33(CL): Shutterstock/Goodluz; p33(CR): Shutterstock/Robert Cumming; p34(a): Corbis/Chris Bott/Splash News; p34(b): Getty/Jennifer Graylock; p34(d): Corbis/Frank Trapper; p34(e): Getty/Gregg DeGuire; p35(c): Corbis/Larry Downing/Sygma; p35(f): Alamy/WENN UK; p35(C): Alamy/Glow Images; p36(BR)(male): Shutterstock/eurobanks; p37: Shutterstock/Maryna Kulchytska; p38(BL): Alamy/Cultura Creative (RF); p39: Alamy/WENN Ltd; p40(TL): Corbis/George Steinmetz; p40(BL): Corbis/Geoff Renner/Robert Harding World Imagery; p41(a): Alamy/Andrey Kekyalyaynen; p41(b): Getty/Ken Walsh; p41(c): Alamy/MBI; p41(d): Corbis/Duncan Smith; p41(e): Getty/Nico Kai; p41(f): Getty/UpperCut Images; p42 L(1): Getty/innovatedcaptures; p42 L(2): Shutterstock/Benoit Daoust; p42 L(3): Shutterstock/Andrey tiyk; p42 L(4): Getty/Fuse; p42 L(5): Getty/Peter Hogstrom; p42(BL): Shutterstock/Eviled; p42 R(1): Getty/Westend61; pp42/43 B(2): Alamy/Anton Petrus; p43(3): Alamy/Andreas von Einsiedel; p47: Getty/SM/AIUEO; p48(TL): Corbis/Andrew Aitchison/InPictures; p48(TR): Getty/Cathy Finch; p48(CL): Corbis/Marcie Malroy/Shestock; p48(CR): Shutterstock/Matt Antonino; p49(a): Alamy/Shaun Higson; p49(b): Alamy/Cultura Creative (RF); p49(c): Shutterstock/Dmitry Kalinovsky; p49(d): Shutterstock/lightwavemedia; p49(e): Shutterstock/Monkey Business Images; p49(f): Getty/kzenon; p49(g): Corbis/Turba; p49(h): Shutterstock/michael jung; p50(TL): Corbis/Wavebreak Media Ltd/lightwave; p50(a): Alamy/Tetra Images; p50(b): Shutterstock/Lestertair; p51(T): Shutterstock/auremar; p51(C): Shutterstock/coloursinmylife; p51(B): Shutterstock/Antonio V Oquias; p55: Alamy/LOOK Die Bildagentur der Fotografen GmbH; p56: Photo Courtesy of www.iLoveEcoChic.com; p58(TR): Corbis/Fairchild Photo Service/Conde Nast; p58(BR): Getty/Mark Robert Milan; p59(TL): Getty/Thomas Concordia; p59(TC): Getty/Gilbert Carrasquillo; p59(CL): Corbis/Edward le Poulin; p59(C): Rex/Gregory Pace/BEI; p59(BR): Corbis/Dream Pictures/Blend Images; p62(1): Shutterstock/Bennyartist; p62(2): Shutterstock/StudioSmart; p62(3): Getty/Kettaphoto; p62(4): Shutterstock/Raulin; p62(5): Shutterstock/PodPad; p62(6): Shutterstock/Ruslan Semichev; p63: Corbis/Matthias Oesterle/Demotix; p64(BL): Alamy/ZUMA Press Inc; p64(BR): Shutterstock/Christian Bertrand; p68(TV screen): Shutterstock/Peter Elvidge; p70: Shutterstock/Admin5699; p71: Corbis/Orjan F Ellingvag/Dagens Naringsliv; p72(L): Alamy/architecture uk; p72(R): Alamy/Hemis; p73(L): Corbis/Fernando Benoechea/Beateworks; p73(R): Corbis/WZ Photography; p74(a): Shutterstock/przis; p74(b): Getty/Tomas Anderson; p74(c): Shutterstock/Michael Warwick; p74(d): Shutterstock/Ozervoc Alexander; p74(C): Shutterstock/Deymos.HR; p74(B): Alamy/Christine Osborne Pictures; p75: Shutterstock/bikeriderlondon; p79: Corbis/David Bathgate; p80(a): Alamy/Martin Bennett; p80(b): Shutterstock/Yampi; p80(c): Shutterstock/J Paget RF Photos; p80(d): Alamy/Elizabeth Whiting & Associates; p80(e): Shutterstock/Yampi; p80(f): Shutterstock/SGM; p80(CR): Shutterstock/arek_malang; p81(1): Shutterstock/Photographee.eu; p81(2): Shutterstock/Photographee.eu; p81(3): Shutterstock/Photographee.eu; pp82/83(a): Corbis/Z/BZM Productions/Ocean; p83(b): Getty/Purestock; p83(c): Getty/Scott Griessel; p83(d): Alamy/Chris Rout; p83(e): Getty/Dan Hallman; p87: Getty/Greg Epperson; p88(Valentina Tereshkova): Alamy/RIA Novosti; p88(rocket): Alamy/

ITAR-TASS Photo Agency; p89(L): Superstock/Album/Oronoz; p89(R): Shutterstock/wavebreakmedia; pp88/89(B/G)(stars): Shutterstock/clearviewstock; p90(CL): Alamy/Moviestore Collection Ltd; p90(CR): Getty/Timothy Allen; p90(BL): Corbis/Ruud van der Lubben/Demotin; p90(BR): Alamy/epa european pressphoto agency; p91(a): Shutterstock/Stefan Holm; p91(b): Shutterstock/Ariwasabi; p91(c): Getty/mediaphotos; p91(d): Alamy/moodboard; p95: Shutterstock/specnaz; p96: Corbis/James W Porter; p97(a): Alamy/Art Kowalsky; p97(b): Shutterstock/Goodluz; p97(c): Getty/Bambu Productions; p98(a): Corbis/Sigrid Olsson/PhotoAlto; p98(b): Corbis/Sarah Kastner/Stock 4B; p98(c): Alamy/Tetra Images; p98(d): Corbis/Hero Images; p98(e): Getty/Izf; p99: Shutterstock/Monkey Business Images; p105(TL): Corbis/John Smith; p105(TR): Getty/Michael DeLeon; p105(C)(Rosa): Corbis/Kevin Dodge/Blend Images; p105(C)(Franco): Getty/Juanmonino; p105(B)(Lidia): Getty/Juanmonino; p105(B)(Hassan): Alamy/Springfield Photography; p106: Shutterstock/Djomas; p108: Shutterstock/Monkey Business Images; p109(L): Shutterstock/arek_malang; p109(R): Shutterstock/Alexander Image; p110(Rosa): Corbis/Kevin Dodge/Blend Images; p110(Franco): Getty/Juanmonino; p110(Lidia): Getty/Juanmonino; p110(Hassan): Alamy/Springfield Photography; p111(Hanan): Alamy/Ton Koene/VW Pics; p113: Getty/Franckreporter; p133(T)(book): Shutterstock/specnaz; p133(T)(water): Shutterstock/Mariyana M; p133(T)(computer): Shutterstock/Jakub Krechowicz; p133(T)(key): Shutterstock/Yegor Korzh; p133(T)(newspaper): Shutterstock/Paul Paladin; p133(T)(knife): Shutterstock/Ethan Boisvert; p133(T)(phone): Shutterstock/Hadrian; p133(T)(ticket): Shutterstock/Nice Monkey; p133(T)(watch): Getty/specnaz; p133(T)(umbrella): Shutterstock/Africa Studio; p133(B)(bag): Shutterstock/Kedrov; p133(B)(chair): Getty/Kettaphoto; p133(B)(clock): Shutterstock/Kastianz; p133(B)(cup):Shutterstock/Everything; p133(B)(football): Alamy/Daniel Sanchez Blasco; p133(B)(glass): Shutterstock/Raulin; p133(B)(guitar): Shutterstock/StudioSmart; p133(B)(lamp): Shutterstock/PodPad; p133(B)(picture): Getty/serezniy; p133(B)(plant): Shutterstock/Ruslan Semichev; p133(B)(plate): Shutterstock/Bennyartist; p133(B)(radio): Alamy/Paul Salmon; p133(B)(suitcase): Shutterstock/GVictoria; p135(TL): Corbis/Wavebreak Media Ltd; p136(1): Alamy/Blend Images; p136(2): Alamy/Cultura Creative (RF); p136(3): Shutterstock/Alexander Raths; p136(4): Alamy/Rubberball; p136(5): Getty/uniquely india; p136(6): Shutterstock/racorn; p136(7): Getty/Yuri_Arcurs; p136(8): Getty/Londoneye; p139(baby): Shutterstock/Mitar Art; p139(graduation): Corbis/Pankaj & Insy Shah/Gulf Images; p139(boy playing): Shutterstock/I Schmidt; p139(marriage): Getty/Brian McEntire; p139(schoolgirl): Getty/Sappington Todd; p139(mother & baby): Getty/Image Source; p139(finishing school): Alamy/Paul Baldesare; p139(retirement): Corbis/Ian Lishman/Juice Images; p139(university students): Getty/Cultura/Frank & Helena; p139(graveyard): Alamy/Chris Howes/Wild Places Photography; p140(swim): Alamy/Radek Detinsky; p140(cook): Shutterstock/wavebreakmedia; p140(paint): Alamy/Greatstock Photographic Library; p140(sing): Alamy/Jeff Morgan 04; p140(dance): Shutterstock/ayakovlevcom; p140(driving): Alamy/Juice Images; p140(volleyball): Alamy/Inmagine; p140(play cards): Alamy/Asia Images Group Pte Ltd; p140(ride horse): Shutterstock/aleksandr hunta; p140(ride bike): Alamy/Keith Morris; p140(run): Shutterstock/Ahturner; p142(TL): Shutterstock/Jacek Chabraszewski; p142(TC): Getty/Paul Poplis; p142(TR): Getty/dziewul; p142(BC): Getty/Steve McSweeny; p142(BC): Getty/Dennis Gottlieb; p142(BR): Alamy/Nicholas Eveleigh/Purestock; p143(TL): Shutterstock/Blue Lemon Photo; p143(TC): Shutterstock/piotr_pabijan; p143(TR): Getty/Devy Masselink; p143(BL): Getty/Bengt-Goren Carlsson; p143(BC): Shutterstock/Worldpics; p143(BR): Corbis/the food passionates; p143(1): Shutterstock/Valentina-G; p143(2): Shutterstock/EM Arts; p143(3): Shutterstock/gresei; p143(4): Shutterstock/flippo; p143(5): Shutterstock/Tim U R; p143(6): Shutterstock/ntstudio; p143(7): Alamy/Keith Leighton; p143(8): Alamy/Bettna Monique Chavez; p143(9): Shutterstock/Jiang Hongyan; p143(10): Shutterstock/Maks Narodenko; p143(11): Shutterstock/Dancestrokes; p143(12): Shutterstock/Admin5699; p153(plane): Shutterstock/Kenishirotie; p153(bike): Alamy/Sergey Borisov; p153(bus): Shutterstock/Art Konovalov; p153(train): Shutterstock/ValeStock; p153(car): Shutterstock/Patryk Kosmider; p153(boat/ship): Alamy/travelbild.com; p153(taxi): Shutterstock/guroldinneden; p153(tram): Shutterstock/Leonid Andronov; p153(metro/underground): Shutterstock/Pio3.

Commissioned photography by Gareth Boden: pp8(all),18(B), 64(T,C) and 65.

We are grateful to The Stephen Perse 6th Form College, Cambridge for their help with the commissioned photography.

The following stills were taken on commission by Mike Stone for Cambridge University Press: pp12, 13, 20, 21, 28, 29, 36, 44, 45, 52, 53, 60, 61, 68, 69, 76, 77, 84, 85, 92, 93, 100 and 101.

Front cover photograph by Superstock/Flirt.

The publishers would like to thank the following illustrators. Mark Bird; Mark Duffin; Sally Elford; John Goodwin (Eye Candy Illustration); Dusan Lakicevic (Beehive Illustration); Roger Penwill (New Division); Gavin Reece (New Division); Martin Sanders (Beehive Illustration); Sean 290 (KJA Artists); David Semple; Marie-Eve Tremblay (Colagene); Andrea Turvey (Eye Candy Illustration); Gary Venn (Lemonade Illustration).

Corpus Development of this publication has made use of the Cambridge English Corpus (CEC). The CEC is a computer database of contemporary spoken and written English, which currently stands at over one billion words. It includes British English, American English and other varieties of English. It also includes the Cambridge Learner Corpus, developed in collaboration with the University of Cambridge ESOL Examinations. Cambridge University Press has built up the CEC to provide evidence about language use that helps us to produce better language teaching materials.

English Profile This product is informed by English Vocabulary Profile, built as part of English Profile, a collaborative programme designed to enhance the teaching, learning and assessment of English worldwide. Its main funding partners are Cambridge University Press and Cambridge English Language Assessment and its aim is to create a 'profile' for English linked to the Common European Framework of Reference for Languages (CEFR). English Profile outcomes, such as the English Vocabulary Profile, will provide detailed information about the language that learners can be expected to demonstrate at each CEFR level, offering a clear benchmark for learners' proficiency. For more information, please visit www.englishprofile.org.

CALD The Cambridge Advanced Learner's Dictionary is the world's most widely used dictionary for learners of English. Including all the words and phrases that learners are likely to come across, it also has easy-to-understand definitions and example sentences to show how the word is used in context. The Cambridge Advanced Learner's Dictionary is available online at dictionary.cambridge.org. © Cambridge University Press, Fourth Edition, 2013 reproduced with permission.